Relating Information Culture to Information Policies and Management Strategies

Denise A.D. Bedford
Georgetown University, USA

Wioleta Kucharska
Gdańsk University of Technology, Poland

A volume in the Advances in Logistics, Operations, and Management Science (ALOMS) Book Series

IGI Global
PUBLISHER of TIMELY KNOWLEDGE

Published in the United States of America by
IGI Global
Business Science Reference (an imprint of IGI Global)
701 E. Chocolate Avenue
Hershey PA, USA 17033
Tel: 717-533-8845
Fax: 717-533-8661
E-mail: cust@igi-global.com
Web site: http://www.igi-global.com

Library of Congress Cataloging-in-Publication Data

Library of Congress Cataloging-in-Publication Data

Names: Bedford, Denise A. D., 1950- author. | Kucharska, Wioleta, 1977- author.
Title: Relating information culture to information policies and management strategies / Denise A. D. Bedford and Wioleta Kucharska.
Description: Hershey : Business Science Reference, 2020. | Includes bibliographical references and index. | Summary: "This book bridges four subject domains, including knowledge and information economies, business and information strategies, business and information cultures, and information management practices"-- Provided by publisher.
Identifiers: LCCN 2020000242 (print) | LCCN 2020000243 (ebook) | ISBN 9781799843153 (hardcover) | ISBN 9781799851707 (paperback) | ISBN 9781799843160 (ebook)
Subjects: LCSH: Knowledge management. | Information technology--Social aspects. | Technological innovations--Management. | Strategic planning. | Organizational change.
Classification: LCC HD30.2 .B45753 2020 (print) | LCC HD30.2 (ebook) | DDC 658.4/038--dc23
LC record available at https://lccn.loc.gov/2020000242
LC ebook record available at https://lccn.loc.gov/2020000243

This book is published in the IGI Global book series Advances in Logistics, Operations, and Management Science (ALOMS) (ISSN: 2327-350X; eISSN: 2327-3518)

British Cataloguing in Publication Data
A Cataloguing in Publication record for this book is available from the British Library.

Advances in Logistics, Operations, and Management Science (ALOMS) Book Series

ISSN:2327-350X
EISSN:2327-3518

Editor-in-Chief: *John Wang* Montclair State University, USA

MISSION

Operations research and management science continue to influence business processes, administration, and management information systems, particularly in covering the application methods for decision-making processes. New case studies and applications on management science, operations management, social sciences, and other behavioral sciences have been incorporated into business and organizations real-world objectives.

The **Advances in Logistics, Operations, and Management Science** (ALOMS) Book Series provides a collection of reference publications on the current trends, applications, theories, and practices in the management science field. Providing relevant and current research, this series and its individual publications would be useful for academics, researchers, scholars, and practitioners interested in improving decision making models and business functions.

COVERAGE

- Services management
- Computing and information technologies
- Finance
- Networks
- Information Management
- Operations Management
- Production Management
- Risk Management
- Decision analysis and decision support
- Organizational Behavior

IGI Global is currently accepting manuscripts for publication within this series. To submit a proposal for a volume in this series, please contact our Acquisition Editors at Acquisitions@igi-global.com or visit: http://www.igi-global.com/publish/.

The Advances in Logistics, Operations, and Management Science (ALOMS) Book Series (ISSN 2327-350X) is published by IGI Global, 701 E. Chocolate Avenue, Hershey, PA 17033-1240, USA, www.igi-global.com. This series is composed of titles available for purchase individually; each title is edited to be contextually exclusive from any other title within the series. For pricing and ordering information please visit http://www.igi-global.com/book-series/advances-logistics-operations-management-science/37170. Postmaster: Send all address changes to above address.

Titles in this Series

For a list of additional titles in this series, please visit:
http://www.igi-global.com/book-series/advances-logistics-operations-management-science/37170

Legal, Safety, and Environmental Challenges for Event Management Emerging Research and Opportunities
Vipin Nadda (University of Sunderland, London, UK) Ian Arnott (University of Westminster, London, UK) and Wendy Sealy (University of Chichester, UK)
Business Science Reference • © 2020 • 158pp • H/C (ISBN: 9781799832300) • US $195.00

Multi-Criteria Decision Analysis in Management
Abhishek Behl (Indian Institute of Technology, Bombay, India)
Business Science Reference • © 2020 • 422pp • H/C (ISBN: 9781799822165) • US $245.00

Handbook of Research on Project Management Strategies and Tools for Organizational Success
Nelson Antonio Moreno-Monsalve (Universidad EAN, Colombia) H. Mauricio Diez-Silva (Universidad EAN, Colombia) Flor Nancy Diaz-Piraquive (Universidad Catolica de Colombia, Colombia) and Rafael Ignacio Perez-Uribe (Universidad EAN, Colombia)
Business Science Reference • © 2020 • 537pp • H/C (ISBN: 9781799819349) • US $285.00

Advancing Skill Development for Business Managers in Industry 4.0 Emerging Research and Opportunities
Sara Fazzin (H-Farm College, UK)
Business Science Reference • © 2020 • 168pp • H/C (ISBN: 9781799820369) • US $185.00

Management and Inter/Intra Organizational Relationships in the Textile and Apparel Industry
Vasilica-Maria Margalina (Technical University of Ambato, Ecuador) and José M. Lavín (CESINE University Centre, Spain)
Business Science Reference • © 2020 • 427pp • H/C (ISBN: 9781799818595) • US $215.00

For an entire list of titles in this series, please visit:
http://www.igi-global.com/book-series/advances-logistics-operations-management-science/37170

IGI Global
PUBLISHER of TIMELY KNOWLEDGE

701 East Chocolate Avenue, Hershey, PA 17033, USA
Tel: 717-533-8845 x100 • Fax: 717-533-8661
E-Mail: cust@igi-global.com • www.igi-global.com

Table of Contents

Preface vii

Section 1
Anchoring Culture in Strategy

Chapter 1
Culture and Strategy 1

Chapter 2
Culture Basics 20

Section 2
Learning to See Strategies

Chapter 3
Seeing Business Strategies 38

Chapter 4
Seeing Information Strategies 58

Section 3
Learning to See Cultures

Chapter 5
Seeing Business Cultures 82

Chapter 6
Seeing Information Cultures 124

Section 4
Documenting Strategies and Cultures

Chapter 7
Balancing Organization Strategies and Cultures 160

Chapter 8
Balancing Unit and Team Level Strategies and Cultures.................................202

Chapter 9
Balancing Individual Strategies and Cultures..235

Section 5
Managing Strategic and Cultural Risks

Chapter 10
Strategic and Cultural Risk 268

Chapter 11
Managing Cultural Risks 286

Chapter 12
Building and Managing Cultural Capacity 296

Appendix: Sample Project Plan for Balancing Cultural Risks.................... 306

About the Authors.. 312

Index.. 313

Preface

OVERVIEW OF THE SUBJECT MATTER

Risk is a significant concern for all kinds of organizations. It is easier to see risks associated with tangible assets such as physical or financial resources than risks associated with intangible assets such as culture. Culture is not recorded on the balance sheet. It is challenging to see business risks that are rooted in culture. Culture affects strategy. This book is designed to help you learn to see your cultures, to understand how they affect strategy, and to achieve a better balance between strategy and culture. The authors focus on risks connected with information cultures and information strategies in a business context. Business and information managers have struggled to meet several challenges in aligning these strategies and cultures. First, culture of any form is not easy to see and understand. Second, there is a need to raise awareness of and develop a deeper understanding of culture among business managers and information managers. Third, the consequences of misalignment or misfit of strategy and culture are well known in the business literature, but there is little guidance on how to resolve the problem. Fourth, this alignment process needs to apply to the information environment of organizations. This means expanding the puzzle to align business and information cultures, align business and information strategies, and ensuring that there is a good ongoing fit between information cultures and business strategies. This means we need to raise awareness of the information capabilities of an organization and also the different levels and types of information cultures. This text addresses all four of these challenges. This text draws upon the information science literature, but it extends it from theory and focused case studies to everyday information management practice.

To accomplish this goal, the authors undertook a deep dive into four subject domains, including knowledge and information economies, business and information strategies, business and information cultures, and information management practices. The most significant aspect of writing this book was synthesizing research and practice across these four domains. The most significant challenge was to present the synthesis in a practical way that might be of value to both business and information managers.

WHERE THE TOPIC FITS IN THE WORLD TODAY

This book is written by two authors who have experienced the failure of information strategies in both a practical and research context. In all cases, the information strategy failures can be attributed to a lack of support or direct opposition from business and information cultures. Both authors are also currently engaged in research into the intersection of business and information cultures.

The structure of the book reflects where we looked for guidance, what we found that helped, what we learned through mistakes, and what we learned from our colleagues. Above all, we learned that you cannot use or borrow someone else's strategy or cultural profile. We learned there is a framework you can use to think through the issues. However, you must work through the framework and consider the issues as they relate to your organization. This book provides a framework that can be leveraged by organizations of any type, of any size, and in any region to develop a vision of a knowledge organization in the 21st century. Above all, we learned that any of the answers to the challenges can be found in the organizational culture literature. The most important advice the authors offer is to learn to see culture in the context of strategy and to try to shape it only in that context. The literature and practical experience suggest that wholesale reshaping of cultures rarely succeeds and creates unintended consequences.

The authors suggest that information strategy and culture must be seen from within and shaped to suit the organization's unique business context. This is not a one-person task that is accomplished by sitting in an office for a few weeks. It is not the purview of information managers. It must be owned and lived by the business side of the organization. This is not just a leadership challenge – it must be owned and lived by every member of the organization. We do not achieve this end game by preaching to ourselves. It is a contact sport, and it must be integrated into the day to day operations of an organization to have an impact – to reach its full potential. The framework offered is intended to help you realize an integrated, adopted and lived vision and strategy.

WHERE THE BOOK FITS IN THE LITERATURE TODAY

The authors define the literature to include the peer-reviewed literature, and the gray literature of business strategies, information strategies, business cultures, and information cultures. The authors intend for the book to fill a significant gap in the business management literature – the ability to shape information culture and business culture to support the organization's information strategies. The authors also hope the book interprets the theoretical research for practical use by business managers. The authors also intend for the book to fill a significant gap in the information strategy and information culture literature – an in-depth discussion of information cultures on a practical level.

The authors anchor the discussion of information cultures in the organizational culture research. This extends the treatment of information culture in the information science literature, which tends to focus on the information behavior aspects. The authors extend the coverage to include information assumptions, beliefs, values, norms, and artifacts. The authors also explore the fragmentation of information cultures across different information management areas of practice.

The authors further hope the text will launch a new discussion of what a supportive information culture looks like and how it relates to business and information strategies. The authors suggest that there is a broader role for business and information management professionals and practitioners to play beyond tactics and support functions. In the 21st century, we have an opportunity to advance the field of knowledge management to a core and trusted business capability. The authors hope this text will contribute to realizing that opportunity.

THE INTENDED AUDIENCE FOR THIS BOOK

The audience for this book includes professionals and practitioners in all of those fields described earlier. The three primary audiences are business managers and organizational executives, information managers, and cultural experts and practitioners. The book is intended for business managers and leaders who are responsible for ensuring the success of business and information strategies, to help them shape their work to better meet the demands of a knowledge economy. The book is intended for information managers who have struggled with these challenges on a practical level and are looking for guidance on what to think about and how to frame it for their organizations. In particular, the book is intended for anyone who is familiar with the field of information management but who needs something beyond the general discussions and the ten-page high-level discussions of strategy. The book is intended for cultural practitioners and researchers who need a deeper understanding of information cultures. The book is also designed to stimulate a discussion and prompt a new perspective on the fundamental role of information in the 21st-century knowledge economy.

STRUCTURE OF THE BOOK

The book is organized into five sections and 12 chapters. Section 1 is comprised of two chapters and introduces the reader to Anchoring Culture in Strategy. Section 2 is comprised of two chapters. This section provides a deep dive into business and information strategies and helps the reader learn how to see the full richness of strategies across their organization. Section 3 is comprised of two chapters. This section offers a deep dive into business and information cultures and helps the reader learn to see the full extent of cultures across their organizations. Section 4 is comprised of three chapters focused on documenting what we have learned to see – business and information strategies and cultures at the organization, the unit, and the team, and the individual level. Finally, Section 5 is comprised of three chapters that cover risk and hazards, risk assessment and building an organization's cultural capacity.

Chapter Summaries

The summaries of all 12 chapters are provided below. The reader will also find extensive references to literature, to thought leaders and practitioners in that topic.

Chapter 1 focuses on cultures and strategies. This chapter describes the knowledge economy and explains how it differs from an agrarian and industrial economy. The authors describe the changing role of information in the knowledge economy and the impact of business information assets on knowledge organizations. The chapter stresses the importance of managing information and business strategies, and of aligning information and business cultures. The authors consider what we need to know to align strategies and cultures. Eight essential questions help the reader to translate these issues into his/her environments.

Chapter 2 defines culture and explains the different conceptual models developed by key researchers in the field. The authors explain why it is important for us to learn how to see our cultures. The chapter breaks the conceptual models down into three basic elements, including assumptions and beliefs, values and behaviors, and artifacts. The authors explain why and how each organization's culture is unique – and walk through the factors that influence our organizational cultures. The chapter reminds us that it is hard to deliberately change an organization's culture because it is inherently dynamic. Each organization should strive to understand how these factors affect our organizations.

Chapter 3 is designed to help the reader see their business strategies. This chapter reminds the reader that strategy is an important leverage point. We need a good inventory of our business strategies before we can align and shape cultures to support the. Strategies at all levels of the organization are important – not just those at the top or leadership level. We need to understand our strategies across all functions and the strategies of individuals. It is important to identify not only explicit and well-formed strategies, but those that are implicit, poorly formed and only partially developed. Aligning culture with poor strategies does will not prevent strategies from failing. In the knowledge economy, business strategies should be assessed in terms of their treatment of information assets.

Chapter 4 is designed to help the reader see their information strategies. In the knowledge economy, we must manage information as a strategic business asset. Information must be an essential component of our business strategies, and the information strategy must speak to the business value of information. Information strategies are often formulated and issued only at the organization level. The authors stress the importance of developing information strategies that pertain to business units, teams, and individuals. The authors present an integrated view of information strategies to mirror and support business strategies. The integrated view is a high-level synthesis of the information science literature and practice.

Chapter 5 is designed to help the reader see their business cultures. In this chapter, we focus on the essential elements of culture and consider the factors that may contribute to shaping an organization's unique culture. The authors caution that this is a rich chapter – the goal is to help business managers make the transition from understanding culture at a theoretical level to seeing and managing it on an everyday practical level. In this chapter, the authors explain what we need to know about business cultures. We define business cultures in terms of their structural and dynamic aspects. The authors define three structural levels, including macro-level (global, national), meso-level (organization, unit), and micro-level culture (individual). For each level, a rich set of dynamic factors are identified. This chapter prepares the manager for describing his/her organization's business culture.

Chapter 6 is designed to help us see our information cultures. This chapter reminds us that we care about information cultures because they affect the organization's ability to define and implement a practical and effective information strategy. Just as business culture supports or impedes business strategy, so does information culture support or impede information strategy. Organizations typically have many information cultures, some of which may be contradictory. Left unaddressed, there is a greater danger posed by information cultures in the knowledge economy. Information culture is reflected in the organization's values, norms, and practices concerning the management and use of information. The information science literature provides insufficient treatment to help us understand the day to day impacts of information cultures on business. It also fails to provide an inclusive description of the range of cultures extant in the information management profession and practice. Just like business cultures, information cultures exist and may vary by level of the organization. The authors call out and describe dynamic factors that affect information cultures at all five levels.

Chapter 7 walks the reader through the documentation of organization strategies and cultures. The goal of this chapter is to identify and manage those risks that relate to information strategies and the business' use of information in the knowledge economy. Business and information managers must find a fit that grows our information and business cultures, and supports our business and information strategies. There is no single tool or rule that you can follow to address the risk. The authors provide a framework the reader can work with to think through and develop a fit that works for you today, in the situation. The authors also provide a seven-step methodology any organization can apply to align strategies and culture in any context. To highlight situations and results of strategy-culture inbalance at the organization level, the authors include nine scenarios drawn from real-life experiences.

Chapter 8 walks the reader through the documentation of unit and team strategies and cultures. The goal of this chapter is to identify methods for reducing the risk of strategic failures at the division, the unit, the community, or the team level. In particular, we are interested in managing those risks that relate to information strategies and the business' use of information in the day to day work and operations of any organization. The framework and methodology we follow to identify misalignments, to develop target lists of strategies at risk are the same at these lower levels. What is different is the breadth and depth of business strategies we have to work with, the nature of the impact of lacking or sub-optimized information strategies at the operational level, and the cultural factors we need to see and shape. We establish a general methodology around the framework at the organization level and promote that methodology throughout the organization. The authors walk through the seven-step methodology, noting that line managers and team members must take ownership of and be engaged in the assessment process. To highlight situations and results of strategy-culture imbalance at the unit and team level, the authors include nine scenarios drawn from real-life experiences.

Chapter 9 walks the reader through the documentation of individual strategies and cultures. Strategies may be formulated and published by senior leaders; they may be supported by line managers and by teams. The success of a strategy comes down to the actions of individuals. In particular, we are interested in managing those risks result from an individual's day to day behaviors and actions. What changes at this level? Two things change. First, who conducts the assessment will change. The individual must take responsibility for knowing the organization's strategies, becoming aware of their strategies, and their own cultures. The individual must drive this process. Second, the individual must have a clear understanding of which individuals are responsible for which strategies. To highlight situations and results of strategy-culture inbalance at the individual level, the authors include nine scenarios drawn from real-life experiences.

Chapter 10 focuses on assessing and managing risk. This chapter explores the concepts of harm and risk and translates them to the strategy and culture context. The peer-reviewed and gray literature speak to generic hazards and threats whose consequences might be amplified by cultural and information behaviors and actions. This chapter takes the discussion of hazards and risks one step further by speaking to specific hazards and threats related to organizations' business and information cultures, and information strategies. The business literature tells us that the rate of strategic failure is somewhere between 60% and 90%. The authors describe several common risk factors that can be addressed by redefining the strategic planning process. The authors translate the standard six-step strategic planning process into an extended method to account for cultural and strategic alignment.

Chapter 11 focuses on assessing cultural risks. Risk assessment is a process that allows us to understand risks, define risk criteria, assess the probability and the consequences of that risk occurring, define a level of risk we can tolerate and afford, and define a cost-effective and efficient mitigation treatment.

The authors provide a risk assessment and analysis method which the reader can use to (1) build cultural risk into your organizational risk management profile; and (2) adapt the organization's risk management profile to include cultural risks. The method builds upon but extends the ISO 31000/31010 risk management methodology to determine the level of cultural risk your organization is carrying. The authors walk through and translate each of the seven steps to account for cultural risks.

Chapter 12 focuses on building the cultural capacity, capabilities, and competencies of an organization. Cultural risks can be managed to create value, or they can be ignored to create liabilities. To manage cultural risks, organizations must have a cultural capacity from which to draw. Building cultural capacity is a three-pronged effort. It means building capacity at a strategic level, at an individual level, and collectively. Cultural capacity is achieved through strategic, collective, and individual actions. This chapter considers how organizations can build cultural capacity strategically, collectively, and individually.

HOW THIS BOOK IMPACTS THE FIELD

The authors intend to provide a holistic picture of information cultures, to help business managers understand those cultures, and to provide a foundation upon which to ground and grow future information culture research. The authors hope the practical coverage of the issues will encourage information professionals to undertake new research into these topics. The authors also intend to offer business managers a text that will help to reduce the rate of failure of information strategies.

The goal of the book is to create a new dialog among business and information managers and organizational culture researchers. We hope the practical treatment will encourage those in the business community engaged in strategy development and organizational standards to expand their coverage and treatment of information cultures and information strategies.

Bridging these perspectives and areas of practice is essential for success in the knowledge economy. This new context calls for a coalescing of perspectives and practices and a new focus on knowledge organizations and economic transitions. Until this dialog begins, each area of practice will operate in isolation. Until this dialog begins, each area of practice will focus on a part of the solution. Until this dialog begins, no one area of practice will effectively address the challenge. The authors hope this book will be a catalyst for that dialog.

NOTE FROM THE AUTHORS

Over the past year the authors have jointly conducted and shared their research, synthesized what they found in the literature, and blended our two different perspectives on organizational culture. This is an on-going learning process for us. It was not possible for us include everything we have learned over the years. Dr. Kucharska's wealth of knowledge and experience with business and corporate environments is only partially represented in this text. For a full representation of her work, we refer the reader to her many peer-reviewed papers. Dr. Bedford's contributions represent forty years of "lessons learned" in a wide range of organizational settings and economic sectors. We hope that the blending of our theoretical knowledge and practical experiences is of value to the reader.

Section 1
Anchoring Culture in Strategy

Chapter 1
Culture and Strategy

ABSTRACT

This chapter describes the knowledge economy and explains how it differs from an agrarian and industrial economy. The authors describe the changing role of information in the knowledge economy and the impact of business information assets on knowledge organizations. The chapter stresses the importance of managing information and business strategies, and of aligning information and business cultures. The authors consider what we need to know to align strategies and cultures. Eight essential questions help the reader to translate these issues into his/her environment.

ROLE OF INFORMATION IN THE NEW ECONOMY

In 2019, there is a consensus about the knowledge economy's basic factors and behaviors and how these differ from the earlier agrarian and industrial economies. In agrarian economies, the basic factors of production were land and resources. In this economy, the nature of work was extraction – whether through agriculture, mining, or other forms of leveraging natural resources. In the industrial economy, the primary factor of production is financial and equipment. In this type of economy, the nature of work is fabrication and manufacturing.

The essence of the knowledge economy is the idea that knowledge capital replaces financial and physical capital as the primary factor of production and the primary source of wealth. The concept of a knowledge economy was first presented by Machlup (1962) in his groundbreaking research into the

DOI: 10.4018/978-1-7998-4315-3.ch001

shifts in the national accounts. Research into and characterizations of the knowledge economy have continued over the decades (Bell, 1976; Porat and Rubin, 1977; Baumol Braunstein Fisher and Ordover, 1980; Antonelli and David, 2015; Drucker, 2013).

In the knowledge economy, the primary factor of production is knowledge – what people know and what they know how to do. Knowledge is the natural resource, and knowledge processes are the means of production in the knowledge economy. New economies never entirely replace earlier economies, but they significantly change those economies.

These early characterizations of a knowledge and knowledge economy are important. However, they do not describe the seismic shift in attitude and practice that has taken place in the last 20 years. In the past sixty years, we have moved from academic research into the knowledge economy to everyday management of businesses struggling to survive in a knowledge economy. Today, knowledge plays a critical role in every organization, every day, in every function and process, and the work of every individual (Kucharska and Bedford, 2019). The world economy is now dominated by knowledge capitalism. Knowledge is recognized as an economically valuable resource. Organizations, teams, and individuals must produce, consume, and leverage knowledge in every aspect of their work. Knowledge is a critical resource of every type of organization in every sector. This means that our business strategies need to be adaptable, agile, and dynamic. Just as we developed business strategies to support business cycles in the industrial economy, today, we must develop business strategies that align with the knowledge economy.

The knowledge economy shifts how we do agriculture, how we do resource extraction, how we manufacture, and how we do innovation. The knowledge economy also significantly shifts who can become a primary economic player. An individual with ideas and knowledge competencies can become a primary player - an individual no longer needs significant financial or physical capital to become a significant producer in the 21st century. This means that who engages in a market is dynamic. It means that an organization's position and role in a market is no longer determined only by the amount of financial and physical capital they control. Information and knowledge workers are independent producers of knowledge and information in these markets. It means that individuals who understand how to leverage their knowledge capital can be competitive. It means that organizations that do not leverage or manage their knowledge capital are at risk in a market. This means that an individual's, a team's, and an organization's business strategy must take knowledge capital into account. This means ensuring that our business strategies leverage information and treat information like a critical knowledge asset. It means that our information strategies must align with and support our business visions and goals. Today we treat information as knowledge capital. Knowledge capital requires much more sophisticated, comprehensive and inclusive strategies (Bontis, 2003; Ceruti Williams Bedford, 2019; Bedford, 2012; Bedford, 2020; Handa Pagani Bedford, 2019; Allee, 2000; Allee, 2009; Allee, 2012; Snowden, 2003).

ROLE OF CULTURE AND STRATEGY IN THE NEW ECONOMY

As we consider the history and evolution of strategy, it becomes apparent that strategy is an industrial economy management method and mental model. Humans have always had their informal strategies – paths and methods they use to achieve their personal and professional goals. But, formal strategies, strategy development, and strategic planning are all methods developed by businesses and organizations to manage paths to goals that leverage more extensive resources than those of a single individual. Strategies are now a formal management tool. While this is the case, it is also true that there is still significant variation in how well organizations do strategies. There is more work to be done in this area. The challenge is that the economic ground is shifting under organizations today. Organizations that have a strong strategy component will need to adapt them to the new economic assumptions and factors. Those organizations that have not yet mastered strategies have an opportunity to reinvent their efforts.

All organizations need to realize that the role of strategies and the players are changing. Strategies are no longer formulated only by the top leadership. In organizations whose cultures are increasingly creative, innovative and participatory – strategies at the unit and the individual level are as important as those at the organization level. In industrial-era management structures, culture has consistently been under-rated, under-estimated, and under-leveraged. As a result, where culture and strategy do not align, culture has always prevailed. Culture will always "eat strategy for breakfast" given the opportunity. This was the case even when strategies are well-formed and well-promoted. If the culture is at odds, the strategy will fail. In the knowledge economy, culture is already playing a dominant role. Managers and individuals need to learn to see cultures and to understand how to leverage them to support strategy.

In the knowledge economy and organizations with shifting behaviors and expectations, we should expect culture to be an increasingly important and perhaps dominant factor in whether and how an organization achieves its business goals. The bottom line – and the authors' motivation for writing this book - is that both strategies and cultures play a much more pivotal role in the knowledge economy. A new role of managers and staff is learning how to align cultures and strategies – at every level of the organization. This book attempts to address some of the issues we need to think about in the 21st century.

ALIGNING BUSINESS AND INFORMATION CULTURES AND STRATEGIES

Culture and strategy are co-dependent. Every organization has a culture that exerts powerful influences on the behavior of units, teams, and individuals. For better or worse, an organization's culture has a significant impact on an organization's ability to carry out objectives. When a team or an organization's culture is not well aligned with its strategy – conventional business wisdom tells us that the "company culture will eat strategy for breakfast" (Peter Drucker cited in Kesterson, 2015, p. 56). It is critical as business strategies adapt, so must cultures. A business strategy that is well designed for the knowledge economy will fail if it exists within an industrial or agricultural era culture. It is critical in the knowledge economy that there is a good fit between the knowledge strategy and the knowledge culture.

How can organizations better align their business and information strategies and cultures? In this dynamic environment, organizations may find that culture is a source of strength or weakness (Schwartz and Davis, 1981). It is essential to know your culture well enough to be able to leverage it to support your strategy. Organizations must be able to "see" their business strategies in a new context. They must be able to "see" their business cultures. Moreover, they must be able to characterize and assess their knowledge strategies and knowledge cultures. Finally, they must routinely assess the goodness of fit of these elements – and design a fit that best suits their business context at any given point in time.

Figure 1. Alignment of strategies and cultures – business and information

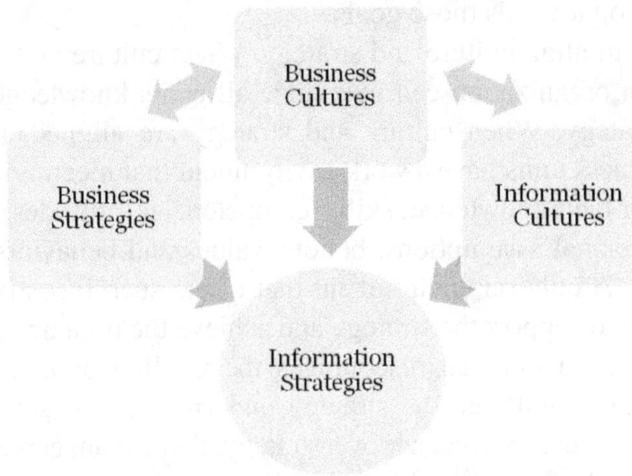

It is the strategic fit of the culture that the organization must solve. However, this is not a one-dimensional challenge. First, we must ensure that all of the business strategies are aligned. A strategy is the firm's overall expression of its main objectives as well as its primary means to accomplish it. The strategic fit must be accomplished at all levels of the organization – enterprise, function or line of business, and individual. Organizations cannot assume that all of their business strategies are in total alignment in a knowledge economy. Strategic fit is the situation in which all the internal and external elements relevant to an organization are aligned with each other and with the business strategy. In a dynamic economy, we must assume that alignment across the organization will also be an agile and dynamic activity.

It is an organization's culture rather than a strategy, which is the key to understanding organizational success. If the culture is right, then the right strategy can be implemented. While strategic alignment is the functional imperative, it is organization culture, which is the critical success factor. In the field of strategic management, culture is seen primarily as a constraint to deep-seated organizational change. Cultural risk helps us to understand when a particular strategy is likely to fail. How do we manage cultural risk? We manage cultural risk by ensuring the culture is best suited to the mission, aims, and business context of the particular organization. There is no perfect culture – the suitable culture is an appropriate pattern of behavior that enables the organization to achieve its goals and fulfill the mission. What set of assumptions, beliefs, values, and behaviors do you need to support your strategy? A suitable culture helps to ensure that the everyday decisions and actions move you towards those goals.

It is crucial to align culture and strategy. When culture and strategy are in harmony, an organization can maximize all of its knowledge capital to achieve its strategy. When culture and strategy are aligned, individuals, teams and business units have a work environment that incentivizes them to contribute their tacit knowledge, skills, competencies, attitudes, procedural knowledge, personal assumptions, beliefs, values and behaviors, networks and reputation. A cultural environment that offers such incentives enables an organization to support the strategy and achieve the organization's goals. A working environment that discourages the pooling of knowledge and information capital will see the strategy undermined and sub-optimized. Culture will always take precedence over strategy. Those managers and workers who understand the culture and how it behaves have the power to shape it to support or undermine strategy. Business managers must understand what affects their culture to ensure it is aligned with and supports your strategy.

It is also true that not even the most robust culture can implement a poorly formed or ill-conceived strategy. Too often, managers develop strategies their companies cannot implement without making significant changes in their corporate cultures? There may be three reasons for this. 1 some Executives do not consider the time and energy and take to match strategy and culture. To others, lack the skills the soft skills necessary for successfully managing strategy and culture together. Three others change either strategy or culture but do not change both together. Weak strategies and weak cultures make weak tools. In the industrial economy, it may have been acceptable to see our organizations as well-tuned machines and to handle change through simple recalibration. This approach does not work in the knowledge economy. Strategy alone cannot create Excellence. Neither can culture. Like a sound mind in a sound body, only by working in harmony can strategy and culture work together to help us achieve business goals.

The nature of the culture strategy fit depends on the strength of the strategy, reaching from extremely vague to extremely precise. If the strategy is extremely vague, it harmonizes with any culture. Only with a precise strategy is there a possibility of a misfit. There are many ways how a strong corporate culture can guide the decisions and behavior of individuals in an organization.

WHAT YOU NEED TO KNOW TO ALIGN CULTURE AND STRATEGY

What do you need to understand to determine whether you have a misalignment? What do you need to know to determine the level of cultural risk you might be carrying? What do you need to see to design a better alignment between strategy and culture? You need to know whether your business and information strategies and cultures are aligned or out of alignment, where the misalignments exist within the organization, the cause of the misalignment, and the degree of risk the misalignment introduces. You also need to know what level of risk you are willing to accept. Once you have an understanding of these issues, you can identify an option for mitigating risk.

The authors pose seven questions that will help the reader work through these issues. The seven questions include:

- Question 1. How might strategy and culture not align?
- Question 2. What factors might cause a misalignment?
- Question 3. How can we assess the risk associated with the misalignment?
- Question 4. What actions might managers take to reconcile culture and strategy?
- Question 5. What do we need to know about business cultures to fit it into your business strategy?
- Question 6. What do you need to know about the business strategy to order to design a supportive business culture?
- Question 7. What do you need to know about the information strategy to align it with business strategy?
- Question 8. What do you need to know about information cultures to align it with business cultures?

QUESTION 1. HOW MIGHT CULTURE AND STRATEGY NOT ALIGN?

There are several situations in which culture and strategy might not align. In some situations, the cause may lie with the business strategy. The strategy might be too vague; it might be a simple statement of principles or vision. In other cases, it may be too precise, prescriptive, and detailed. In this case, it more closely resembles tactics or methods than actual strategies. In these cases, the best formed or conceived knowledge culture cannot compensate for a poor strategy. In some situations, the strategy may be very well formed, but the challenge is on the cultural side. A culture that is too rigidly controlled at the top levels of the organization may not allow sufficient creativity or flexibility for strategies to be effectively or efficiently implemented. At the other end of the spectrum, an organization's culture may be anarchic and offer little coordinated support for the strategy. Alignments may result in any of these situations. These misalignments may be compounded if they persist across levels of the organization.

Table 1. Possible strategy and culture misalignments

	Vague Strategy or Principles Only	Well-Formed Strategy	Prescriptive Strategy or Tactics
Rigid Culture	High Risk	Moderate Risk	High Risk
Well Managed Culture	Moderate Risk	Low Risk	Moderate Risk
Anarchic or Chaotic Culture	High Risk	Moderate Risk	High Risk

We usually use strategy to navigate change in the world of business. In the knowledge economy, though, this may not be sufficient. We must consider culture. To correct a misalignment, we must consider how culture and strategy fit and support each other. If you have a "Strategy X" what kind of a "Culture Y" do you need? What kind of a culture do you have now, and how does it need to shift? If you have a 'Culture Y', how should you design your 'Strategy X'? What factors do you need to think about in terms of strategy and the primary factors that will affect "the fit"?

It is important to note that while we can characterize a strategy as well-formed or poorly formed, it is more challenging to characterize the nature of organizational culture. It is important to state early on that it is not the intent of the authors to characterize an organization's culture as good or bad. Rather, it is essential to understand how the nature of the culture supports or impedes the strategy. An organization may assess its culture and have a stellar rating from an academic perspective, but if that culture does not support the strategy or align with the business environment, that rating has little business value.

QUESTION 2. WHAT FACTORS MIGHT CAUSE A MISALIGNMENT?

There are many situations in which a misaligned might develop. We offer a few to demonstrate how common this might be. Consider an organization that has a strong historical culture developed decades ago by its founders in an industrial economy. Strategy and culture might have been aligned then, but the business environment has changed so dramatically that new strategies are needed. The new strategy conflicts with the culture. Or, a company grows at a rapid rate, and its strategy has simply outpaced its culture. To keep up with the new business environment, the organization has hired 45% of its original staffing levels – all under the age of 35. Another common situation might be that an organization has failed to keep pace with its business environment, and senior executives must change both the strategy and the culture to rescue the organization from bankruptcy and failure. Consider an organization with a well-established and aligned business culture and strategy which is caught in a market shift. In this case, both the strategy and the culture may need to shift to remain viable in the new market. Organizations will always need to develop new business strategies. As noted earlier, strategies can be expected to change more rapidly in the knowledge economy than in other economies. Strong cultures must adapt to changing environments if they do not adapt, they will wither. If they over adapt, changing too many fundamental aspects at once, they may die. If a new strategy means the culture must change too quickly or too much, both the strategy and the culture might fail. It is always essential to calibrate strategy and culture to suit a situation. Fine-tuning strategy and culture provide the key to survival in the knowledge economy. (Hickman – Creating Excellence)

QUESTION 3. HOW CAN WE ASSESS THE RISK ASSOCIATED WITH A MISALIGNMENT?

Managers would need to know how much cultural risk is there in my portfolio of businesses, each with its strategy and approach to implementation. How is this risk spread across the business? What are the specific sources of cultural risk, and do any patterns emerge across my portfolio? If too many important business units are at significant cultural risk, is the total corporate strategy in danger? The degree of cultural risk depends on the answers to these questions. How important is each organizational approach to the success of the strategy? How compatible is each approach with the division's current culture? Significant risks result from organizational approaches that are highly important to the success of the pro strategy but are not compatible with the existing culture. In assessing the importance of each organizational approach to the strategy we have found it important to consider several key points.

- What specific behavior is the organizational approach designed to encourage?
- How will the Key Management task be affected? How will import relationships be affected?
- How this behavior is linked to critical success factors?
- What specific customer needs our requirements is the behavior intended to satisfy?
- What competitive advantage will be gained in the market?
- What impact will such Behavior have on?
- What impact will this Behavior have on external factors?
- How much change is involved?
- How adaptable is the culture?
- How skilled is the management in managing culture?
- How much change is envisioned, and how realistic is it given the current culture?

QUESTION 4. WHAT ACTIONS MIGHT MANAGERS TAKE TO RECONCILE CULTURE AND STRATEGY?

Anything that makes the implementation of strategy more compatible with the culture or reduces the strategic significance of the behavior tends to reduce cultural risk. In most situations, when a misalignment is identified, the question management most often asks is - should you change the strategy or the culture? Rather, the question is not that simple. There are four common options (Dennison Hooijberg Lane and Lief, 2012; Campbell, 1992; Tosti, 2012), including (1) they simply ignore the culture; (2) they attempt to change the culture to fit the strategy; (3) they change the strategy to fit the culture; and (4) they adopt the culture to suit the strategy in a given context (Figure 2). The challenges and consequences of each of these options are discussed below.

Figure 2. Four options to correct a strategy culture misalignment

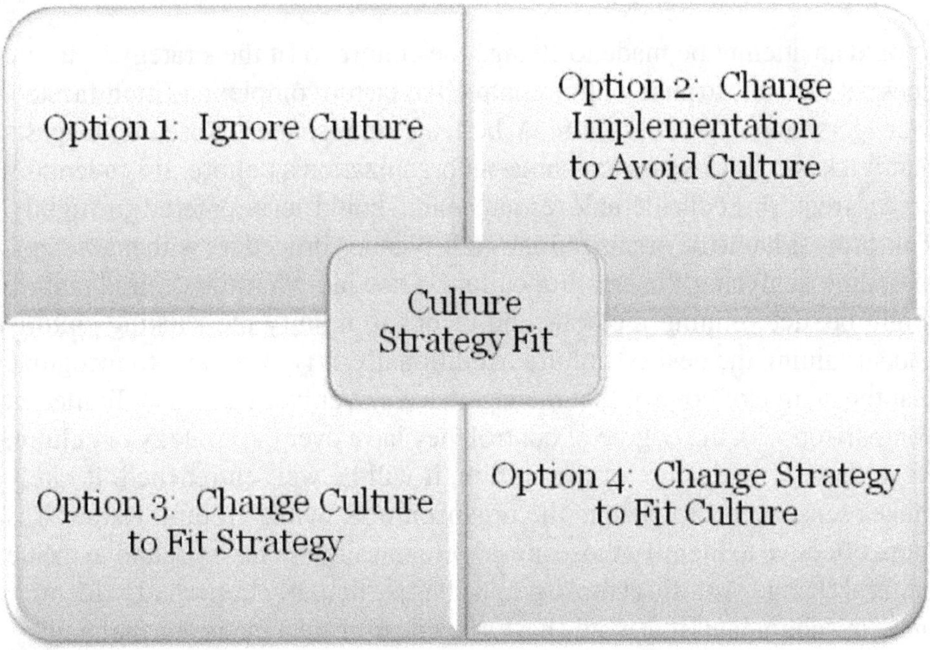

Option 1. Ignore the Culture

Can the impact of an organization's culture be safely ignored? Should ways be sought to manage around the culture? It is rarely a good strategy to ignore culture. Ignoring culture may have significant consequences for strategy – strategic proposals may be rejected as too radical and too inconsistent with the organization's function cultures or professional cultures to warrant a risk. Culture can seldom be ignored when making management decisions or changes in the knowledge economy. Whether consciously or unconsciously, most managers and decision-makers consider culture. Ignoring culture puts the strategy and the organization's survival at risk. We know that culture will always overcome strategy, so this is not just a neutral option without consequences - it is, in fact, a negative result. Organizations will continue to put resources into strategy development and strategic planning, but those resources will be wasted – because they will generate little or no benefit. Also, there is a strong possibility of a negative psychological and cultural impact when strategies do not succeed. A cursory cost-benefit analysis of this option would suggest there is little or no benefit but continued high costs and risks.

Option 2. Change the Culture to Fit the Strategy

Should an attempt be made to change the culture to fit the strategy? Culture does not succumb to push-button control. It is far too complex and multifaceted. Managers cannot control culture. At best, they may shape it. Research suggests that it takes 6 to 15 years to change an organization's culture. It is a lengthy process requiring considerable resources and should not be entered into lightly. This process has to be organized as a well-planned procedure with main steps, including analyzing the existing culture, knowing what the desired culture might be, determining methods and tactics to modify the existing culture, and sustaining the desired culture. Additionally, it is important to recognize that the degree of control that managers have over culture is very limited in comparison with the degree of control they have over the strategy or culture. Regardless of the nature of the culture, it will be well-entrenched. It rarely makes sense to try to change the organization's whole culture. Rather it is more effective to identify those areas were misalignments exist and to tackle cultural change or shifts at those points. It is particularly important to identify those misalignments that would have a business-critical impact on the strategy. An organization's culture is most effectively changed by gradually reducing the perceived differences between current and desired cultures, by increasing the value that the culture places on adaptability and enhancing the ability of managers involved to affect the change.

In short, changing the culture is a long term effort. Changing the culture is incredibly expensive in terms of time and effort. There is an opportunity cost to those people who are charged to change the culture – if the change does not happen, there may be negative consequences to them. Culture is not a monolithic thing – an organization has multiple cultures – so any effort to change the culture in a single, all-encompassing effort is likely to fail. Each element, each level of the culture must be changed and adapted. There may also be a backlash to attempting to change the culture wholesale and directly – elements of the culture may "dig in" or become more entrenched. If the cultural change is associated with a single individual and that individual leaves, the change may be abandoned. Cultural change needs to be top-down, bottom-up, middle-in and middle-out. Because of the long-term nature of cultural change, such an attempt is unlikely to have a positive impact on strategy in the short term. From a cost-benefit perspective, this option has very high one-time costs and some potential benefits. However, the probability of success is low. The potential for future recurring costs is also high.

Option 3. Change the Strategy to Fit the Culture

Should strategy be changed to one that is more compatible with the existing culture? Changing the strategy to suit the culture brings cultural risk to a manageable level. However, it puts strategy at risk. Strategies are developed to ensure that the organization can succeed in the market in its industry and sector and deliver value to its stakeholders. If you adapt the strategy to suit the internal culture, what level of business risk will you incur? Strategies should take into consideration internal capacity and capabilities but also the external environment in which it must perform and succeed. This option compromises the organization's performance potential and its ability to adapt to the external environment to suit the internal culture.

From a business perspective, this option is less desirable than Option 1. In Option 3, you will sacrifice your business strategy to favor culture. While there may not be a "bad" or a "good" culture per se, cultures can be characterized as being supportive or in opposition to strategy. The cost of adopting a suboptimal strategy, to avoid adapting or changing culture carries significant business risks. From a cost-benefit perspective, the real business costs of sub optimizing strategy are high. And, the benefit is low or negative. In this scenario, the business runs the risk of actually losing value.

Option 4. Adapt the Culture to Suit the Strategy in a Given Context

This is the best option because it allows you to design a solution for a given context and a given point in time. Ideally, this option allows an organization to integrate cultural analysis at the start of the strategy development process. What does it mean to take this option? To take this option, it means understanding the goals that the strategy is designed to achieve and how those strategies will help you to achieve those goals. It means considering the cultural implications of each possible strategy – wherever they may be found across the organization. It means developing an understanding of the cultures of the units, teams, and individuals who will support each strategy.

To take this option, you will need to understand what your cultural risks are and how to asses them. You'll need to be able to calculate the cultural risks for each strategy and the cultural change that is needed to support each strategy. This means determining the probability of success of any attempt to change the culture, however small. It means building the cultural adjustment costs and benefits into the strategic planning process. It means ensuring that you have cultural support individuals assigned to the mission or project. It also means raising awareness of the importance of cultural adjustment and adaptation across the organization, and ensuring it is part of every project plan.

From a cost-benefit perspective, this is perhaps the most balanced of all four options. There is a cost to any strategy of adjusting the culture, but the costs are balanced by the probability of benefit and value. The benefit takes the form of an effective strategy and business outcome. Over the long term, there is also a benefit to the organization because units and individuals have had an opportunity to see that adaptation is possible and that they can grow with the organization.

Questions 5, 6, and 7 presume that the reader will select the most effective option for their organization. Experience and research suggest this will be Option 4. However, these questions are important, regardless of which option you chose to follow.

QUESTION 5. WHAT DO WE NEED TO ABOUT CULTURE TO FIT IT TO STRATEGY?

While the strategy is our primary focus, culture is the dominant factor. It is the greatest challenge. To be effective in aligning culture to support our business strategies, we need to know what it is. We need to be able to "see it" – to make it visible and manageable – if we expect to shape it. We need to know how to create an objective picture of it at all levels of the organization. We need to know what factors shape it and how these factors play out in a given context and at a given point in time. And, we need to know where cultures are in harmony and where they are in conflict. You need to know (1) which cultures are you trying to change; (2) which culture is dominant; (3) whose assumptions and beliefs you are trying to change; (4) whose values and behaviors are you changing; and (5) how your culture relates to culture.

Most managers are comfortable with the idea that their organizations have a cultural dimension. They are though unsure about what that word means in a business context and what they could make of a better understanding of their organizations. Most managers lack culture awareness – simply because this is not part of their education or training. Managers should heighten their cultural awareness and learn to see the cultures at play in their organizations and units. Cultural awareness must always precede understanding, developing, changing, and perfecting a culture. A good culture takes time to build, and it must be able to evolve with changing conditions (Hickman – Creating Excellence).

QUESTION 6. WHAT DO YOU NEED TO KNOW ABOUT THE BUSINESS STRATEGY TO DEFINE SUPPORTIVE CULTURES?

Remember that we're taking strategy as our starting point. We need to understand enough about our strategy to know where cultures present a risk. What do we need to know about strategy to align it with culture? We need to know what our strategy is – at all levels and in all areas of operation. We need to know how to find strategies across the organization – to make them visible. We need to know how to create a whole organization description of our business strategies. We need to know how they fit together and where there are gaps or conflicts.

QUESTION 7. WHAT YOU NEED TO KNOW ABOUT YOUR INFORMATION STRATEGY FOR ALIGNMENT

Aligning business cultures and strategies is a complex effort. In the knowledge economy, our task is doubly complex because we must extend our reach beyond business cultures and strategies to include knowledge and information strategies. To succeed in the knowledge economy, we need to know what knowledge and information strategies are in place, where we have gaps, and where we have misalignments. In the new economy, we must increase our awareness of the role that information plays in organizations, and consider how to integrate information strategies and cultures with the business level. This is not a trivial task because knowledge and information strategies may be embedded in other strategies, they may be implicit to the way we work, and they may reflect our basic assumptions and beliefs, or not part of any formal business strategy. An organization may have vague or visionary information strategies – for which there are no or only loose methods for implementing. They may be interpreted in a variety of ways. Alternatively, they may be embedded only in the everyday operations and practices of information professionals. The approach we use for discovering and aligning business strategies and cultures can, and should, be applied to information strategies.

QUESTION 8. WHAT YOU NEED TO KNOW ABOUT YOUR INFORMATION CULTURE FOR ALIGNMENT

Information cultures have all of the same challenges and opportunities of business cultures. However, information cultures may be grounded in two distinct sets of assumptions and beliefs. The first set reflects the business view of the information. The second reflects the information professional's view. These two views are often at odds in organizations. This is a common source of failure for adopting and promoting information strategies.

TAKING EFFECTIVE ACTION - INTEGRATING CULTURAL ANALYSIS AND STRATEGY DEVELOPMENT

As we noted in Figure 1, our focus is on the effective implementation of a knowledge and information strategy. Our chances of success will be improved if those knowledge and information strategies are well aligned with business strategies, business cultures, and information cultures. We have suggested that the most effective approach to aligning these elements is to focus on strategy and to identify and adjust culture to support those strategies. How does this translate to knowledge and information strategies? At a high level, this means:

- Finding and understanding your business strategies wherever they exist
- Identifying the cultural support implications of each strategy
- Developing an understanding of the cultures of the units, teams, and individuals who will support each strategy
- Identifying your cultural risks and assessing their impact on strategy
- Identify the cultural change that is needed to support each strategy
- Building the cultural risks, need, adjustment costs and benefits into the strategic planning process
- Ensuring that you have cultural support individuals assigned to the mission or project and awareness of the importance of cultural adjustment and adaptation across the organization, and ensuring it is part of every project plan.

The remaining chapters in this text are designed to guide you through these considerations.

CONCLUSION

After reading this chapter, you should be able to:

- Explain the role of information in the knowledge economy
- Explain why it is essential to align cultures and strategies
- Explain why it is essential to integrate business and information strategies
- Describe what we need to know to align culture and strategy
- Describe the four options for reconciling culture and strategy differences
- Explain how to integrate cultural analysis in the strategy development process

REFERENCES

Allee, V. (2000). The value evolution: Addressing larger implications of an intellectual capital and intangibles perspective. *Journal of Intellectual Capital*, *1*(1), 17–32. doi:10.1108/14691930010371627

Allee, V. (2009). *The future of knowledge*. Routledge. doi:10.4324/9780080507156

Allee, V. (2012). *The knowledge evolution*. Routledge. doi:10.4324/9780080509808

Antonelli, C., & David, P. (2015). *The economics of knowledge and the knowledge driven economy*. Routledge.

Baumol, W. J., Branunstein, Y., Fisher, D. M., & Ordover, J. A. (1980). *Manual of pricing and cost determination of organizations engaged in dissemination of knowledge*. Academic Press.

Bedford, D. (2012). Expanding the definition and measurement of knowledge economy-integrating triple bottom line factors into knowledge economy index models and methodologies. In *Proceedings of the European Conference on Intellectual Capital* (pp. 67-74). Academic Press.

Bedford, D. A. (2012). The role of knowledge management in creating transformational organizations and transformational leaders. *Journal of Knowledge Management Practice, 13*(4), 32–44.

Bell, D. (1976, May). The coming of the post-industrial society. *The Educational Forum, 40*(4), 574–579. doi:10.1080/00131727609336501

Bontis, N. (2003). Intellectual capital disclosure in Canadian corporations. *Journal of Human Resource Costing and Accounting, 7*(1), 9-20.

Campbell, A. (1992). *The power of missions: Aligning strategy and culture.* Planning Review.

Ceruti, M., Williams, A., & Bedford, D. (2019). Knowledge Organizations. In *Translating Knowledge Management Visions into Strategies.* Emerald Publishing Limited London. doi:10.1108/978-1-78973-763-920191004

Drucker, P. (2013). *Managing for the Future.* Routledge. doi:10.4324/9780080938059

Drucker, P. F. (1971). *Drucker on management.* Management Publications.

Handa, P., Pagani, J., & Bedford, D. (2019). *Knowledge Assets and Knowledge Audits (Working Methods for Knowledge Management).* Emerald Publishing Limited London.

Kesterson, R. K. (2015). *The Basics of Hoshin Kanri.* CRC Press, Taylor & Francis.

Kucharska, W., & Bedford, D. A. D. (2019). Knowledge Sharing and Organizational Culture Dimensions: Does Job Satisfaction Matter? *Electronic Journal of Knowledge Management, 17*(1), 1–18. doi:10.2139srn.3406496

Kumar, K. (1978). *Prophecy and progress: The sociology of industrial and post-industrial society.* New York: Penguin Books.

Machlup, F. (1962). *The production and distribution of knowledge in the United States* (Vol. 278). Princeton university press.

Porat, M. U., & Rubin, M. R. (1977). *The information economy: Definition and measurement* (Vol. 77, No. 12). The Office.

Snowden, D. (2003). Innovation as an objective of knowledge management. Part I: The landscape of management. *Knowledge Management Research and Practice*, *1*(2), 113–119. doi:10.1057/palgrave.kmrp.8500014

Tosti, D. T. (2007). Aligning the culture and strategy for success. *Performance Improvement*, *46*(1), 21–25. doi:10.1002/pfi.035

ADDITIONAL READING

Cameron, K. (2008). A process for changing organization culture. Handbook of organization development, 14(5), 2-18.

Choo, C. W., & Bontis, N. (Eds.). (2002). *The strategic management of intellectual capital and organizational knowledge*. Oxford University Press on Demand.

Denison, D., Hooijberg, R., Lane, N., & Lief, C. (2012). *Leading culture change in global organizations: Aligning culture and strategy* (Vol. 394). John Wiley & Sons.

Godin, B. (2008). The knowledge economy: Fritz Machlup's construction of a synthetic concept. *Project on the history and sociology of S&T statistics working paper*, (37), 33.

Hesselbein, F. (1997). *The Organization of the Future. The Drucker Foundation Future Series* (p. 94104). San Francisco, CA: Jossey-Bass Inc., Publishers.

Kander, A. (2005). Baumol's disease and dematerialization of the economy. *Ecological Economics*, *55*(1), 119–130. doi:10.1016/j.ecolecon.2004.10.008

Osberg, L., Wolff, E. N., & Baumol, W. J. (1989). *The information economy: The implications of unbalanced growth*. IRPP.

Wolff, E., & Baumol, W. J. (1989). Sources of postwar growth of information activity in the United States. In The information economy: The implications of unbalanced growth (pp. 17-46).

Chapter 2
Culture Basics

ABSTRACT

This chapter defines culture and explains the different conceptual models developed by key researchers in the field. The authors explain why it is essential for us to learn how to see our cultures. The chapter breaks the conceptual models down into three essential elements, including assumptions and beliefs, values and behaviors, and artifacts. The authors explain why and how each organization's culture is unique – and walk through the factors that influence our organizational cultures. The chapter reminds us that it is hard to deliberately change an organization's culture because it is inherently dynamic. Each organization should strive to understand how these factors affect our organizations.

CULTURE – DEFINITIONS AND CHARACTERIZATIONS

Culture is difficult to recognize – it is difficult to see and expose our underlying assumptions and beliefs, our values and behaviors, and to interpret our cultural artifacts. Culture is complex – as a collective asset, it is an aggregation of the cultures of individuals, business units, and the entire membership of the group or organization. Culture is refined and expanded by each individual in the organization. Culture is dynamic and continuously evolving. Culture is multi-directional. Culture is both the way we do things around here and what we do when we think no one is looking. Culture is the code, the core Logic, the software of the mind that organizes the behavior of the people, and

DOI: 10.4018/978-1-7998-4315-3.ch002

the lessons that we have learned that are important enough to pass on to the next generation (Denison, 1990; Denison Hooijberg Lane and Leif, 2012).

Culture is viewed as a shared mental model that influences how individuals interpret behaviors, and they often behave without their being aware of the underlying assumptions. Culture is learned, reinforced, and handed on as learning to the Next Generation and new members of groups. Culture has a purpose in terms of achieving common objectives. Perceive success will reinforce the culture and make it stronger. An organization or group will develop its distinct patterns of behaviors and beliefs to support the culture and the internal socialization process.

CULTURE – THE BODY OF KNOWLEDGE

Organizational culture has been defined in many ways by various authors and researchers. There is general agreement that organizational culture can be referred as a set of values, beliefs, and behavior patterns that form its core identity and shape everyday behaviors (Deal and Kennedy, 1982; Jones, 1983; Schein, 1992; Kotter and Heskett, 1992; Pheysey, 1993; Van der Post, 1998; Deshpande and Farley, 1999). Hofstede defines culture as the collective programming of the mind that distinguishes the members of one category of people from another. The fundamental expression in this definition is the collected programming. It describes a process to which each of each one of us has been subjected since birth. When parents returning from the hospital carry you over the threshold, they have often already made their first culturally-based decision.

Frost defines culture to mean rituals, myths, stories, legends, interpretation of events, ideas, and experiences that are influenced and shaped by the groups within which they live. Organizational culture includes values and assumptions about social reality. Culture provides the shared rules governing cognitive and affective aspects of membership in an organization, and the means whereby they are shaped and expressed. Culture is not primarily inside people's heads, but somewhere between the heads of a group of people, workgroup interactions, in board meetings, but also in material objects. Culture then is central and describes our behaviors, social events, institutions, and processes. Culture is the setting in which these phenomena become comprehensible and meaningful. Culture provides group members with a shared understanding, feelings of clarity, Direction, meaning, and purpose.

The most notable researcher, though, is Edgar Schein. Schein (1992) defined organizational culture as a pattern of underlying assumptions invented, discovered, or developed by a given group as it learns to cope with its problem of external adaptation and internal integration. These values are then taught to new members in the organization as the correct way to think and feel about those problems. For Schein (1992), culture is the total of all the shared, taken for granted assumptions that a group has learned throughout its history. Also, culture is determined to be the residue of success. Culture is also the structure and control system to generate behavioral standards. Corporate culture has to be kept strictly apart from similar-looking concepts like corporate identity, organizational climate, or the national culture. Corporate culture is the implicit, invisible, intrinsic, and informal consciousness of the organization which guides the behavior of the individuals and which shapes itself out of the behavior.

Schein defines culture in a particularly useful way for organizational management. Shine defines organizational culture as a pattern of shared underlying assumptions that was learned by a group as it solved his problems of external adaptation and internal integration, which has worked well enough to be considered valid and, therefore, to be taught to new members as the correct way to perceive, think, and feel about those problems. Shein's classic approach divides culture into three levels. He argues that basic underlying assumptions lie at the root of culture and our unconscious, taken-for-granted beliefs, perceptions, thoughts, and feelings. Espoused values are derived from the basic underlying assumptions and the espouse justification of strategies, goals, and philosophies. Finally, at the top level are artifacts which are defined as the visible yet hard to decipher organizational structures and processes.

Here we should reference Dennison's Iceberg model. Only about 10% of an iceberg is visible above the water. 90% is below the surface. Nevertheless, the inertia of the part that is beneath the surface is what will sink your ship. It is often the parts of the culture that we cannot see that will get us into trouble. This figure also reminds us that culture is learned. It is filled up from the accumulated principles that we learn as we survived together over time. The lessons from the past shape our survival strategies for the future. Our mindset and worldview shape the way we use the lessons of the past to forge the strategies of the future.

Managers tend to see culture as normative values and beliefs which enforce a relatively homogeneous, fixed set of behaviors. Because culture is fossilized at habit, it resists change and frustrates strategy formulation and implementation. Strategy constitutes an essential constellation of meanings, and strategic management is a cultural process aimed at altering managers' interpretations about the fundamental nature and purpose of their organizations and their roles in it. Senior executives seeking strategic changed need to pay more attention to what messages they are seeking to communicate and how these messages are likely to be received.

The concept of culture has been around for a long time. Strategic planning was the realization that no brilliant strategy can succeed if you can implement it. Webster's definition of culture stresses the act of developing desired traits with expert care and training. With this emphasis on implementation, culture building offers Executives a tool for turning well-formulated strategies into results. Culture building requires a renewed application of some soft management skills, but that does not mean it is a simple or straightforward matter. Just as any living organism thrives in a delicately balanced environment, so does a corporate culture that exists within a finely-tuned system. Corporate culture is the way we do things around here. However, a robust and thriving culture is even more than the way things get done. It is also the unique ways people unify behind a common purpose, deliver Superior performance, and pass skills along to others. A calibrated and aligned culture is an asset that supports strategy - at all levels.

Most attempts to define organizational culture leave managers who have tried it at a loss. The usual result is a list of eight or ten phrases describing the informal rules that govern the interaction of management team members. This may be useful until an attempt is made to judge from the list whether a proposed strategy will find that the culture is amenable to accept execution. In this case, managers have no method for thinking through the relationship between culture and the critical success factors on which strategy is based. We must recognize that the essential elements of an organization determine its everyday behaviors and actions. The management philosophy and control can also describe an organization's culture.

SEEING THE ELEMENTS OF CULTURE

There are several characterizations and models of organizational culture. In this section, the authors provide a high-level review of some of the more notable researchers Organizational culture is also the dominant values espoused by an organization or a set of values and assumptions that underlie the statement: "This is how we do things around here" (Deal and Kennedy, 1982; Quinn et al., 2015). According to Van de Post et al. (1998), culture is, to the organization, what personality is to the individual (Alexander Seidman and Seidman, 1990).[1] These definitions have in common the view that culture consists of some combination of artifacts (also called practices, expressive symbols, or forms), values and beliefs, and underlying assumptions that organizational members *share* about appropriate behavior (Cooke and Rousseau, 1988; Gordon and DiTomaso, 1992; Corbett and Rossman, 1989; Rousseau, 1990; Schall, 1983; Schein, 1992; Schwartz and Davis, 1981). There is some consensus that organizational culture is holistic, historically determined, and socially constructed, and it involves beliefs and behavior, exists at a variety of levels, and manifests itself in a wide range of features of organizational life (Hofstede, 1998; Neuijen, Ohayv, and Sanders, 1990; Pettigrew, 1990).

Choe (1993), Schwartz and Davis (1981), and Scholz (1987) found a strong relationship between corporate strategy and culture. Choe found that firms pursuing the prospectors' strategy tend to have a developmental culture, and those with defensive strategies tend to have a hierarchical culture. Rashid Anantharaman and Raveendran (1997) also found that there was an association between organizational strategy and culture, which is consistent with the findings by Choe (2003).

McGuire Dow and Argheyd (2003) believe that corporate cultures are real, are often taken for granted, extremely controlling of our behaviors, and are signals of slow change in business environments that are not experiencing significant disruption. Sadri and Lees (2001), a positive corporate culture could provide immense benefits to the organization, and thereby a leading competitive edge over other firms in the industry. However, a negative culture could harm organizational performance as it could deter firms from adopting the required strategic or tactical changes. Such type of culture could inhibit future changes in an organization.

Denison (1990) examined the relationship between corporate culture and performance. Corporate culture was based on the perceptions of organizational practices and conditions to characterize the organizational culture. He found that the organization with participative culture performed better than other cultural types.

While specific models and characterizations may differ, the essential elements of organizational culture are consistent across researchers. Organizational culture includes an organization's assumptions and beliefs, fundamental values, behaviors, and artifacts (Schein, 1984; Schein, 1990).

In this text, the authors take these three elements as the foundation. Culture is manifested in rituals and routines, stories and myths, symbols, power structures, organizational structures, and control systems. .An organization's culture is comprised of three things, including: (1) assumptions and beliefs; (2) values and norms; and (3) artifacts (Figure 1). Think of assumptions and beliefs as the fundamental things an organization believes in – it is essential guiding principles. Think of values and norms as act and behave in order to

Figure 1. Three elements of culture

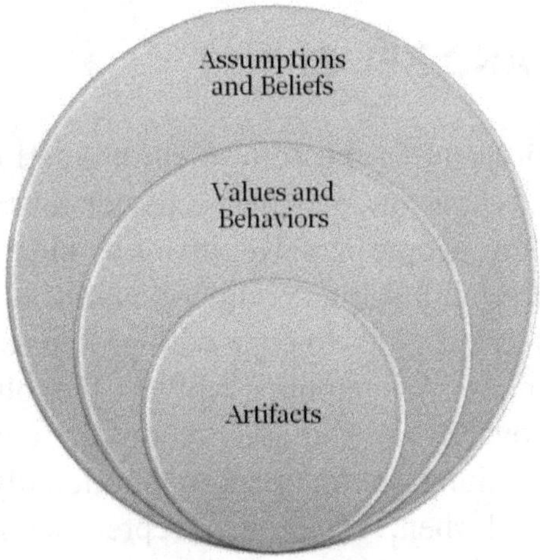

live up to those beliefs and principles. Think of artifacts as the things – whether implicit or explicit – that remind and reinforce those beliefs and behaviors.

We can begin with what is most visible and gradually pull back or expose the layers of culture – from artifacts to behaviors and values to assumptions and beliefs. Alternatively, we can begin with the most basic and persistent forms of culture – starting with assumptions and beliefs – and move to what is most visible and alterable. Regardless of which way you view them, the three elements are inherently connected and interdependent. How do we learn to see our assumptions and beliefs? How do we learn to see our values and behaviors? Furthermore, how do we learn to see our cultural artifacts?

We need to have a deep and holistic understanding of our organizational culture – before we can attempt to align it with or fit it to any of our strategies. Where do we begin to develop our understanding of culture? How do we begin to expose and see our cultures? There are two ways to approach the elements of culture. One approach is from what is most apparent – the artifacts that we can see – and to work backward to peel back the levels of culture until we arrive at assumptions and beliefs. A second approach is to begin with, deep-seated assumptions and beliefs and track how these are manifested in behaviors, values, and artifacts. Which approach you adopt to build your understanding depends on your preferences and context. Because these two approaches are common, the cultural elements are often modeled as building blocks. Rather than assume a progression one way or the other, the authors present the elements of culture as interconnected spheres (Figure 1).

ASSUMPTIONS AND BELIEFS

Underlying assumptions are at the core of culture and represent the belief systems that individuals have toward human behavior, relationships, reality, and truth. They describe how people perceive situations and make sense of events, activities, and human relationships. Assumptions and beliefs are formed over time as people develop strategies to cope with problems and pass along the strategies to new members. Assumptions evolve as the solution to the problem is repeated over and over again. Our assumptions are embedded in what we pay attention to, what things mean, react to emotionally, and what actions we are likely to take and when. Assumptions represent our cognitive stability and our defense mechanisms. Different cultures make different assumptions about others based on their values. If people are treated consistently in terms of certain underlying assumptions, they come eventually to behave according to those assumptions in order to make their world stable and predictable.

Not all assumptions are mutually compatible or consistent. If a group holds the assumption that all good ideas and products ultimately come from Individual effort, it will not readily assume that groups can be held responsible for the results. Or those individuals will put a high priority on group loyalty. If a group assumes that the way to survive is to conquer nature and manipulate the environment aggressively, it cannot have the same time as soon. The notion that business should be profitable, that schools should educate, or that medicine should prolong life is assumptions. They do not rise to the level of cultural values.

Beliefs lead to attitudes, which in turn lead to intentions and behaviors. Beliefs are underlying assumptions about the world and how it works. Because many facets of physical and social reality are difficult or impossible to experience personally or to verify, people rely on others they identify with and trust to help them decide what to believe and what not to believe. Beliefs that have been held for a long time without being violated or challenged may be taken so much for granted that we are no longer aware of them. This is why organizational members frequently fail to realize what a profound influence culture has on them. This is why it can be difficult to "see" our cultures.

VALUES AND BEHAVIORS

Values in and of themselves are a reflection of underlying assumptions. Awareness of and support for values increases where those values are clear and evident. Values are the social norms that define the rules that govern how people behave. We see values in the way that individuals behave in their everyday work environments and their work practices. Values tell us why people behave the way they do. Values are also underlying assumptions that have an implicit *ought to.* Schein (1988) observed that values vary across organizations, and members cared more intensely about some values than others. Schein distinguishes between pivotal and peripheral values.

Pivotal values are central to an organization's functioning; members are required to adopt and adhere to the behavioral norms derived from these values and are typically rejected from the organization if they do not (e.g., Chatman, 1991; O'Reilly and Chatman, 1996). Pivotal values include (1) actual values, and (2) corrective values. Actual values. These often include the cultural traits and behaviors that are supported throughout the organization. These are observable. These articulate the unique cultural enablers and Central aspects of the core culture of the organization in the company's language. Corrective values. These are the essential values that seek to lessen the impact of implicitly or explicitly recognized culture. The organizations with the most cohesive cultures, such as cults and prisons, could embrace pivotal values that are so widely adopted and enforced that they preclude the emergence of peripheral values, and, by implication, subcultures (O'Reilly and Chatman, 1996; Schein, 1961; Van Maanen and Barley, 1984). Most business organizations, however, do not operate with only one culture (Trice and 8 Beyer, 1993). A more likely profile is a strong culture firm that emphasizes both a set of pivotal values essential to its functioning and identity, as well as a set of peripheral values that are less relevant to every individual or unit. While Schein discussed the role of pivotal values for organizations, he did not consider their potential role in subcultures.

Peripheral values are desirable but are not believed by members to be essential to an organization's functioning. Members are encouraged to accept peripheral values but can reject them and still function fully as members. Thus, members' degree of conformity to peripheral norms can vary considerably. Peripheral values include (1) aspirational values, and (2) fashionable values. Aspirational values are lofty but achievable goals and sometimes not so achievable. Fashionable values these are current popular ones include being green, embracing Corporate social responsibility, or focus on diversity. These types of values may display prominently on banners in an advertisement but are not always embraced by the organization and embedded in the values.

Pivotal and peripheral values may be more relevant to some parts of the organization than to others. Specifically, peripheral values may be relevant to subcultures within an organization while being less relevant to the identity and functioning of members of the dominant organizational culture. Organizations with strong pivotal values can also sustain peripheral values on which members' agreement and intensity vary. In strong cultures widely-shared, intensely-held core values were pervasive across the organization. However, individual operating units are given the autonomy to determine how to operate daily. An organization's credo might say one thing, but the operating culture might have a slightly different character and set of values. In supportive cultures, subunits can act on the values that are important to them but peripheral to the functioning of the organization, leaving the pivotal core values of the organization intact (O'Reilly and Tushman, 1997).

Bloor and Dawson (1994) observed that pivotal values included high professional standards and a commitment to client rehabilitation. Workers within the organization simultaneously embrace core values but also focused on ethical behavior and client advocacy. Because there is the agreement that the pivotal values are essential and the peripheral values they adopted did not interfere with the organization's pivotal values workers' beliefs did not detract from the strength of the dominant organizational culture. Strong pivotal and varying peripheral cultural values can coexist.

Every organizational culture is molded and governed by certain norms and values. It is necessary to distinguish between openly stated or explicit beliefs and unstated or implicit ones. In a healthy, open, and creative organizational culture, there will be a minimal discrepancy between explicit and implicit assumptions and beliefs. In a weak organizational culture, the stated and unstated assumptions and beliefs are often in conflict. For instance, management makes per claim its interest in encouraging creativity and initiative, but simultaneously an unstated Norm May imply that no one should question what the boss decides. Official Personnel policy May Express a wish to support self-development and Improvement among employees, where his company practices may fall far short of this ideal.

BEHAVIORS

Behaviors and habits are what an external Observer can discern. The organization implicitly or explicitly communicates them through its advertising, physical premises, rituals, myths, habits, structure, and work processes. Common behaviors might include work practices, language, and communication, the way we dress, and how we relate to one another. Behaviors may be represented as work behaviors, like learning styles, in the language we use and the way we communicate, in the way we dress or present ourselves, and our relationships.

The work practices are where the organization's culture meets business strategy and execution. Combining these two perspectives results in a dynamic cultural model. This point is essential to Option 4. Work practices are core organizational behaviors. They are central to organizational and operational routines and habits that have been established to run the organization. Decision-making processes are obviously heavily influenced by the espoused values and corresponding justification. Work practices include the organizational structure and hierarchy, both formal and informal, decision-making processes, organizational skills and capabilities, workflow processes, and Performance Management reward and compensation systems. National cultures profoundly impact organizational work practices. The work practices and operational habits themselves are artifacts and provide further insight. Additionally, the handling of an existential crisis or heroic effort may also shed light on deeply held beliefs (Hammerisch and Lewis, 2012).

Mental processes and learning styles are other indicators of behavior. What can we learn by observing the way a group of individuals thinks and learn? How do they approach problem-solving? Do they take a practical and experiential approach, or do they begin with abstract and conceptual models? How does a group or an organization typically process information? Do they take a flexible or legalistic approach to weigh alternatives? Does the organization or group encourage everyone to learn and strive to develop to their full potential, or are only the "high fliers" or "high performers" supported? What can we learn from observing who communicates with whom? Is there an inherent class structure built into the culture? Is there a hierarchy, or are some individuals segregated from others based upon their classification or hiring status?

Language and communication systems, methods, or practices are the third indicator of behavior. Language and communication differentiate one group from others; in other words, for the verbal and nonverbal methods of communication, gestures, and body language, is there specialized terminology? What is the primary language - in terms of dialect, accent, flying, acronyms, or other variations to improve interactions? Information workers tend to be computer literate and technologically sophisticated. There may be a standard set of behaviors and a common linguistic register in use in mobile communication tools and applications.

Dress, presentation, outer garments, adornments, body decorations, or lack thereof is another indicator of behavior. What are the dress requirements for daily work and events? Are there formal or informal guidelines for business meeting attire, for laboratory work, for fieldwork?

Relationships are an essential indicator of behavior. How are individual and organizational relationships determined? What is a typical group arrangement? What are the evident designations, rank, or protocols that are honored?

ARTIFACTS

Artifacts are tangible and visible objects that reflect and reinforce culture. Artifacts are things we can see, hear, and feel. They are visible products and things – language, technology, products, creations, and styles of clothing, manners of address, stories we tell and organizational myths, art, technology, heroes, rituals, and ceremony. We can physically observe a building's physical workspaces - the rituals the advertising the organizational charts and documented worst processes or artifacts. These elements are easy to observe but difficult to decipher. They are easy to observe but may be difficult to decipher by outsiders. They may be ambiguous symbols. They include the design of the physical space, facades, and buildings (Deal and Kennedy, 1982; Hofstede, 1991; Trice and Beyer, 1984; Wuthnow and Witten, 1988).

How can we "see" our artifacts? How do we interpret them? How do others interpret them? How do artifacts affect or define culture? Do the artifacts support a productive culture? What may need to change? An organization May reveal significant information about its embedded values from visible artifacts. Is the boss in a large corner off is? Can an individual's status in the hierarchy be determined based on the size and position of their desk or office? By the type of car they drive? Is an organization's headquarters located in a modest building in an industrial area, or is it an iconic building on a prominent plot in the center of town? This type of information about the company and its people can tell us much about deeply rooted beliefs (Hammerich and Lewis, 2012)

INTERPLAY OF CULTURAL ELEMENTS

While we can understand and "learn to see" each of the three elements of organizational culture, it is also critical to understand how they build upon and relate to each other. We may be able to discover our assumptions and beliefs by reviewing our organizational visions or codes of ethics, but are these consistent across all levels and areas of the organization? Do our cultural artifacts reinforce our assumptions and beliefs, or do they tell us something more deep-seated about what we truly believe? Do our values come through in our behaviors? Moreover, do they embody our espoused beliefs? Where these three elements are not aligned, the culture will be fractured. While every organization has at least one culture, most organizations will have many cultures – subcultures, group cultures, and individual cultures. In this text, we are less concerned with whether a culture is productive or unproductive and more interested in whether and how to fit it to the business strategy. Culture in and of itself is neither positive nor negative. Our interest in culture

Figure 2. The interplay of factors and culture in an organization

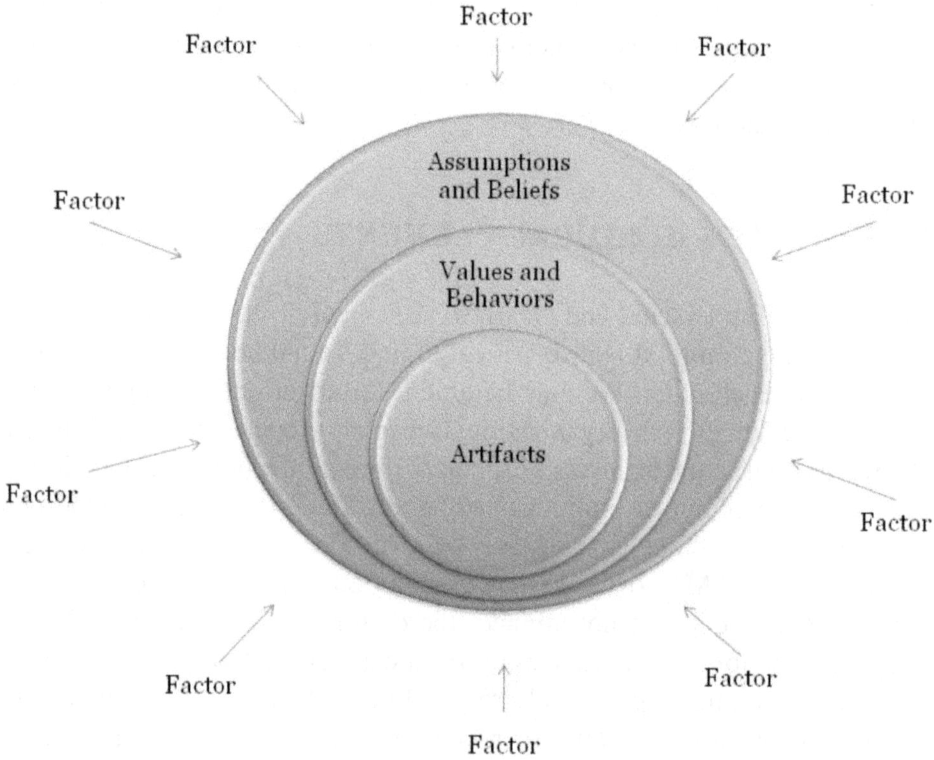

is in how it aligns with and reinforces strategy. This means that we need to ensure that each of the three elements of our culture aligns with and "fits" the elements of our strategies.

In order to shape and align culture with a strategy, we need to know what factors shape an organization's culture at any given point in time. While it is hard to change, it is dynamic and continuously changing based on these critical factors. To manage the culture, we need to understand these factors. This is what translates the theory into practice for a manager. How do we make these abstracts concepts real, practical, and actionable for managers? We need to translate them into an organizational context and describe them in business terms. Chapter 3 presents a practical structure for seeing an organization's culture.

CONCLUSION

After reading this chapter, you should be able to:

- Define culture and organization cultures
- Describe the most common organization culture models
- Explain what we mean by assumptions and beliefs
- Explain what we mean by values and behaviors
- Explain what we mean by artifacts
- Explain how these cultural elements interact

REFERENCES

Alexander, J. C., Seidman, S., & Seidman, S. J. (Eds.). (1990). *Culture and society: Contemporary debates.* Cambridge University Press.

Alvesson, M. (2012). Understanding organizational culture. *Sage (Atlanta, Ga.).*

Chatman, J. A. (1989). Matching people and organizations: Selection and socialization in public accounting firms. In Academy of Management proceedings (Vol. 1989, No. 1, pp. 199-203). Briarcliff Manor, NY: Academy of Management.

Choe, J. M. (2003). The effect of environmental uncertainty and strategic applications of IS on a firm's performance. *Information & Management, 40*(4), 257–268. doi:10.1016/S0378-7206(02)00008-3

Cooke, R. A., & Rousseau, D. M. (1988). Behavioral norms and expectations: A quantitative approach to the assessment of organizational culture. *Group & Organization Studies, 13*(3), 245–273. doi:10.1177/105960118801300302

Corbett, H. D., Firestone, W. A., & Rossman, G. B. (1987). Resistance to planned change and the sacred in school cultures. *Educational Administration Quarterly, 23*(4), 36–59. doi:10.1177/0013161X87023004005

Corbett, H. D., & Rossman, G. B. (1989). Three paths to implementing change: A research note. *Curriculum Inquiry, 19*(2), 163–190. doi:10.1080/03626784.1989.11075322

Deal, T. E., & Kennedy, A. A. (1982). *Corporate cultures*. Reading, MA: Addison Wesley.

Denison, D., Hooijberg, R., Lane, N., & Lief, C. (2012). *Leading culture change in global organizations: Aligning culture and strategy* (Vol. 394). John Wiley and Sons.

Denison, D. R. (1990). *Corporate culture and organizational effectiveness*. John Wiley and Sons.

Gordon, G. G., & DiTomaso, N. (1992). Predicting corporate performance from organizational culture. *Journal of Management Studies, 29*(6), 783–798. doi:10.1111/j.1467-6486.1992.tb00689.x

Hammerich, K., & Lewis, R. D. (2012). Fish can't see. *Water (Basel)*, 121–131.

Heskett, J. L., & Kotter, J. P. (1992). Corporate culture and performance. *Business Review (Federal Reserve Bank of Philadelphia), 2*(5), 83–93.

Hofstede, G. (1998). Attitudes, values and organizational culture: Disentangling the concepts. *Organization Studies, 19*(3), 477–493. doi:10.1177/017084069801900305

Jones, G. R. (1983). Transaction costs, property rights, and organizational culture: An exchange perspective. *Administrative Science Quarterly, 28*(3), 454–467. doi:10.2307/2392252

Lewis, R. (2010). *When cultures collide*. Nicholas Brealey Publishing.

McGuire, J., Dow, S., & Argheyd, K. (2003). CEO incentives and corporate social performance. *Journal of Business Ethics, 45*(4), 341–359. doi:10.1023/A:1024119604363

Neuijen, B., Ohayv, D. D., & Sanders, G. (1990). Measuring organizational cultures: A qualitative and quantitative study across twenty cases. *Administrative Science Quarterly, 35*(2), 286–316. doi:10.2307/2393392

O'Reilly, C. A., & Chatman, J. A. (1996). *Culture as social control: Corporations, cults, and commitment*. Academic Press.

O'Reilly, C. A. III, & Tushman, M. L. (2008). Ambidexterity as a dynamic capability: Resolving the innovator's dilemma. *Research in Organizational Behavior, 28*, 185–206. doi:10.1016/j.riob.2008.06.002

O'Reilly, C. A. III, & Tushman, M. L. (2008). Ambidexterity as a dynamic capability: Resolving the innovator's dilemma. *Research in Organizational Behavior, 28*, 185–206. doi:10.1016/j.riob.2008.06.002

Pettigrew, A. (1990). *Organizational climate and culture: Two constructs in search of a role*. Academic Press.

Pheysey, D. C. (2002). *Organizational cultures: Types and transformations*. Routledge. doi:10.4324/9780203028568

Quinn, R. E., Bright, D., Faerman, S. R., Thompson, M. P., & McGrath, M. R. (2015). *Becoming a master manager: A competing values approach*. John Wiley and Sons.

Rashid, M. Z. A., Anantharaman, R. N., & Raveendran, J. (1997). Corporate cultures and work values in dominant ethnic organizations in Malaysia. *Journal of Transnational Management Development*, 2(4), 60–72.

Rousseau, D. M. (1990). Assessing organizational culture: The case for multiple methods. *Organizational Climate and Culture, 153*, 192.

Sadri, G., & Lees, B. (2001). Developing corporate culture as a competitive advantage. *Journal of Management Development, 20*(10), 853–859. doi:10.1108/02621710110410851

Schall, M. S. (1983). A communication-rules approach to organizational culture. *Administrative Science Quarterly, 28*(4), 557–581. doi:10.2307/2393009

Schein, E. H. (1961). Management development as a process of influence. *Industrial Management Review (pre-1986), 2*(2), 59.

Schein, E. H. (1984). Coming to a new awareness of organizational culture. *Sloan Management Review, 25*(2), 3–16.

Schein, E. H. (1988). Organizational socialization and the profession of management. *MIT Sloan Management Review, 30*(1), 53.

Schein, E. H. (1990). Organizational culture: Vol. 45. *No. 2*. American Psychological Association.

Schein, E. H. (1992). *Organizational culture and leadership. Jossey-Bass.*

Scholz, C. (1987). Corporate culture and strategy—The problem of strategic fit. *Long Range Planning*, *20*(4), 78–87. doi:10.1016/0024-6301(87)90158-0

Schwartz, H., & Davis, S. M. (1981). Matching corporate culture and business strategy. *Organizational Dynamics*, *10*(1), 30–48. doi:10.1016/0090-2616(81)90010-3

Trice, H. M., & Beyer, J. M. (1993). *The cultures of work organizations.* Prentice-Hall, Inc.

Van der Post, W. Z., De Coning, T. J., & Smit, E. V. D. M. (1998). The relationship between organisational culture and financial performance: Some South African evidence. *South African Journal of Business Management*, *29*(1), 30–40. doi:10.4102ajbm.v29i1.768

Van Maanen, J., & Barley, R. S. (1984). Occupational Communities: Culture and Control in Organizations,(w:]. *Research in Organizational Behavior.*

Wuthnow, R., & Witten, M. (1988). New directions in the study of culture. *Annual Review of Sociology*, *14*(1), 49–67. doi:10.1146/annurev.so.14.080188.000405

ADDITIONAL READING

Alvesson, M. (2012). Understanding organizational culture. *Sage (Atlanta, Ga.).*

Deshpandé, R., & Farley, J. U. (1999). Executive insights: corporate culture and market orientation: comparing Indian and Japanese firms. *Journal of International Marketing*, *7*(4), 111–127. doi:10.1177/1069031X9900700407

Section 2

Learning to See Strategies

Chapter 3
Seeing Business Strategies

ABSTRACT

This chapter focuses on business strategies and reminds the reader that strategy is an important leverage point. We need a good inventory of our business strategies before we can align and shape cultures. Strategies at all levels of the organization are essential – not just those at the top or leadership level. We need to understand our strategies across all functions and the strategies of individuals. It is essential to see and understand all of the forms that a strategy might take, including those that are well-formed, documented, and published; and those that are hidden, false, learned, or only partially developed. Aligning culture with poor strategies will not prevent strategies from failing. In the knowledge economy, business strategies should be assessed in terms of their treatment of information assets.

WHY WE CARE ABOUT STRATEGY

Strategies and the strategic planning process is an essential point of leverage for ensuring that our business and information cultures support our business goals. In order to leverage strategies, we need to know how we define a strategy, what kinds of strategies we have, how to find them, and see them across the organization. The word – strategy – is an essential and frequently used term. People use the word strategy to refer to a formal statement, a planning or management process, or a general agenda or a business approach. Most organizations have a rich repertoire of strategies – some formal and explicit, some informal and tacit, and others invisible but understood.

DOI: 10.4018/978-1-7998-4315-3.ch003

"Seeing" strategies in this way reminds us that culture and strategy play out at all of the same levels. Strategy and culture must align and support one another at all three levels – the organization, the unit or team, and the individual. A risk exists at every level. Addressing risk at only one level will not have a sustainable effect.

Figure 1. Business strategies in the framework

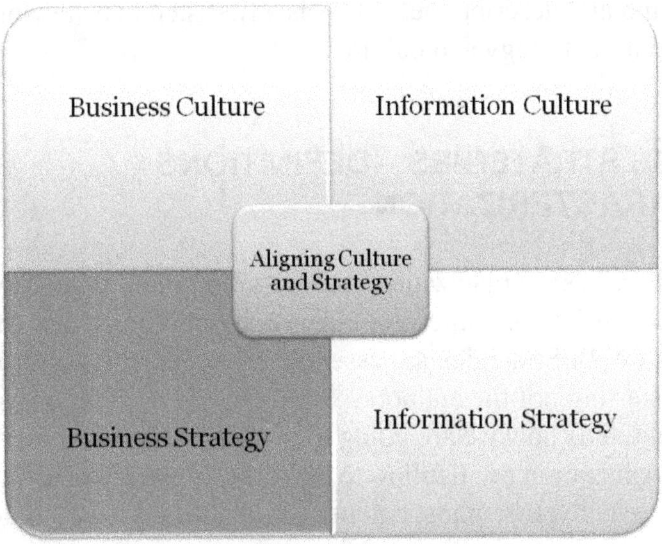

The challenge of designing a good fit is more complicated than merely ensuring that the top-level organization strategy and cultures align. Additionally, it is essential to understand and "see" the organization's business strategies at all three levels because we cannot assume that all strategies and all cultures will be in harmony. If we assume that all strategic planning and strategy translation is harmonized, and design a fit to the culture from that assumption, there may be unforeseen conflicts and risks.

We cannot assume that only those explicit documents that are labeled as strategies are the only ones driving our organizations forward. We cannot assume that only those strategies that are created by senior leaders – at the enterprise level – are the essential strategies. Strategies exist at every level of the organization. A strategy is such a standard management method – we might assume that some type of strategy will support anything an organization might manage.

All of these strategies are potential points of leverage for aligning culture. Nevertheless, trying to align culture with all of these strategies will be challenging and may not produce a value that balances the cost. It is essential to identify those strategies that have the most significant business value and impact, and also the greatest cultural risk. While the essential strategies will vary across organizations, there is a transparent methodology any organization can use to find and describe them. This is a first step in achieving a balance and alignment of strategy and culture.

BUSINESS STRATEGIES – DEFINITIONS AND CHARACTERIZATION

A strategy describes an organization's business direction and goals. We develop strategies to translate and interpret our visions, missions, and cultures into actions (Figure 2). Strategies are essential management tools, but they are neither the starting nor the endpoint. Strategies do not tell us where we are going – they tell us how we are going to get there. The strategy is the large-scale plan organization's will follow to make the dream happen. Strategies are often confused with other management tools that we say have 'strategic value'

Figure 2. Where strategies fit in the planning

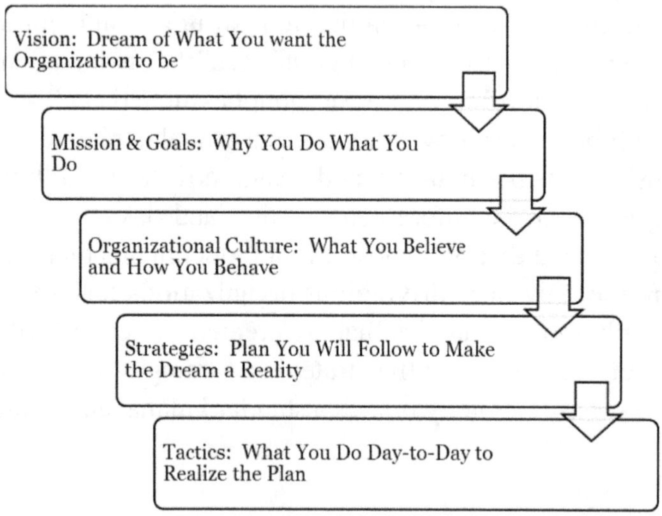

such as annual or quarterly plans, budgets, project plans, work breakdown structures, and tactics are not strategies.

Strategies are interpreted and translated into tactics. Tactics are specific actions we take to implement our strategy. Tactics describe how the organization does what it does. They focus on real-time, day-to-day operations. They play a role in establishing an environment in which our strategies will succeed and sustain. How well we fit our strategies and cultures will be assessed and measured by our day to day tactics.

Strategy formation involves synthesis and definition. Strategic planning is an organization's process of defining its strategy and making decisions on allocating its resources to pursue this strategy. Strategic planning became prominent in corporations during the 1960s and is a standard management tool is every form and aspect of business today. In most cases, strategic planning is the responsibility of senior managers. However, the evolution of organizations to less hierarchical structures and the broader assignment of decision making throughout an organization has made strategic planning and strategy development a popular tool at all levels of the organization. This is an essential observation for our concerns because it means that wherever strategies are developed, there is a risk that they may clash with culture. Regardless of how we arrive at our strategy, to succeed it must be aligned with our business cultures. Where strategy and culture are not aligned, strategic plans and tactics will be at risk.

Organizations arrive at strategies through many paths. Some organizations begin with an understanding and expression of the organization's mission. An organization's mission is the embodiment of the organization's vision. Other organizations may combine the tasks of setting goals and strategies by defining strategic goals and creating a context for strategic actions.

Strategies are like shoes – one size does not fit all. There may be general sizes and designs, but in the end, we shape them to fit our feet. Some companies use a top-down, autocratic approach, where the plan gets created by a small group of senior managers and handed down to the rest of the organization. Some prefer a more democratic approach, with employees at all levels contributing their ideas and input to the plan. Most companies employ a hybrid of these two models.

LEVELS AND TYPES OF STRATEGIES ACROSS THE ORGANIZATION

An organization's business goals are achieved by the effective execution of different business strategies. While every employee, partner, and stakeholder of the company focus on fulfilling business objectives, their activities are defined by various business strategies according to their level in the organization. Virtually anything that an organization manages will have a strategy because strategies are essential management tools. They permeate an organization.

We need to have a good understanding of the kinds of business strategies the organization produces and implements. It is the logical and natural points of alignment that provide the most significant opportunities for us to shape culture to support strategy. Cultural shifts or adjustments are more likely to be supported if there is a clear and distinct business rationale for the adjustment. Changing culture for the sake of change will rarely succeed. However, identifying small adjustments or fits to achieve a strategy is likely to be seen as part of the strategic planning and implementation process. We can present the change as just an element of what we do to achieve our business goals.

Perhaps the most effective way to begin finding our strategies is to look at the organization's administrative structure. As we look for strategies, remember that the goal is to understand where we have opportunities to fit the culture to support the strategy. This could be a very intense process – particularly in a large organization where you're likely to find many strategies - focus on those strategies that have the highest value to the organization. This may mean focusing on areas that are core operations of the organizations – those business units that are essential to producing value and sustaining the business. Fitting culture to strategy in these areas will help the organization to prosper.

ORGANIZATION LEVEL STRATEGIES

The corporate level is the highest and broadest representation of the business strategy. It is the business plan which sets the guidelines of what the organization wants to achieve, and how the business expects to achieve it. It sets the mission, vision, and corporate objectives for everyone. Business strategies are defined at the organization level – to address how the organization expects to achieve its highest level business goals. Common strategies at the organization level might include marketing strategies, technology strategies, general management strategies, and innovation strategies. Consider that each of these types of strategies would also leverage many more targeted strategies (Table 1).

Table 1. Examples of organizational and targeted strategies

Primary Strategy	Targeted Strategies
Marketing Strategies	• Product Strategies • Pricing Strategies • Product Promotion Strategies • Advertising And Distribution Strategies • Branding Strategies • Business Development Strategies • Customer Service Strategies • Customization Strategies
Pricing Strategies	• Algorithmic Strategies • Price Discrimination Strategies
Technology Strategies	• Technology Related Product Strategies • Internal Information Technology Sharing Strategies • Decision Automation Strategies • Decision Support Strategies • Digital Transformation Strategies • Gasification Strategies • Information Strategies • Visualization Strategies • Architecture Integration Strategies • Knowledge Management Strategies • Technology Modernization Strategies • Process Automation Strategies • Process Improvement Strategies • Process Integration Strategies • Artificial Intelligence Strategies
Cost Reduction Strategies	• Productivity Improvement Strategies • Operational Efficiency Improvement Strategies • Cost Mitigation Strategies • Cost Reduction Strategies

Similarly, innovation strategies may be defined and communicated at the organization level, but interpreted and applied at the function, process, and individual level. Creativity may be a mission or goal of the whole organization. However, creativity strategies may be more critical to our core operational units rather than to our financial accounting or human resource management functions. However, when the organization level innovation strategy and culture align, we may see strategic gains in all units.

In addition to organization-level strategies, most organizations have function level strategies that are designed to be implemented across the organization. The most common of these are human resource strategies. Human resource strategies include leadership development strategies, training strategies, staff development strategies, learning strategies, recruitment strategy, diversity strategy, and non-discrimination strategy.

UNIT OR TEAM LEVEL STRATEGIES

The business unit level strategies vary across the organization. We should expect each function to have one or more unit-specific strategies, and new process-related strategies. Different business functions produce different products and services and may have different operations. At the functional level, we are likely to see strategies developed annually – and aligned with tactical plans, project plans, individual work programs, and agendas.

Functional level strategies focus on the day to day actions and decisions needed to deliver unit level and organization level strategies, on maintaining relationships between different departments and fulfilling functional goals. This is the most critical level for aligning culture and strategy – because this is the level at which strategies are or are not most often realized.

Management strategies at this level address what the organization does - the directing and controlling operations. Strategies at this level are likely to include benchmarking strategies, best practice strategies, business transformation strategies, business capability management strategies, change management strategies, delegation strategies, job rotation strategies, management by exception strategies, preventive action strategies, process reengineering strategies, and risk management strategies.

Specialized function or unit strategies might also include

- Human resource management strategies
- Learning and training strategies
- Facilities management strategies
- Security management strategies
- Communication management strategies
- Budget strategies
- Information management strategies.

All of these strategies, though, must align with and support the overall business goals and visions laid out in strategies at the organization level.

INDIVIDUAL LEVEL STRATEGIES

Most discussions of strategy do not focus on or consider strategies defined and implemented by individuals. At this level, strategies often take the form of personal business behaviors. We are unlikely to find strategies explicitly described as such. These strategies may be found in an individual's performance goals and objectives and documented in their annual review agreements and appraisal process. Understanding strategies at this level is more challenging, but these strategies are essential to understanding the big picture. This may be particularly true for individuals who hold critical positions or are high performers in the organization.

What does this mean in terms of alignment? It means that we want first to consider how the cultural factors at that level fit the strategy. Are there conflicts or disconnects between the strategies developed for the whole organization and the organization's overall culture? Are the human resource level strategies aligned with the espoused values and behaviors of unit managers? Does the information technology strategy align with the unit level cultures across the organization? How well does the accounting strategy align with the espoused values and behaviors of unit managers? If you walked through the methodology outlined in Chapter 1, you will have a good holistic picture of your organization's culture. You are now ready to develop a picture of your organization's business strategies. This section gives us an idea of what kinds of strategies we might find.

LEARNING TO SEE BUSINESS STRATEGIES THROUGHOUT THE ORGANIZATION

As we noted earlier, organizations may take different paths to develop strategies. Strategies – in part or whole - may also integrated into other documents such as mission statements, organizational goals, organizational value statements, organizational codes of ethics, organizational plans, department or unit plans, and procedural documents. Ideally, an organization will have clearly defined, managed and labeled strategies – at all levels. Practically, though, it will be necessary to discover strategies or elements of strategies. It is not necessary to have a complete inventory of business strategies or plans in order to design a good fit for culture. You need to have a good enough inventory – one that gives you an understanding of how culture might support or impede the realization of those strategies.

Traditionally, strategy has been defined to include plans, goals, objectives, game plans, action programs, policies and explicitly formulated business programs (Andrews, 1987; Ansoff, 1987; Chandler, 1962; Hofer and Schendel, 1978; Learned et al., 1965; Lorange and Vancil, 1977; Ohmae, 1982; Porter, 1996; Steiner, 1969). These formal strategies reflect management's aspirations about the organization's future and are written down and openly announced to organization members, even though this is not always stated in direct terms (Mintzberg and Waters 1982). Most of us are familiar with the formal realized strategies, but they can take many forms. To support our goal of culture strategy alignment, we need to understand what strategies we have and how we develop them. We need a full accounting of the organization's strategies and its approach to strategic planning to see how it aligns with the culture. We also need full accounting as a foundation for discovering how information strategies align or conflict with the business strategy. You need to know what to look for and where to look. Where should you start to look? First, look at your organization chart – every function every activity will have a strategy. What are some examples of common organizational strategies? From a strictly business perspective, we might find and look for:

Once you know where to look, you will need to know what to look for. Not everything that is called a strategy is a strategy. Moreover, not all strategies are packaged and presented as such. You need to be able to see all of the strategies that may be in place or practice. Strategies will be packaged differently by each organization. The strategy may be distinct – it may stand on its own – or it may be part of a larger strategy. A strategy may be implied or referenced in planning or budgeting documents. Just like cultural values and behaviors, a strategy may be formally defined and espoused, but implemented or realized differently. Steensen (2014) has conducted extensive research into non-formal strategies. He characterizes what he has found into four types of strategies, including (1) shared; (2) hidden; (3) false; (4) learned; and (5) realized (Figure 3). Descriptions and interpretations of Steensen's characterizations are provided below. In mapping Steensen's characterizations to levels of strategy and considering them in the context of culture, the authors suggest these characterizations are not exclusive, i.e. a hidden strategy may also be a false strategy.

Figure 3. Representation of Steensen's strategy wheel

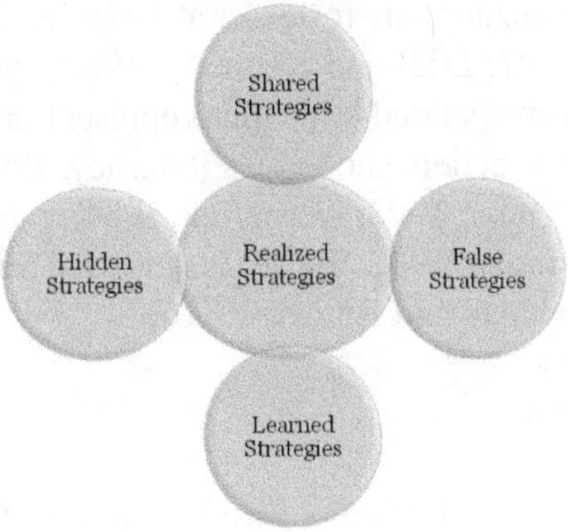

Shared Strategies

Steensen defines shared strategies as ideas or preferred approaches that may be "shared" or communicated to others in the course of doing business. In the context of this text, a shared strategy might best be understood as an individual's expression or interpretation of an organization or business level strategy, or it may be an expression of their personal goals and business ambitions. If it is an interpretation or expression of a broader organization, unit or team strategy it may reinforce that strategy, it may adapt that strategy, or it may be an opposing strategy. If it is an expression of their personal ambitions, it may be entirely disconnected from either of those strategies (Campbell and Yeung, 1991; Collins and Porras, 1996; Hamel and Prahalad, 1989; Smircich and Stubbart, 1985; Weick, 1987). Where a shared strategy is an interpretation of the organization or business strategy, it may be an important translation or explanatory tool which helps others to understand what those strategies mean and how to turn them into actions (Pfeffer, 1981; Peters, 1978). These kinds of "shared strategies" may also add value to the formal strategy and provide important feedback to those who formulated them. They may actually be an important element of the strategy communication and translation process (Chaffee, 1985; Johnson and Roberts, 1993).

Those "shared strategies" that interpret and translate formal unit, team or community strategies may be the most important for organizations to consider when creating a holistic picture of their organizational strategies – simply because this is where strategies are turned into action. This is the point at which we must align culture and strategy. It is also the level at which we see such an overlap and blending of culture and strategy, where shared strategies take the form of organizational stories, oral histories, and business myths (Barry and Elmes, 1997; Deal and Kennedy, 1982; Weick, 1987). At this level and in these forms, shared strategies represent and reinforce a unit's collective assumptions, beliefs and values ((Barney, 1991, 2002; Collis and Montgomery, 1997; Peteraf, 1993; Wernerfelt, 1984), capabilities (Day, 1994; Stalk, Evans, and Shulman, 1992; Teece, Pisano, and Shuen, 1997; Sanchez and Heene, 1997; Prahalad and Hamel, 1990).

Hidden Strategies

Steensen's second characterization of informal strategies focuses on hidden strategies. In the context of this text, a hidden strategy most clearly aligns with strategies at the individual level. These most often represent the unexpressed assumptions, beliefs, values and behaviors (Mintzberg and Waters, 1985; Goold and Campbell, 1988; Hax, 1990; Peattie, 1993). Hidden strategies may not be entirely unexpressed – they may come through in an individual's behaviors, decisions, and actions. They may not be fully expressed in a written or verbal form – but they are easily recognized as a hidden agenda. Hidden strategies may be intentional or unintentional. They may be deliberate behaviors intended to achieve an individual's long term career goal (Peters, 1978; Pfeffer, 1981) (Sminia, 2005). They may be intentionally designed to safeguard a unit, team or community from an external or internal threat (Andrews, 1987; Heil, Day, and Reibstein, 1997; Peattie, 1993). In this situation, a protective strategy may be highly effective and essential to achieving a business goal – if they were made explicit or known, their value would be reduced or destroyed. Or, they may simply be a practical strategy an individual must adopt to survive in an unstable business environment (Mintzberg 1978; Mintzberg, 1983; Mintzberg, 1987; Quinn, 1980; Quinn, 1982). These forms of hidden strategies may be essential in dynamic or tumultuous organizational or business environment (Mintzberg, 1990).

False Strategies

Steensen defines a false strategy as one that is intentionally false and deliberately designed to deceive. According to Steensen's interpretation, false strategies are most often created to send messages to external competitors – similar to counter-intelligence activities. In the context of strategy and culture, though, we suggest that false strategies may be found internally and may not be distinct from some forms of hidden strategies described above. One attribute that sets a false strategy apart from the other types of informal strategies, though, is their intention to provoke actions. Consider an internal senior leader who wishes to provoke the actions of another senior leader – to encourage their competitor to take a false path that in the end leaves them vulnerable to failure (Peattie; 1993). False strategies may be effective external tools, but they can be destructive tools when used internally. Internal false strategies are a cultural alarm – it means that we have a destructive internal structure. False strategies in external markets may have been an effective competitive intelligence strategy in an industrial economy (Porter, 1980) because they could tell us about a competitor's basic behavior. However, these actions are less likely to be effective in a knowledge economy, simply because of the increasing ease of discovering an organization reputation (Porter (1985; James, 1984; Heil et al.,1997) and corporate culture. Such false strategies today will rarely be effective at outwitting a competitor (Mintzberg, 1987)

Learned Strategies

Learned strategies may best be described by the business adage 'how we do things around here' or 'how things work here'. Learned strategies may also be understood to overlap with or resemble organizational patterns of behavior – an element of culture. They represented a unit, team, or community's understanding of how to survive or prosper in the organizational climate. These kinds of informal strategies are critical to see and understand because they help us to understand how any organization is likely to respond to change. And, change is an essential element of a knowledge organization and a knowledge economy. An organization may never define and communicate a formal business strategy related to changing conditions, but everyone in the organization 'has learned how to detect and survive the change' (Mintzberg, 1978; Mintzberg and Waters, 1985). As noted for other informal strategies, learned strategies have a strong relationship to organizational culture – in the form of behaviors (Stacey ; 1996). Managers of business units, teams and communities are a good place to begin looking for learned strategies – because it is at this level that decisions are often made (Weick and Roberts 1993; Pfeffer and Salancik, 1978). Decisions – particularly those that involve rewards, recognitions, hiring, promotions, firing, budget and resource allocations – teach us more about the actual strategy than any written or formally pronounced strategy (Bower and Doz, 1979; Hamel, 1996); Mintzberg, 1990; Quinn, 1978; Huber, 1991). In a knowledge economy, learned strategies (distringuished from learning strategies…) help us to understand the organization's capacity to respond and adapt to change and its capacity for innovation (Bierly and Hamalainen, 1995; Johnson, Melin, and Whittington, 2005; Johnson and Huff, 1998).

Realized Strategies

Finally, Steensen describes a fifth type of informal strategy – realized strategies. Simply put, we define a realized strategy as the collective actions of an organization – the holistic behavior that is inherent to 'how we do things around here' (Katz and Kahn, 1966; Pettigrew, 1977; Mintzberg, 1978). It is the strategy we might interpret if we were to collect all of an organization's decisions over a period of time and deduce its strategy – without having access to its formal, written or officially communicated strategies. It is a pattern of behaviors that represents the fundamental assumptions, beliefs and values of the organization over that time (Mintzberg, 1987; Johnson, 1987; Quinn, 1982, Stacey (1996; Whittington, 1996, 2006; Jarzabkowski, Balogun, and Seidl, 2007; Jarzabkowski and Whittington, 2008; Wilson and Jarzabkowski, 2004; Hodgkinson, Johnson, Whittington, and Schwarz, 2006; Whittington, Molloy, Mayer, and Smith, 2006; Statler, Jacobs, and Roos, 2008). A realized strategy provides deep insights and a critical intersection point for organizational culture. Discovering realized strategies over time and across the entire organization is critical for aligning culture and reducing cultural risk.

Formal and Informal Strategies

Steensen and all of the other important researchers remind us that it is important to understand not only the formal, official, and communicated strategies, but all of the other informal strategies at play in an organization. In fact, it is often the informal strategies that most closely align with and present the greatest opportunities for reducing cultural risks. Informal strategies can also tell us a lot about whether our strategies are effective or ineffective. The more informal strategies we discover or observe, the greater the likelihood that we have substantial cultural risks and misalignments. In Chapters 7, 8 and 9 the authors have shared twenty-seven scenarios that illustrate real-world examples of informal strategies – at the organization, the unit, team and community, and the individual level. The wealth of scenarios suggests that more time should be devoted to discovering, explaining, and understanding informal strategies and the risks they present.

CREATING A HOLISTIC VIEW OF BUSINESS STRATEGIES

A holistic view allows us to see all of the connections and dependencies among all of our strategies. Before you can design a solution that aligns strategies and cultures, you need to learn to see your strategies. The authors acknowledge that culture is often invisible and tacit, but we likely assume that strategies will be explicit, documented, and easy to see. In fact, how an organization develops and communicates its strategies is often reflective of its culture – meaning if the culture is anarchic, you are likely to find many and different strategies – some documented some shared and unstated. It is important to discover the greatest strategic risks, and to consider how you might better balance culture and strategy at those points. You do not need to fit the culture to every strategy in the organization. If you make the adjustment at key points and demonstrate value, other points of misalignment will be easier to see and to fit. Chapters 7, 8 and 9 will help guide you through the alignment process at each level of the organization

CONCLUSION

After reading this chapter, you should be able to:

- Explain why we care about business strategy
- Define different types of forms of business strategies
- Describe the levels and types of strategies you can find across the organization
- Explain how we discover business strategies across the organization
- Explain how to create a holistic view of business strategies for your organization

REFERENCES

Andrews, K. R. (1987). *The concept of corporate strategy. Homewood: Irwin. Ansoff, H. I. (1965). Corporate strategy*. New York: McGraw-Hill.

Ansoff, H. I. (1987). The emerging paradigm of strategic behavior. *Strategic Management Journal*, *8*(6), 501–515. doi:10.1002mj.4250080602

Barney, J. B. (1991). Firm resources and sustained competitive advantage. *Journal of Management*, *17*(1), 99–120. doi:10.1177/014920639101700108

Barry, D., & Elmes, M. (1997). Strategy retold: Toward a narrative view of strategic discourse. *Academy of Management Review*, *22*(2), 429–452. doi:10.5465/amr.1997.9707154065

Bierly, P. E., & Hamalainen, T. (1995). Organizational learning and strategy. *Scandinavian Journal of Management*, *11*(3), 209–224. doi:10.1016/0956-5221(95)00011-J

Bower, J. L., & Doz, Y. (1979). Strategy formulation: A social and political process. In D. E. Schendel & C. W. Hofer (Eds.), *Strategic management* (pp. 152–166). Boston: Little Brown.

Campbell, A., & Yeung, S. (1991). Creating a sense of mission. *Long Range Planning*, *24*(4), 10–20. doi:10.1016/0024-6301(91)90002-6 PMID:10114092

Chaffee, E. E. (1985). Three models of strategy. *Academy of Management Review*, *10*(1), 89–98. doi:10.5465/amr.1985.4277354

Chandler, A. D. (1962). *Strategy and structure: Chapters in the history of the industrial enterprise* (12th ed.). Cambridge, MA: The MIT Press.

Collins, J. C., & Porras, J. I. (1996). Building your company's vision. *Harvard Business Review*, *74*, 65–77.

Collis, D. J., & Montgomery, C. A. (1997). *Corporate strategy: Resources and the scope of the firm*. Chicago: Irwin.

Day, G. (1994). The capabilities of market-driven organizations. *Journal of Marketing*, *58*(4), 37–53. doi:10.1177/002224299405800404

Deal, T. E., & Kennedy, A. A. (1982). *Corporate cultures: The rites and rituals of corporate life*. Reading, MA: Addison-Wesley.

Goold, M., & Campbell, A. (1988). *Strategies and styles: The role of the centre in managing diversified corporations*. Oxford: Blackwell.

Hamel, G. (1996). Strategy as revolution. *Harvard Business Review, 74*, 69–81. PMID:10158475

Hamel, G., & Prahalad, C. K. (1989). Strategic intent. *Harvard Business Review, 67*, 63–77. PMID:10303477

Hax, A. C. (1990). Redefining the concept of strategy and the strategy formation process. *Planning Review, 18*(3), 34–40. doi:10.1108/eb054290

Heil, O. P., Day, G. S., & Reibstein, D. J. (1997). Signaling to competitors. In G. S. Day & D. J. Reibstein (Eds.), *Wharton on dynamic competitive strategy*. New York: John Wiley and Sons, Inc.

Hodgkinson, G., Johnson, G., Whittington, R., & Schwarz, M. (2006). The role of strategy workshops in strategy development process: Formality, communication, coordination and inclusion. *Long Range Planning, 39*(5), 479–496. doi:10.1016/j.lrp.2006.07.003

Hofer, C. W., & Schendel, D. (1978). *Strategy formulation: Analytical concepts*. St. Paul: MN West Publishing Company.

Huber, G. P. (1991). Organizational learning: The contributing processes and the literatures. *Organization Science, 2*(1), 88–115. doi:10.1287/orsc.2.1.88

James, B. G. (1984). *Business wargames*. Harmondsworth: Penguin Books Ltd.

Jarzabkowski, P. (2003). Strategic practices: An activity theory perspective on continuity and change. *Journal of Management Studies, 40*(1), 23–55. doi:10.1111/1467-6486.t01-1-00003

Jarzabkowski, P., Balogun, J., & Seidl, D. (2007). Strategizing: The challenges of a practice perspective. *Human Relations, 60*(1), 5–27. doi:10.1177/0018726707075703

Jarzabkowski, P., & Whittington, R. (2008). A strategy-as-practice approach to strategy research and education. *Journal of Management Inquiry, 17*(4), 282–286. doi:10.1177/1056492608318150

Johnson, G. (1987). *Strategic change and the management process*. Oxford: Basil Blackwell.

Johnson, G., & Huff, A. S. (1998). Everyday innovation everyday strategy. In G. Hamel, C. K. Prahalad, H. Thomas, & D. O'Neill (Eds.), *Strategic flexibility: Managing in a turbolent environment*. Chichester: John Wiley and Sons, Ltd.

Johnson, G., Melin, L., & Whittington, R. (2005). Micro strategy and strategizing: Implications for strategy process research. In S. W. Floyd, J. Roos, C. D. Jacobs, & F. W. Kellermanns (Eds.), *Innovating strategy process*. Oxford: Blackwell Publishing.

Katz, D., & Kahn, R. L. (1966). *The social psychology of organizations*. New York: Wiley.

Learned, E. P., Christensen, C. R., Andrews, K. R., & Guth, W. D. (1965). *Business policy: Text and cases*. Homewood, IL: Irwin.

Lorange, P., & Vancil, R. F. (1977). *Strategic planning systems*. New York: Prentice-Hall Inc.

Mintzberg, H. (1978). Patterns in strategy formation. *Management Science, 24*(9), 934–948. doi:10.1287/mnsc.24.9.934

Mintzberg, H. (1983). *Power in and around organizations*. Englewood Cliffs, NJ: Prentice-Hall Inc.

Mintzberg, H. (1987). The strategy concept 1: Five Ps for strategy. *California Management Review*, *30*(1), 11–24. doi:10.2307/41165263

Mintzberg, H. (1990). The design school: Reconsidering the basic premises of strategic management. *Strategic Management Journal, 11*(3), 171–195. doi:10.1002mj.4250110302

Mintzberg, H., & Waters, J. A. (1982). Tracking strategy in an entrepreneurial firm. *Academy of Management Journal, 25*, 465–499.

Mintzberg, H., & Waters, J. A. (1985). Of strategies, deliberate and emergent. *Strategic Management Journal*, *6*(3), 257–272. doi:10.1002mj.4250060306

Ohmae, K. (1982). *The mind of the strategist: The art of Japanese business*. New York: McGraw-Hill.

Peattie. (1993). Strategic planning: Its role in organizational politics. *Long Range Planning, 26*, 10-17.

Peteraf, A. (1993). The cornerstones of competitive advantage: A resource-based view. *Strategic Management Journal, 14*(3), 179–191. doi:10.1002mj.4250140303

Peters, T. J. (1978). Symbols, patterns, and settings: An optimistic case for getting things done. *Organizational Dynamics, 7*(2), 3–23. doi:10.1016/0090-2616(78)90035-9

Pettigrew, A. M. (1977). Strategy formulation as a political process. *International Studies of Management & Organization, 7*(2), 78–87. doi:10.1080/00208825.1977.11656228

Pfeffer, J. (1981). Management assymbolic action: The creation and maintenance of organizational paradigms. *Research in Organizational Behavior, 3*, 1–52.

Pfeffer, J., & Salancik, G. (1978). *The external control of organizations: A resource dependence perspective*. New York: Harper and Row.

Porter, M. E. (1980). *Competitive strategy: Techniques for analyzing industries and competitors*. New York: The Free Press.

Porter, M. E. (1985). *Competitive advantage: Creating and sustaining superior performance*. New York: The Free Press.

Porter, M. E. (1996). What is strategy? *Harvard Business Review, 74*, 61–78. PMID:10158475

Prahalad, C. K., & Hamel, G. (1990). The core competence of the corporation. *Harvard Business Review, 28*, 79–92.

Quinn, J. B. (1978). Strategic change: Logical incrementalism. *Sloan Management Review*, 7–21.

Quinn, J. B. (1980). Managing strategic change. *Sloan Management Review*, 3–20.

Quinn, J. B. (1982). Managing strategies incrementally. Omega. *International Journal of Management Sciences, 10*, 613–627.

Roos, J., Victor, B., & Statler, M. (2004). Playing seriously with strategy. *Long Range Planning, 37*(6), 549–568. doi:10.1016/j.lrp.2004.09.005

Sanchez, R., & Heene, A. (1997). Reinventing strategic management: New theory and practice for competence-based competition. *European Management Journal, 15*(3), 303–317. doi:10.1016/S0263-2373(97)00010-8

Sminia, H. (2005). Strategy formation as layered discussion. *Scandinavian Journal of Management, 21*(3), 267–291. doi:10.1016/j.scaman.2004.09.002

Smircich, L., & Stubbart, C. (1985). Strategic management in an enacted world. *Academy of Management Review, 10*(4), 724–736. doi:10.5465/amr.1985.4279096

Stacey, R. D. (1996). *Strategic management and organizational dynamics* (2nd ed.). London: Pitman Publishing.

Stalk, G., Evans, P., & Shulman, L. (1992). Competing on capabilities. *Harvard Business Review, 70*, 57–69. PMID:10117369

Statler, M., Jacobs, C. D., & Roos, J. (2008). Performing strategy—Analogical reasoning as strategic practice. *Scandinavian Journal of Management, 24*(2), 133–144. doi:10.1016/j.scaman.2007.11.006

Steensen, E. F. (2014). Five types of organizational strategy. *Scandinavian Journal of Management, 30*(3), 266–281. doi:10.1016/j.scaman.2013.10.003

Steiner, G. A. (1969). *Top management planning*. New York: The Macmillan Company.

Teece, D. J., Pisano, G., & Shuen, A. (1997). Dynamic capabilities and strategic management. *Strategic Management Journal, 18*(7), 509–533. doi:10.1002/(SICI)1097-0266(199708)18:7<509::AID-SMJ882>3.0.CO;2-Z

Weick, K. E. (1987). Organizational culture as a source of high reliability. *California Management Review, 29*, 112–127.

Weick, K. E. (1995). *Sensemaking in organizations*. Thousand Oaks, CA: Sage Publications.

Wernerfelt, B. (1984). A resource based view of the firm. *Strategic Management Journal, 5*(2), 171–180. doi:10.1002mj.4250050207

Whittington, R. (1996). Strategy as practice. *Long Range Planning, 29*(5), 731–735. doi:10.1016/0024-6301(96)00068-4

Whittington, R. (2006). Completing the practice turn in strategy research. *Organization Studies, 27*(5), 613–634. doi:10.1177/0170840606064101

Whittington, R., Molloy, E., Mayer, M., & Smith, A. (2006). Practices of strategising/organising: Broadening strategy work and skills. *Long Range Planning*, *39*(6), 615–629. doi:10.1016/j.lrp.2006.10.004

Wilson, D. C., & Jarzabkowski, P. (2004). Thinking and acting strategically: New challenges for interrogating strategy. *European Management Review*, *1*(1), 14–20. doi:10.1057/palgrave.emr.1500008

Chapter 4
Seeing Information Strategies

ABSTRACT

In the knowledge economy, we must manage information as a strategic business asset. Information must be an essential component of our business strategies, and the information strategy must speak to the business value of information. Information strategies are often formulated and issued only at the organization level. The authors stress the importance of developing information strategies that pertain to business units, teams, and individuals. The authors present an integrated view of information strategies to mirror and support business strategies. The integrated view is a high-level synthesis of the information science literature and practice.

WHY WE CARE ABOUT INFORMATION STRATEGIES

Information is a critical business asset–, particularly in the knowledge economy. In the knowledge economy, there is a complex information landscape. The opportunities for creating, access, discovering, and consuming information have multiplied. Information management has emerged as both a discipline and an essential tool of modern management. This notion should be at the heart of a university's information strategy.

In the knowledge economy, organizations, units, teams, and individuals must manage their information assets. Strategies are essential tools for managing any kind of asset. In order for information strategies to be effective, they must be aligned with business strategies and supported by both information and

DOI: 10.4018/978-1-7998-4315-3.ch004

Figure 1. Information strategies in the framework

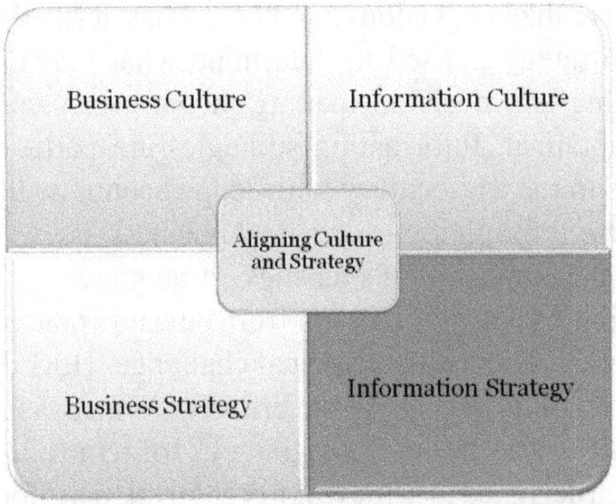

business cultures. Information strategies are the critical points of leverage for aligning information in the knowledge economy.

Information strategies are the focal point for this book because there is a high rate of failure of practical operationalization. One of the most significant causes of failure is a lack of alignment of information strategies to (1) business strategies and to (2) information cultures. To address these points of failure, we need to know (1) what strategies we have, (2) how they align with the organization's business strategies, (3) how they align with the information culture.

To accomplish ties, we need to know what we mean by an information strategy, what kinds of information strategies exist across the organization, were to look for them, and how to see them regardless of whether they are explicit or implicit. In the end, we need to have an accurate accounting of the organization's information strategies.

INFORMATION STRATEGY – DEFINITIONS AND CHARACTERIZATIONS

What is an information strategy? An information strategy tells us how the business uses, treats, and values information. The purpose of an information strategy is to highlight the extent to which a modern, complex organization depends on information, in all of its guises, and to consider how this strategic asset should be managed. An information strategy describes how the organization will realize the visions and goals it has defined for information.

Information Strategy is used to determine what information is crucial for the functioning and decision making in the organization and how to build it and maintain it. Information strategies are particularly important for organizations in the 21st-century knowledge economy. In the knowledge economy, business information is a critical business asset. As such, it must be addressed by the organization's business strategies.

The information strategy derives not from business practices but business goals and principles. This is the principal challenge. How do organizations ensure that information management, broadly defined, is integrated into, facilitates, and influences the business strategy? **Information Strategy** refers to a long-term plan designed to achieve An organization's information strategy tells us how the organization expects to manage and leverage its business information assets. It is an integral part of the organization's business strategy. The information strategy references and supports the organization's vision, mission, and goals. An organization's information strategy must always be consistent with and integrated with other business strategies.

The central argument here is that a business process and its information infrastructure cannot and should not be separated in terms of strategic thinking and planning. This argument applies at the level of individual processes like learning and teaching or research, and it also applies to the development of the overall organizational business strategy. It applies to understand the information requirements of the vertical business process as well as more fundamental questions such as the quality, reliability, and stewardship of information. In this chapter, we will first discuss the structural (e.g., business-level alignment) aspects of information strategies. Then we will discuss how information management affects all aspects of business strategies.

Our first task is to align information strategies in a way that allows us to "see" them as equivalent to and an integral part of the organization's business strategies.

LEARNING TO SEE INFORMATION STRATEGIES ACROSS THE ORGANIZATION

Information strategies cannot and should not be a free-standing, self-contained strategy.

The information strategy should be designed as a matrix that aligns with the organization's horizontal and vertical business processes. Strategies for managing information should be integral elements of every business strategy. An information strategy, whether broad or narrow in scope, requires a strategic context. We must avoid information requirements planning with no strategic purpose having been defined and no management framework in place. The converse—a strategy that does not consider information resources—is equally unhelpful. Information requires a strategy every bit as much as a strategy requires information.

We should learn to see information strategies at the same levels we look for business strategies and that we learn to see business culture, including meso-level, macro-level, and the micro-level. This approach puts information assets at risk in many ways. It leaves information management to the discretion of individual managers and workers. It may give rise to a variety of unpredictable and unsustainable practices across the organization. It may give rise to a variety of practices over time. It may leave information management practices vulnerable to transitory technologies – and short term gains. Too often, business approaches information management as a means of managing information or technology tactics and tools. This means there is not a top-down or big picture – a collective organization vision or expectation. Also, we may find that where information strategies are fragmented or represented as tactics, they may not be given the status or regard afforded to business strategies

The challenge is to integrate this process into strategic planning as a high-level, cross-cutting theme. As the corporate plan seeks to pull the various process-specific strategies together into an integrated whole, so a parallel mechanism would seek to establish an integrated information strategy comprised of the following:

- A "General Information Strategy" addressing the horizontal issues:
- The information sub-strategies that are incorporated into the central vertical strategies such as learning and teaching and research
- Standards and expectations for individual-level information behaviors and strategies.

ORGANIZATION LEVEL STRATEGIES

The organization-level information strategy is overarching and inclusive. It describes the broad set of principles that are the foundation of the organization's definition, valuation and treatment of information, its fundamental assumptions and beliefs about information, its best practices, business rules, and policies. Organization level information strategies are inclusive, and they apply to everyone in the organization. It follows that the process of developing and managing these parent strategies will require an inclusive approach, with the process owner working with the information services or IT department and any other identified sources of expertise in the matters at hand.

Organization level strategies focus on the strategic aspects of information as defined across the organization. Organization level information strategies should be inclusive. They require input from and coordination across all business units. This level of an information strategy is the baseline from which all sub-strategies are developed.

Where does information management live in the organization? At this level, the most visible indication of an information management role or strategy lies with a Chief Information Officer. There may also be other information roles scattered across the organization. Those strategies which are dedicated to information are most often found at the macro level or in selected business functions, i.e., those functions dedicated to information professionals and areas of information practice. Research suggests that information strategies from these units often represent important professional principles and standards, or information management practices and tactics. Discovering information strategies at these lower levels may often mean extracting and deducing them from tactics, decisions, actions, and procedural documents. The challenge we face is to weave together all the variations and forms of information strategies into a single working foundation.

The central theme for aligning all information strategies at the organization level is the rationale for leveraging information that generates business value. Businesses continually consider the value of their inputs, their processes, their outputs, and their outcomes. Business information is a fundamental input to every process; they are part of every business transformation and inherent to every product and service. Ideally, business units continually review the information they create, use, and produce in every business process. This continual review provides an opportunity to ask whether the information we are using is the best value we could have, is it being used in the business to generate the level of value we expect and is it contributing to the value of our outputs and outcomes.

The dictionary defines value as the importance, worth, usefulness, utility, or benefit of something. Value can also mean the monetary worth of something. To establish a monetary value means we can put or set a price on something or to cost it out. Business value is an informal term that includes all forms of value that determine the health and well-being of the firm in the long run, including employee value, customer value, supplier value, channel partner value, alliance partner value, managerial value, and societal value. Many of these forms of value are not directly measured in monetary terms. Much of the work in the field of knowledge management traces back to the ideas of Drucker (1999). Drucker was an early proponent of business value as the proper goal of a firm, especially that a firm should create value for customers, employees – as knowledge workers, and distribution partners. Drucker's management by objectives was a goal-setting and decision-making tool to help managers at all levels create business value.

How do businesses establish a value proposition for a capital asset? Can we translate these methods to information assets? Business value is an informal concept, and there is no consensus, either in academic circles or among management professionals, on its meaning or its role in effective decision-making. While it is true that it is an informal business concept, some methods are in everyday use to assign value to physical and financial capital assets. The challenge we face for determining the value of business information, though, is that the business does not ask these questions, and too often, information management practitioners and professionals do not answer them in a business manner.

How might information managers approach the question of value? What can we learn from the literature (Al-Fedaaghi, 22013; Allee, 2008; Andriessen, 2004; Bontis et al., 2007; Cummins, 2003; Hand and Lev, 2004; Housel and Nelson, 2005; Kirschenmann, 2001; Lev, 2003; Sullivan and Sullivan, 2000)? What are the conventional approaches for assigning or estimating the business value of an information asset? What does value look like? How do economists and business managers define value? Can we interpret the most common types of business value for knowledge capital? There are four common types of business value (Fig. xx), including (1) net present value; (2) time value as money; (3) internal rate of return; and (4) required rate of return.

Net present value is the difference between the present value of cash inflows and the present value of cash outflows over a period of time. It is used in capital budgeting and investment planning to analyze the profitability of a projected investment or asset. It is the value of all future cash flows (positive and negative) over the entire life of an investment discounted to the present. For example, if a company decides to open a new product line, they can use net present value to determine if the projected future cash inflows will cover the future costs of starting and running the project. This definition of value translates very well to information. The challenge is to ensure that the individuals who make decisions about the acquisition or creation of the information assets asset think in these terms. Ideally, the "investor" makes a formal net present value assessment. Consciously making an informal assessment is a good option – as a starting point in a path to a formal assessment.

Time value as money is grounded on the assumption that the asset – in this case, money – has a time value. If you were to save this money today, what would be its value at a certain point in the future? To calculate this, analysts use the net inflation interest rate. This suggests that the present value of a future sum of money is less the further away in time the sum is due to be expended or received. How does this translate to knowledge capital? The challenge here is that knowledge loses value if it is stored or taken out of circulation. Knowledge does not earn interest by not being used. Knowledge only gains interest through use and being in circulation. And, leveraging information does not deplete it or reduce its availability information replicates and creates new equity the minute it is used or put into circulation

The internal rate of return is used to estimate the profitability of potential investments. It is a discount rate that makes the net present value of all cash flows from a particular project equal to zero. How does this translate to knowledge capital? When we hire a person or establish a new network connection or define a new business process, we make a judgment call on the value that new investment is likely to generate. We may not be conscious of the fact that we are doing that, but individuals do it every day. The question is, what would it take to formalize this thought process?

Furthermore, is how we do it today sufficiently rigorous for the organization to trust it? When a business manager chooses an individual as a new hire, do they think about how that individual's tacit knowledge will contribute to the long-term profitability of the organization? Or, do they simply choose someone to fill an open job to ensure the work is performed? It is more likely that a business manager thinks about the profitability that will result from a new operation or an improved operation. In some businesses where relational capital is a valuable asset such as in real estate (i.e., potential clients), insurance (i.e., potential clients), or politics (i.e., potential donors or supporters), the future profitability of a new connection is an essential part of the "investment decision."

The required rate of return is the minimum return an investor expects to achieve by investing in an asset. We define the required rate of return by adding a risk premium to the interest percentage that could be gained by investing excess funds in a risk-free investment. How does this translate to knowledge capital? Value might be determined by what we would expect to accrue from hiring an individual if we only leverage their skills and competencies in a single business process. Alternatively, a different value might accrue if we invested in that individual in a way that encouraged them to grow all eight types of information assets and if those assets were allocated across multiple processes. The investment asset is an individual – and the "excess funds" is the full range of capital they possess. What is the excess value we accrue if that person brings their reputation and their personal network? Or when the individual has a significant positive effect on the organizational culture of the unit?

At present, the business managers or business process managers do not associate these concepts of value with the information assets they use to generate products and services. The information management literature, too often assumes it is not possible to establish a base from which to estimate value. While it may be difficult to assign value to intangible assets, it is not impossible. Where value seems indeterminate, it is possible to define value by a structured interview with critical decision-makers regarding the strategic intent of the information produced, what tangible value it presents to those doing the work, and to the organization, and what kinds of improvements decision-makers can realize if they only knew what they needed to know. Such interviews must be structured so that they speak to concerns of management and should be consistent in order to reconcile different perceptions of value. However, the resulting input will be invaluable not only to attribute value to the information assets themselves but to identify more tangible measures of value that can be coupled with the less tangible assets. In this way, intangible assets like meetings, discussions, social forums can also be audited for organizational impact. Value propositions and value estimation are always relative – it is relative to the value of the business. Any attempts by information managers working outside of the business context to establish business value will fail.

Business strategies at the organization level may contain few if any, references to information. This is because business managers often treat information as a byproduct of business processes. Business information is not treated as a thing of value. The authors provide a set of guiding questions to help you think through how information might be referenced in your business strategies. These questions include:

1. Which of the four value strategies does your organization prefer?
2. Are these valuation strategies referenced in the organization level strategies?

3. Do you find references to them in the unit or function level strategies?
4. To whom does value accrue?
5. Who owns revenues generated from value? Where are these issues addressed in business strategies?
6. Who owns the profits generated by value? Moreover, where are these issues addressed in strategies?
7. Can we trace the source of ownership and determine who derives value? How does this guide us to a strategy?
8. Can we trace the costs associated with managing the asset? Where do these strategies live?
9. Can we determine whether costs will be offset or recovered over time through the generation of higher value? At what level will the recovery occur?
10. Can we trace the expenses associated with acquiring the asset? Are they offset by the value generated? Who manages these strategies?

UNIT AND TEAM LEVEL INFORMATION STRATEGIES

One of the essential requirements of an information strategy is to ensure that every strategic plan – at every unit - whether explicit or implicit – includes a reference to business information. Ideally, every business unit should have a clearly defined strategy for managing and leveraging business information. Moreover, ideally, each of these strategies is aligned with and is supportive of the organization level information strategy. These strategies should set out the extent and nature of their dependency on information resources and explain how they are to be managed (Afifi and Weiner, 2004; Broadbent, 1991; Espejo and Watt, 1988; Galliers and Leidner, 2014; Hicks Culley and McMahon, 2006; Reponent, 1994; Trauth, 189; Weir et al., 2007; Yang and Fan, 2016). Unit level strategies help to ensure those information strategies are embedded in the day-to-day, vertical management processes. It is at these levels that we find a consistent interpretation of, treatment of, and reference to information interrelatedness, consistency, quality, ownership, currency, and general management. This means that you need to look for information strategies – explicit and implicit – in every business unit or function. What are some examples of the kinds of business strategies we might find at the organization level?

The business and information management literature is rich with examples of failed information management strategies. While the reasons for these failures may be many and varied, it is clear that chief among them is the notion that information strategies are somehow separate from business processes. The most reliable method of ensuring that an information strategy will fail is to simply call it an information management strategy and to make no effort to link it to business goals, strategies, and value. Information management strategy development at the unit level should be lead by the business process owners. The strategic planning process should be inclusive. These strategies should not be formulated or implemented solely by information professionals outside the business unit. It follows that parallel strategies that do not support the business goals or conflict with those of other units are discouraged, or at least viewed as temporary envisioning or thought exercises that should feed back into unit and organization information strategy.

The conceptual framework the authors propose assumes we will find or develop a formal strategy for each critical business area. This means we need to conduct a review of strategies for each business unit and develop a holistic view of information at the unit level. The benefit of this approach is that it places responsibility and accountability for managing information assets where they are used – in the hands of business managers. Each business unit assumes an ownership role and responsibilities for each information strategy.

The most common type of information strategy we will find at the unit level is produced by information professionals and practitioners. These strategies represent established practices in historical areas of information management practice. Information professionals see information management as a core function. Common information strategies today might include strategies that align with operational units such as:

- Technology strategies (Chen et al., 2010; Harper and Utley, 2001; Lederer and Sethi, 1991)
- Library strategies (Greenstein and Thorin, 2002; Rowley, 2011; Smith, 1983)
- Information security strategies (Anderson and Choobineh, 2008' Ahmed Maynard and Park, 2014; Luiijf et al., 2011)
- Intellectual property or copyright strategies (Gallie and Legros, 2012; Gollin, 2008; Geller, 1998)
- Customer relationship information management strategies (Ling and Yen, 2001; Payne and Frow, 2005)
- Records or document management strategies (Chartaby, 1991; Daum, 2007)

- Archives management strategies (Whittaker and Hirschberg, 2001; Kemoni, 2009; Bantin, 1998; Wactlar and Christel, 2002)
- Information disclosure strategies (Ferreira and Rezende, 2007; Merkl-Davies and Brennan, 2007; Hotz and Xiao, 2013)
- Language or translation strategies in multilingual organizations (Gambier, 2010; Martin, 2000)
- Art and multimedia collection strategies (Waltl, 2006; Chan and Cope, 2015)
- Knowledge management strategies that also cover information (Bedford, 2015; Eden, 1992; Feurer and Chaharbaghi, 1995; Fredrickson, 1986)
- Information architecture strategies (Burda et al., 2007; Godinez et al., 2010)

Information strategies might also focus on specific types or formats of information, including:

- Web content management strategies
- Social media strategies
- Digital information asset strategies
- Audiovisual information asset strategies
- Art and physical artifact asset strategies
- Content management strategies
- Data management strategies

Most often, though, we will find information strategies that align with the information life cycle (Bedford, 2019). There are many information life cycle models, including those focused on information systems development, information technology use, data life cycles, knowledge life cycles, publications life cycles, research life cycles, document and records life cycles, and content life cycles. For illustration purposes, the authors use a working life cycle model (Table 1) that includes eight stages, including: (1) idea generation; (2) information creation and capture; (3) securing and classifying information; (4) organizing and describing information; (5) finding and discovering information; (6) accessing and using information; (7) retaining and disposing of information; (8) destruction of information.

Table 1. Strategies related to the eight stages of information life cycle

Life Cycle Stage	Life Cycle Focus	Related Information Strategies
1	Idea Generation and Business Innovation Strategies	· Innovation strategies · Ideation strategies · Copyright strategies · Trademark strategies
2	Information Creation and Capture Strategies	· Information versioning · Information translation · Information capture strategies · Information identification strategies · Records declaration strategies · Information storage strategies · Information repository strategies · Information description strategies · Information quality strategies
3	Security and Classifying Information Strategies	· Information security classification strategies · Access strategies · Use and user privilege strategies · Disclosure strategies · Information modification strategies · Business information continuity strategies · Information inspection strategies · Information authentication strategies · Watermarking strategies · Information risk management strategies · Redaction strategies
4	Organizing and Describing Information Strategies	· Information description strategies · Information cataloging strategies · Metadata strategies · Metadata management strategies · Topical classification strategies · Functional classification strategies · Indexing strategies · Master data management strategies · Filing scheme strategies · Records classification strategies
5	Finding and Discovery Strategies	· Search Strategies · Browse and navigation strategies · Discovery strategies
6	Using and Sharing Information Strategies	· Publishing strategies · Availability of information strategies · Accessibility of information strategies
7	Preserving and Disposing of Information Strategies	· Records management and control strategies · Evidentiary strategies · Regulatory strategies · Financial compliance strategies · Information authentication strategies · Preservation strategies · Conservation strategies
8	Information Destruction Strategies	· Retention strategies · Physical destruction strategies · Electronic destruction strategies

INFORMATION STRATEGIES AT THE INDIVIDUAL LEVEL

We have a sense of the focus and makeup of an organization and a unit-level strategy. We can recognize strategies at these levels because we have a wealth of examples from the business and the information science literature. We have good practice models that help us understand what to expect in terms of an explicit information strategy or an implicit information strategy. We do not have these same reference models or examples at an individual level. Nevertheless, this is a critical level to "see" and understand because it is where organization and unit level strategies are implemented or ignored in day to day actions. In the end, it is the actions of individuals and their information behaviors that determine whether those other higher-level information strategies are realized.

The closest we come in the information science literature to characterizing individual information strategies are in individual information behaviors and personal information management habits. The literature is abundant on these topics, but it is not designed or discussed in a way that translates easily to a practical management context. This is a challenging topic for the authors to cover because it is at the same time (1) a manifestation of and explicit representation of an unstated or implicit strategy; and (2) a defined element of information culture. The overlap of these two concepts demonstrates how interdependent these issues are, and how essential it is to learn to "see" these strategies regardless of their form. In the end, the authors find five different dimensions of individual information strategies that should be taken into account when assessing the state of an organization's overall information strategies. These five dimensions include:

- Generalized information behaviors
- Capacity for information use and management
- Demographic-grounded information behaviors
- Business rationales for information behaviors
- Information behaviors influenced by the business environment

The authors review some of the basic behaviors to help the reader "see" strategies at this level. We caution, though, that these behaviors are illustrative – and we recommend that you expand your review before characterizing your organization at this level.

Table 2 references a few of the more common characterizations of information behaviors drawn from the information science literature. We

Table 2. Generalized information behaviors

Behavior	Information Behavior Effects
Information integrity	Use of information in a trustful and principled manner – what people should and should not do
Information formality	Willingness to use and trust organizational information over informal sources
Information control	Information about performance is continually leveraged to manage and monitor performance
Information transparency	Openness in reporting and presentation of information on errors and failures, allowing individuals to learn from mistakes
Information sharing	Willingness to share information in an appropriate and collaborative way
Practicality	Individuals ability to think about how to obtain and use new information in order to respond to business challenges
Information packaging	Information use as repackaging existing information in a different form and format for accessibility
Information flows	Information use that supports transmission to or exchanges with others
New information creation	Creation of new ideas and meanings
Shaping judgments and decisions	Guides decision-making activities
Influencing others	Influencing the behaviors of others

can observe each of these behaviors for any individual, at any point in time, in any context (Marchand Kettinger and Rollins 2001; Todd 1999). These information behaviors are defined in terms of their positive effects. In any work environment, individuals might demonstrate positive or opposite behavior. They might demonstrate information integrity, or they might treat the information in an unprincipled or mistrustful manner. Information sharing or reader is to determine what the nature of information behavior is at the individual level and to determine whether it is likely to support or impede the unit and organization level information strategies.

As noted earlier, there are two dominant views of information in any organization. The first is the view of information from a business perspective. The second is the view of information from the information professional and practitioner's perspective. While these two views may diverge at the organization and the unit levels, they converge at the individual level. Individuals have innate information behaviors that they bring to the organization each day (Figure 2). These behaviors are adapted and modified by the business context (Figure 2). It is essential for individuals and managers to "see" how these two sets of factors interact in their organizations. What we know from research and experience is that the mix of factors will produce variations within and across units. Moreover, we know that this is a critical level of behavior to affect in order to ensure proper vertical and horizontal alignment of information strategies throughout the organization.

Figure 2. Factors influencing individuals capacity for information

- Ability to ask questions and formulate problems
- Ability to consider multiple viewpoints
- Ability to continuously learn and knowledge capacity
- Ability to create, innovate or imagine
- Ability to leverage information in all of its forms
- Ability to listen and understand
- Ability to see alternatives
- Ability to ask for help and advice
- Ability to temper opinions
- Capacity for interaction and collaboration
- Capacity for thoughtful communication
- Personal Information Experiences
- Regard for accuracy
- Regard for risk-taking

Figure 3. Information practices common to demographics

- Age group
- Business experience and training
- Formal education and training
- Years from last formal education
- Gender
- Information experience and training
- National assumptions and beliefs about information
- National information policies
- Cultural beliefs about information
- Professional training and associations

What factors affect our information management behaviors? To "see" these factors, we must consider both how an individual's innate view of information translates to behaviors and strategies, and how their characteristics influence behaviors. Table xx illustrates the two dimensions (Serrat, 2012; Pikas, 2007; Olson, 1982)

In most cases, an individual's information behaviors and actions will be influenced by their business behaviors and environments. Table 3 identifies some of the most commonly cited factors that most often determine these actions (Choo Bergeron Detlor Heaton, 2008).

Table 3. Rationales for business information behaviors

Rationale for Behavior	Information Behavior Effects
Enlightenment	Used to develop a context or sense of a situation by looking for similar situations, history, and comparable experiences
Problem Understanding	Used to develop a better comprehension of a problem
Instrumental Use	Helps the individual determine what to do and how to do it
Factual Use	Used to determine the facts of a situation or event, defines practical reality
Confirmational Use	Used to verify another form of knowledge or piece of information
Projective Use	Used to predict what is likely to happen in the future
Motivational Use	Used to initiate or sustain personal actions or to determine a future course of action
Personal or Political Use	Used to develop relationships, enhance the status, reputation and personal goals

What factors in the work environment might influence an individual's information behaviors (Johnston and Carrico, 1988; Voida Harmon Al-Ani, 20011; Caudle Gorr Newcomer, 1991)? This is an area of extensive treatment in information science and business management literature. Unfortunately, this literature is not aligned with elements or levels of culture. The authors attempt to collate these factors for the reader (Figure 4).

Figure 4. Business factors that may influence information behaviors

- Ability to develop personal information management tools and methods
- Co-adoption of information management tools and methods by peers
- Expected use in business and it's business transformation
- Formal information training
- Information is critical and core to the business process
- Integration of information management tools and support systems
- Nature of work role (e.g., legal, regulatory, financial, instructional, consulting, production, manufacturing, and so on)
- Nature of the work environment (e.g., office, laboratory, in the field, direct client interaction, and so on)
- Organizational systems and tools available
- Personal overhead and overload for using information management tools and methods
- Personal return on investment or reward for information management
- Practices of coworkers in the unit – peer pressure and peer practice
- Preference for personal versus shared information collections
- Rate of change of information management tools and methods
- Suitability of information management tools to business tasks
- The importance of the task
- Visibility and availability of information management tools

Information strategies are not well understood or researched in either the business management or the information science literature. While there is a wealth of practical experience and advice, most of that guidance is grounded in failure rather than success. The authors ground the peer-reviewed literature, the gray literature, and practical experience in the context of business strategies – to provide structure and a foundation for future work.

CONCLUSION

After reading this chapter, you should be able to:

- Explain why we care about information strategies
- Describe information strategies and explain the different forms they might take in an organization
- Explain how we can discover information strategies
- Explain the relationship between information management practices and information strategies

REFERENCES

Afifi, W. A., & Weiner, J. L. (2004). Toward a theory of motivated information management. *Communication Theory*, *14*(2), 167–190. doi:10.1111/j.1468-2885.2004.tb00310.x

Allee, V. (2008). Value network analysis and value conversion of tangible and intangible assets. *Journal of Intellectual Capital*, *9*(1), 5–24. doi:10.1108/14691930810845777

Anderson, E. E., & Choobineh, J. (2008). Enterprise information security strategies. *Computers & Security*, *27*(1-2), 22–29. doi:10.1016/j.cose.2008.03.002

Andriessen, D. (2004). IC valuation and measurement: Classifying the state of the art. *Journal of Intellectual Capital*, *5*(2), 230–242. doi:10.1108/14691930410533669

Bantin, P. C. (1998). Strategies for managing electronic records: A new archival paradigm? An affirmation of our archival traditions? *Archival Issues*, 17–34.

Bedford, D. A. (2015). The knowledge management information landscape—Awareness, access, use and value of sources. *Journal of Information & Knowledge Management*, *14*(02), 1550002. doi:10.1142/S0219649215500021

Bedford, D. A. D. (2019). Strategic Management of Business-Critical Information Assets. In *Advances in Information Quality and Management*. Hershey, PA: IGI Global.

Bontis, N., Bart, C. K., Nazari, J. A., & Herremans, I. M. (2007). Extended VAIC model: Measuring intellectual capital components. *Journal of Intellectual Capital*, *8*(4), 595–609. doi:10.1108/14691930710830774

Broadbent, M. (1991, January). Information Management: Strategies and alliances. *Aslib Proceedings*, *43*(1), 1–11. doi:10.1108/eb051192

Burda, B., Crompton, J., Sardoff, H. M., & Falconer, J. (2007). Information architecture strategy for the digital oil field. In *Digital Energy Conference and Exhibition*. Society of Petroleum Engineers. doi:10.2118/106687-MS

Caudle, S. L., Gorr, W. L., & Newcomer, K. E. (1991). Key information systems management issues for the public sector. *Management Information Systems Quarterly*, *15*(2), 171–188. doi:10.2307/249378

Chan, S., & Cope, A. (2015). Strategies against architecture: Interactive media and transformative technology at the Cooper Hewitt, Smithsonian Design Museum. *Curator (New York, N.Y.)*, *58*(3), 352–368. doi:10.1111/cura.12118

Chartaby, K. (1991). Records Management—Quo Vadis? *Records Management Journal*, *3*(4), 108–113. doi:10.1108/eb027067

Chen, D. Q., Mocker, M., Preston, D. S., & Teubner, A. (2010). Information systems strategy: Reconceptualization, measurement, and implications. *Management Information Systems Quarterly*, *34*(2), 233–259. doi:10.2307/20721426

Choo, C. W., Bergeron, P., Detlor, B., & Heaton, L. (2008). Information culture and information use: An exploratory study of three organizations. *Journal of the American Society for Information Science and Technology*, *59*(5), 792–804. doi:10.1002/asi.20797

Cummins, J. G. (2003). A new approach to the valuation of intangible capital (No. w9924). Cambridge, MA: National Bureau of Economic Research. doi:10.3386/w9924

Daum, P. (2007). Evolving the records management culture: From ad hoc to adherence. *Information & Management*, *41*(3), 43.

Eden, C. (1992). Strategy development as a social process. *Journal of Management Studies*, *29*(6), 799–812. doi:10.1111/j.1467-6486.1992.tb00690.x

Espejo, R., & Watt, J. (1988). Information management, organization and managerial effectiveness. *The Journal of the Operational Research Society*, *39*(1), 7–14. doi:10.1057/jors.1988.2

Ferreira, D., & Rezende, M. (2007). Corporate strategy and information disclosure. *The RAND Journal of Economics*, *38*(1), 164–184. doi:10.1111/j.1756-2171.2007.tb00050.x

Feurer, R., & Chaharbaghi, K. (1995). Strategy development: Past, present and future. *Management Decision*, *33*(6), 11–21. doi:10.1108/00251749510087614

Fredrickson, J. W. (1986). The strategic decision process and organizational structure. *Academy of Management Review*, *11*(2), 280–297. doi:10.5465/amr.1986.4283101

Galliers, R. D., & Leidner, D. E. (2014). *Strategic information management: Challenges.* Academic Press.

Gambier, Y. (2010). Translation strategies and tactics. Handbook of Translation Studies, 1, 412-418.

Geller, P. E. (1998). From patchwork to network: Strategies for international intellectual property in flux. *Duke J. Comp. & Int'l L., 9*, 69.

Godinez, M., Hechler, E., Koenig, K., Lockwood, S., Oberhofer, M., & Schroeck, M. (2010). *The art of enterprise information architecture: a systems-based approach for unlocking business insight.* Pearson Education.

Gollin, M. A. (2008). *Driving innovation: intellectual property strategies for a dynamic world*. Cambridge University Press. doi:10.1017/CBO9780511805394

Greenstein, D., & Thorin, S. E. (2002). *The Digital Library: A Biography. Strategies and Tools for the Digital Library.* Washington, DC: Digital Library Federation, Council on Library and Information Resources.

Hand, J. R., & Lev, B. (Eds.). (2003). *Intangible assets:Values, measures, and risks.* Oxford: Oxford University Press.

Harper, G. R., & Utley, D. R. (2001). Organizational culture and successful information technology implementation. *Engineering Management Journal, 13*(2), 11–15. doi:10.1080/10429247.2001.11415111

Hicks, B. J., Culley, S. J., & McMahon, C. A. (2006). A study of issues relating to information management across engineering SMEs. *International Journal of Information Management, 26*(4), 267–289. doi:10.1016/j.ijinfomgt.2006.03.006

Hotz, V. J., & Xiao, M. (2013). Strategic information disclosure: The case of multiattribute products with heterogeneous consumers. *Economic Inquiry, 51*(1), 865–881. doi:10.1111/j.1465-7295.2010.00340.x

Housel, T. J., & Nelson, S. K. (2005). Knowledge valuation analysis: Applications for organizational intellectual capital. *Journal of Intellectual Capital, 6*(4), 544–557. doi:10.1108/14691930510628816

Johnston, H. R., & Carrico, S. R. (1988). Developing capabilities to use information strategically. *Management Information Systems Quarterly, 12*(1), 37–48. doi:10.2307/248801

Kemoni, H. N. (2009). *Management of electronic records*. Review of empirical studies from the Eastern, Southern Africa Regional Branch of the International Council on Archives (ESARBICA) region.

Kirschenmann, P. P. (2001). "Intrinsically" or just "instrumentally" valuable? On structural types of values of scientific knowledge. Journal for General Philosophy.

Lederer, A. L., & Sethi, V. (1991). Critical dimensions of strategic information systems planning. *Decision Sciences, 22*(1), 104–119.

Lev, B. (2003). Remarks on the measurement, valuation, and reporting of intangible assets. *Economic Policy Review, 9*(3), 17–22.

Ling, R., & Yen, D. C. (2001). Customer relationship management: An analysis framework and implementation strategies. *Journal of Computer Information Systems, 41*(3), 82–97.

Loshin, D. (2004). Issues and opportunities in data quality management coordination. *Information & Management, 14*(4), 14.

Loshin, D. (2010). *Master data management*. Morgan Kaufmann.

Loshin, D. (2010). *The practitioner's guide to data quality improvement*. Elsevier.

Luiijf, H. A. M., Besseling, K., Spoelstra, M., & De Graaf, P. (2011). Ten national cyber security strategies: A comparison. In *International Workshop on Critical Information Infrastructures Security* (pp. 1-17). Springer.

Marchand, D. A., Kettinger, W., & Rollins, J. D. (2001). *Making the invisible visible: How companies win with the right information, people, and IT*. John Wiley & Sons, Inc.

Merkl-Davies, D. M., & Brennan, N. M. (2007). Discretionary disclosure strategies in corporate narratives: Incremental information or impression management? *Journal of Accounting Literature, 27*, 116–196.

Olson, M. H. (1982). New information technology and organizational culture. *Management Information Systems Quarterly, 6*, 71–92. doi:10.2307/248992

Payne, A., & Frow, P. (2005). A strategic framework for customer relationship management. *Journal of Marketing, 69*(4), 167–176. doi:10.1509/jmkg.2005.69.4.167

Pikas, C. K. (2007). Personal information management strategies and tactics used by senior engineers. *Proceedings of the American Society for Information Science and Technology, 44*(1), 1–21. doi:10.1002/meet.1450440214

Reponen, T. (1994). Organizational information management strategies. *Information Systems Journal, 4*(1), 27–44. doi:10.1111/j.1365-2575.1994.tb00041.x

Rowley, J. (2011). Should your library have an innovation strategy? *Library Management, 32*(4/5), 251–265. doi:10.1108/01435121111132266

Serrat, O. (2017). On knowledge behaviors. In knowledge solutions (pp. 979-984). Springer.

Smith, B. (1983). Marketing Strategies for Libraries. *Library Management, 4*(1), 1–54. doi:10.1108/eb054863

Sullivan, P. H. Jr, & Sullivan, P. H. Sr. (2000). Valuing intangibles companies – An intellectual capital approach. *Journal of Intellectual Capital, 1*(4), 328–340. doi:10.1108/14691930010359234

Todd, R. J. (1999). Back to our beginnings: Information utilization, Bertram Brookes and the fundamental equation of information science. *Information Processing & Management, 35*(6), 851–870. doi:10.1016/S0306-4573(99)00030-8

Trauth, E. M. (1989). The evolution of information resource management. *Information & Management, 16*(5), 257–268. doi:10.1016/0378-7206(89)90003-7

Voida, A., Harmon, E., & Al-Ani, B. (2011, May). Homebrew databases: Complexities of everyday information management in nonprofit organizations. In *Proceedings of the SIGCHI Conference on Human Factors in Computing Systems* (pp. 915-924). ACM. 10.1145/1978942.1979078

Wactlar, H. D., & Christel, M. G. (2002). Digital video archives: Managing through metadata. *Building a national strategy for digital preservation: Issues in digital media archiving, 84*, 99.

Waltl, C. (2006). Museums for visitors: Audience development-A crucial role for successful museum management strategies. *Intercom, 2006*, 1–7.

Weir, C. R., Nebeker, J. J., Hicken, B. L., Campo, R., Drews, F., & LeBar, B. (2007). A cognitive task analysis of information management strategies in a computerized provider order entry environment. *Journal of the American Medical Informatics.*

Whittaker, S., & Hirschberg, J. (2001). The character, value, and anagement of personal paper archives. *ACM Transactions on Computer-Human Interaction, 8*(2), 150–170. doi:10.1145/376929.376932

Yang, T., & Fan, W. (2016). Information management strategies and supply chain performance under demand disruptions. *International Journal of Production Research, 54*(1), 8–27. doi:10.1080/00207543.2014.991456

ADDITIONAL READING

Ahmad, A., Maynard, S. B., & Park, S. (2014). Information security strategies: Towards an organizational multi-strategy perspective. *Journal of Intelligent Manufacturing, 25*(2), 357–370. doi:10.100710845-012-0683-0

Al-Fedaghi, S. (2013). Information management and valuation. *International Journal of Engineering Business Management, 5*, 1. doi:10.5772/52800

Gallié, E. P., & Legros, D. (2012). French firms' strategies for protecting their intellectual property. *Research Policy, 41*(4), 780–794. doi:10.1016/j.respol.2011.12.008

Karimi, J., & Konsynski, B. R. (1991). Globalization and information management strategies. *Journal of Management Information Systems, 7*(4), 7–26. doi:10.1080/07421222.1991.11517901

Kearns, L. R., Frey, B. A., Tomer, C., & Alman, S. (2014). A study of personal information management strategies for online faculty. *Journal of Asynchronous Learning Networks, 18*(1). doi:10.24059/olj.v18i1.296

Martín, R. M. (2000, December). Translation Strategies. In *Investigating Translation: Selected Papers from the 4th International Congress on Translation, Barcelona, 1998* (Vol. 32, p. 129). John Benjamins Publishing.

McKnight, W. (2013). *Information management: strategies for gaining a competitive advantage with data.* Newnes.

Winter, A., Haux, R., Ammenwerth, E., Brigl, B., Hellrung, N., & Jahn, F. (2010). Health information systems. In *Health Information Systems* (pp. 33–42). London: Springer. doi:10.1007/978-1-84996-441-8_4

Section 3
Learning to See Cultures

Chapter 5
Seeing Business Cultures

ABSTRACT

In this chapter, the authors focus on the essential elements of culture and consider the factors that may contribute to shaping an organization's unique culture. The authors caution that this is a rich chapter – the goal is to help business managers make the transition from understanding culture at a theoretical level to seeing and managing it on an everyday practical level. In this chapter, the authors explain what we need to know about business cultures. They define business cultures in terms of their structural and dynamic aspects. The authors define three structural levels, including macro-level (global, national), meso-level (organization, unit), and micro-level (individual) culture. For each level, a rich set of dynamic factors are identified. This chapter prepares the manager for describing his/her organization's business culture.

WHAT WE NEED TO KNOW ABOUT BUSINESS CULTURES

Chapter 2 provided a foundation for understanding the essential elements of culture. Our challenge in Chapter 3 is to explain how those essential elements translate to the cultures of organizations, teams, and individuals. The elements of culture become visible to us as structural and dynamic factors. By structural factors, we refer to the levels or structure of an organization. An individual is our most basic instance of culture – but in an organizational context, these elements compound and expand with each successive layer. An organization's culture is constructed over layers – beginning with the individual, the team, the community, the business unit, the organization, and

DOI: 10.4018/978-1-7998-4315-3.ch005

the organization's national and geographic location. In this text, we refer to these layers as structural elements. Cultural research also tells us that there are dynamic factors that shape an organization's culture at each of these layers. In this text, we refer to these as dynamic factors.

Figure 1. Business cultures in the framework

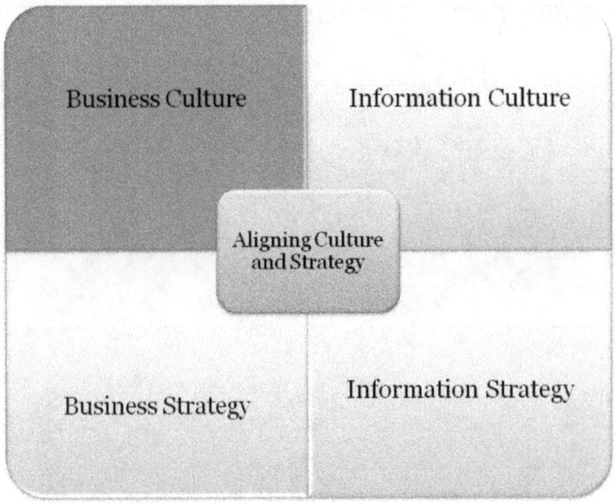

We need to have a general understanding of the dimensions of organizational culture, including its structural and dynamic elements. Managers need to understand and describe our organization's culture is from m a structural perspective – by levels. Managers need to understand and describe our organization's culture in terms of its dynamic factors. Changing or shifting an organization's culture involves everyone – not just senior leadership. This means that everyone - needs to be able to "see" culture in a way that allows them to manage it. In this chapter, we present a reference model of an organization's culture that will serve as a tool for strategy development and alignment.

DIMENSIONS OF ORGANIZATIONAL – STRUCTURAL AND DYNAMIC ELEMENTS

There are two essential dimensions to any business culture - the structural elements (e.g., the organizational levels) and the dynamic elements (e.g., the

Figure 2. Seeing culture from the structural perspective

factors) that will define the business culture of an organization (Figure 2). The structural dimension of culture pertains to the hierarchy of nested levels - beginning with the individual, the teams they belong to, the business units they work in, the informal communities they participate in, the organization they support, and the countries or locations where they live and work.

Culture as a shared meaning system can be formed at each one of these levels. The business culture is formed by factors at play in three general levels, including (1) the macro level; (2) the meso-level; and (3) the micro-level. The macro-level is comprised of global and national cultures. The meso-level culture is made up of the organizational culture and the unit or group culture. The micro-level culture focuses on the culture of the individual. While the authors describe the role of all three levels, the primary focus of this text is on the meso and micro level cultures. These levels are the most relevant to business and information management strategies.

Figure 3. The context for seeing the structural and dynamic factors of culture

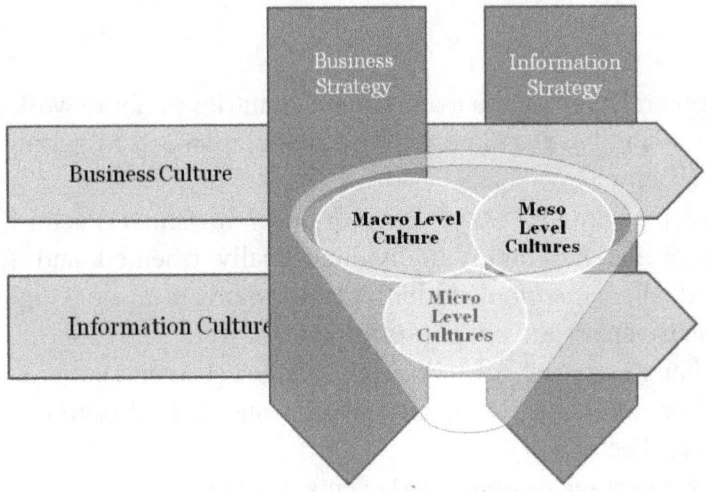

The dynamic dimension pertains to the factors that influence each level and define that level. While structural elements exist in every organization and are "visible" to everyone, dynamic factors are unique. Every organization's culture is unique because it is defined by the interrelationships of these factors at each level. In order to design a fit of culture to strategy, we need to understand how these dynamic factors influence the organization.

Organizations need to "see" the full scope of our organizational culture and to understand it sufficiently well to "shape" or "fit" it to support strategy. The following sections of this chapter walk the reader through a process of discovering and describing your organization's business culture. The most effective approach to characterizing an organization's culture is to look at each level in-depth and to examine the dynamic factors at each level. The authors begin with a review of the dynamic factors that characterize the macro level, the meso level, and the micro levels of an organization. At the end of this review, it should be clear how to develop a practical description of your organization's culture.

NATIONAL CULTURE DYNAMIC FACTORS

National cultures include factors that shape all of the cultures an individual encounters or shapes. For illustration purposes, the authors have identified eleven factors (Figure 4) you should be able to "see" at the national level, including:

- Our general approach to *work* – some countries prefer to work in teams while others have a more individualistic approach to getting the job done (Factor 1)
- Whether we are *process-oriented* or *people-oriented* (Factor 2)
- Whether we are highly individualistically oriented and focus on individual *competition* and individual rewards or place a higher value on cohesiveness and *collaboration* (Factor 3)
- Whether we are *risk-takers* or *risk-avoiders* (Factor 4)
- Whether we value *financial rewards* and compensation or *social rewards* (Factor 5)
- How we *manage meetings* and events (Factor 6)
- What we consider to be effective *leadership characteristics* (Factor 7)
- Our underlying assumptions and beliefs about the *role of managers and workers* (Factor 8)
- Our underlying assumptions and beliefs *of engagement and social behavior* (Factor 9)
- How we approach *decision making* and whether we are comfortable with *open discussions and debates* (Factor 10)
- How we *learn*, where we learn and whom we learn from – a reflection of national education philosophies (Factor 11)

When we think of national cultures, most people will think of cultural artifacts – those visible representations that distinguish one culture from another. The most easily recognized artifacts of national culture might include how we dress, our art and crafts, how we build our homes, or the food we eat. These are ways that cultures distinguish themselves from one another. However, national cultures run much more profound than artifacts, and they are much more pervasive. National cultures also include essential beliefs and assumptions, behaviors, and values. Our national cultures are what we learn from our families, our communities, and our upbringing. They are the first cultures that each of us develops, and they are the cultures that remain throughout our lives. According to Hofstede, these primary cultures determine

Figure 4. Dynamic factors at the national culture level

the mental models, assumptions, and beliefs we acquire during the first ten years of our lives. Of all the structural levels of culture, it is the national culture that aligns most clearly with the lowest level of culture – assumptions, and beliefs. We note that these are not only the most pervasive and long-lasting, but that they are the hardest to change. A wise organizational manager will understand that it is essential to shape but not attempt to change a national culture.

While they occupy a high level in our conceptual model, they echo in dynamic factors at every subsequent level. These factors are among the most extensively researched and documented in the cultural, business, and communication literature (Lewis, 2010).

GLOBAL CULTURE DYNAMIC FACTORS

The increasing complexity of the workplace and the need to coordinate and mobilize resources within and across geographical borders increase the cultural complexity of our work environments. The formation of highly interdependent teams enables organizations to span geographical and cultural boundaries. (Berson, Erez, and Adler, 2004). The international environment creates a new cultural identity – one that blends the national culture and organizational culture. An international identity means that people develop a sense of belongingness to a universal organizational culture by adopting the values and behaviors of the organization while still retaining their assumptions, beliefs, behaviors, and values of their national cultures (Arnett, 2002). From a high-level view, this looks like multiple cultures (Arnett, 2002). Though, individuals in international organizations or who work in a global environment adopt multiple identities. How well these identities and cultures align depend on the similarity of the global and their local cultures. A good fit between the local and global cultures facilitates the integration of global and local identity.

The cultures of international organizations may create tensions between the local culture and the organization or universal culture. (Naisbitt, 1994). Oddly, the international culture has the most significant impact on the individual because it is at the individual level that these two different cultures must align (Tajfel and Turner, 1979). The international culture level means aligning dynamic factors at the national level with the dynamic factors at the organizational level. This means learning to see how the eleven national factors (Figure 4) interact with and influence the nine factors at the organization level (Figure 5)

ORGANIZATIONAL LEVEL DYNAMIC FACTORS

Nested within the national culture is the level of organizational culture, often defined as a set of beliefs and values shared by members of the same organization, which influence their behaviors (Schein, 1992; Miron, Erez, and Naveh, 2003; O'Reilly, Chatman, and Caldwell, 1991; Rousseau, 1990; Schneider, Salvaggio, and Subirats, 2002). The organization-level culture is what is officially sanctioned, presented to the external business environment, and promoted it internally. The organizational culture is a result of all the decisions made and all the actions taken in an organization over time. Culture is slowly formed by people interacting and by repeating behaviors that lead to success as defined by the organization. Cultural leadership comes from the top. Continuous and consistent leadership is an excellent starting point for building strong cultures. The organization level may set the "espoused values" related to information culture, but it is rarely the case that these are reflective of firmly held beliefs and assumptions, and are rarely manifested in day to day behaviors or artifacts.

Through an extensive review of the literature, the authors identified nine factors that play a role in defining the organization's culture, including:

- Leadership Style
- Life Cycle Stage of the Organization
- Geographic Location
- Ethics and Rewards
- Business Sector and Industry of the Organization
- Business Goals of the Organization
- Position of the Organization in the Market
- Internal Structure of the Organization
- Management Control Systems.

Figure 5. Dynamic factors that affect the organization level culture

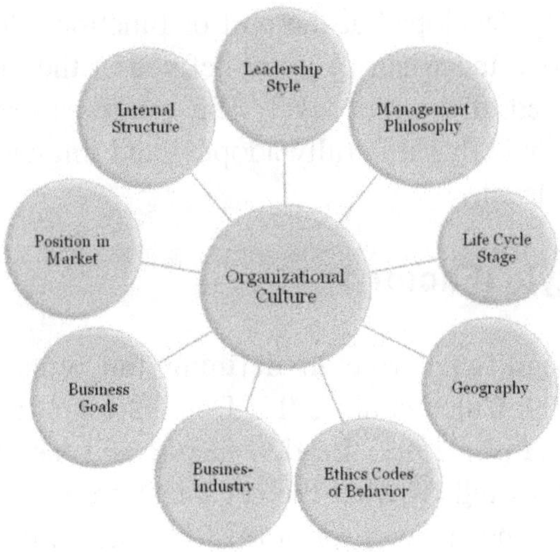

These are the factors we understand and shape to align culture and strategies. The literature provides descriptions of these factors and explains how each might shape culture (Figure 5). In this section, the authors provide enough information about each factor to help the reader "see" the factors and learn how they might help to define culture in a given context and at a given point in time. We discuss these factors because they affect our business and information strategies and because the way we fit cultures and strategies is dependent upon these factors.

The image of organizations as having a multidimensional culture (Gregory, 1983), and only rarely sharing a single, overarching set of beliefs and system of meanings, complicates the role of culture in shaping problem setting and strategies for action.

One aspect that defines an organizational subculture is that the members share a set of problems commonly defined to be the problems of all, and routinely take actions based on collective understandings to the group (Van Maanen and Barley, 1985). If an organization comprises multiple, perhaps cross-cutting cultures (e.g., if occupational and hierarchical subcultures are salient), then whose problem interpretations and actions will matter, and will some interpretations and strategies for actions may overrule others?

The majority of cultural research focuses on organizations. We know more about the culture at this level than at any other level in an organization. While researchers may call out factors and levels, research is not generally extended to those dimensions. Our challenge is that those information strategies are rarely developed or implemented at the whole organization level. They are more frequently developed at the unit or functional level. Information strategies fail most often when they are defined at the organization level, but not implemented at the unit level. The true measure of a successful information strategy is that it is fully adopted and implemented at the unit and the individual level.

Leadership Style (Factor 1)

Leaders play a significant role in defining the organizational culture (Baumgartner, 2009; Culen et al., 2012; Den Hartog et al., 1999; Hofstee, 1984; House and Mansor, 1999). Leaders inspire and energize people – their behaviors and values tell us what the organization assumes and believes. Their behaviors set the standard or norm for others. Leaders demonstrate a sound ethical compass. In the ideal situation, they demonstrate effective communication skills, show us how they learn and how to mentor and coach others, demonstrate the right balance of risk-taking and risk avoidance, show us how to ask for and offer help, and their ability to adapt to and accept change, their charm and ability to influence and motivate people. Through their daily behaviors, leaders telegraph the organization's lived assumptions, beliefs, and values. What cues might you look for to understand this effect?

Shein tells us that leaders in embed their beliefs, values, and assumptions in an organization. More specifically, leaders embed culture by (1) paying attention to, measuring and controlling; (2) reacting to critical incidents and organizational crises; (3) allocating budgets and resources; (4) the roles models they project, what they teach, how they coach others; (5) allocating rewards and assigning status; and (6) recruiting, selecting, promoting and shedding staff.

- To "see" the leader's beliefs, we might pay attention to what they *measure and* regularly control, what they *notice*, what they *comment on*, the kinds of *questions* they ask, the *remark*s they make, what a leader continuously supports.
- Leaders demonstrate their behaviors and norms by how they react to *critical incidents and crises* - do they handle incidents consistently and with control, or do they treat each event or crisis differently? Does the leader create crises? Does he/she leverage crises to create anxiety and uncertainty?
- We can see a leader's beliefs in what they fund and support. How are *budget decisions* made? Is input on budget decisions encouraged or discouraged?
- What kind of a *role model* do leaders project? Do they share their knowledge and experience with others? Do they sponsor, coach, or mentor others? Whom do they mentor? Is there a difference in what leaders communicate formally and what they say informally?
- How do leaders *allocate rewards*? Who do they promote and advance? How do leaders assess performance? Does the leader expect value in return for rewards or status? What is punished?
- What criteria or characteristics do leaders value when they are *recruiting staff*, *selecting* new staff, *promoting* staff, and *off-boarding*

Figure 6. Cultures aligned with life cycle stages of the organization

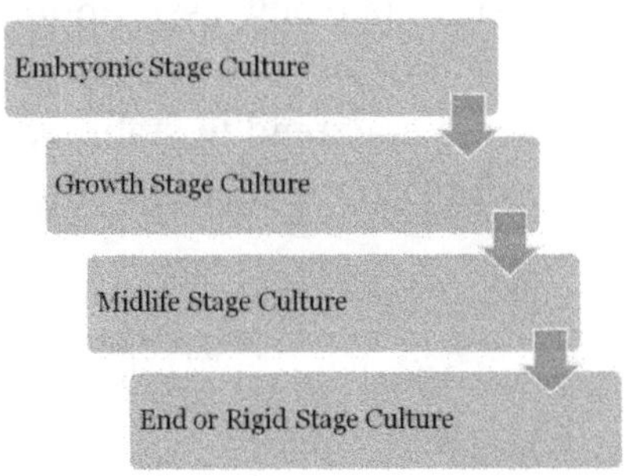

staff? Does the leader bring all of "his/her people" with him when he takes a new role? What kinds of relationships do leaders establish with their subordinates?

- An autocratic leader reserves complete authority and allows subordinates a little freedom. A democratic leader shares authority with followers and seeks consensus. A participatory leader advocates or delegates authority totally to a work unit. The in its members have complete control or freedom to resolve a crisis or producing innovation.

Life Cycle Stage of the Organization (Factor 2)

What cues might you look for to understand this effect? Each stage has a different effect on the organization's culture.

- The early or embryonic stage culture is characterized by an innovative and expansive, a growth orientation, and an intense focus on stakeholder orientation, risk-taking, empowerment, trust, agility, and short-term orientation.
- The growth stage culture focuses on expansion with intent to expand products and services, a focus on scale and efficiency, a focus on process, and disciplined innovation. This stage may also shift to a culture that values budgeting, planning and execution, market orientation, revenue generation, cost management, relationship building, and quality.
- A midlife stage culture may focus on growth and change as functions and subunits mature. Subcultures may develop. Leadership and cultural dynamics come to the fore, and there may even be shifts in culture if new leaders come onto the scene. At this stage, you may have differentiation of cultures – where many of the original founding managers and leaders are still engaged, but new leaders are also bringing in external cultures. This stage may see an expansion in the business outlook – and stimulate new assumptions, beliefs, values, and behaviors.
- In the final stages, cultures may tend to stabilize and become rigid – if the organization is winding down, there is little incentive to revitalize the culture.

Geographic Location and National Culture of the Organization (Factor 3)

How might the location of the organization affect the culture? We noted earlier that national cultures have a significant effect on organizational cultures through the behaviors of individuals. Where an organization is located may tend to strengthen these cultural characteristics, where there is a higher concentration of individuals from that culture (Boya Cigiller et al., 2004; Hein and Brinley, 2004; Hofstede, 1983; Lewis, 2010; Lewis, 1999; Lewis, 2003; Morris and Peng, 1994; Murakami and Singelis, 2002; Schwartz, 1992; Smith Dugan and Trompenaars, 1990; Smith Trompenaars and Duggan, 1995). Today organizations may have one or more locations in different countries. Where an organization was founded may reflect the dominant culture. The founder's national cultures may reflect the dominant culture. The host country's culture may also play a dominant role in each location. An organization that has its headquarters and founding culture in Pennsylvania but has field offices around the world – will have multiple national cultures at play, a dominant host country culture, and a harmonizing global culture. The geographic location may:

- Be reflected in the history and traditions of the organization, the predominant beliefs, and assumptions of the organization.
- Affect the administrative and internal structure of the organization;
- Affect the number of reporting layers in the organization and the administrative practices of the organization;
- Affect power relationships – how leaders and authorities behave and govern;
- How people organize themselves and *work together* to accomplish the organization's goals.

Ethics and Standards of Behavior (Factor 4)

Ethics is an essential dimension of organizational culture. Ethics concerns the general nature of good and evil and right and wrong and the moral obligations or choices of individuals. Ethics establishes the norms for governance, values, and behaviors – it speaks to an essential element of culture. How might ethics and

- Organizations may have codes of ethics, or they may take their ethical cues informally and indirectly from the behaviors and actions of leaders.\;
- Organizational ethics and behaviors may also be determined by the nature of the functions or professions that make up an organization – professional codes of ethics or standards of behaviors. For example, a hospital will have embedded values aligned with the medical profession – the Hippocratic Oath, privacy, and confidentiality considerations. An organization devoted to managing financial resources may have an entirely different set of ethics – all grounded on the production of profit and transactions;
- Organizations also reflect the professional ethics associated with trades and professionals that define their core operations and capabilities.
- Ethics may be espoused or actual, enforcement systems and mechanisms may support them, or they may simply be plaques on the wall.
- How unethical behaviors or immoral behaviors are punished or rewarded tells us a lot about the culture of an organization;

This factor may interact with and be influenced by leadership cultures. The ethical standards and norms that leaders set at all levels of the organization are defining elements of their culture.

Function or Industry Focus of the Organization (Factor 5)

What can we learn about the organization's culture from its business functions that define it or the economic sector in which it operates? The economic sector determines what an organization makes or what value it offers to its stakeholders (Grimshaw, 1995; Leung et al., 2005; Moore, 2014; Shermont and Krepcio, 2008; Soares Farhangmehr and Shoham, 2007; Trompenaars, 1996). The culture of a fashion retailer will differ from the culture of a community non-profit that provides safety nets for local populations. Two fashion retailers, though, may have similar cultures, as may community social service organizations. Organizations in the same economic sector will share cultural norms and values which may be dictated by the external environment. In some cases, the functional or sector culture may override national cultures. Automotive companies have a strong engineering culture. They also have a robust production-oriented culture. Pharmaceutical companies may tend to exhibit values and behaviors consistent with the medical profession because research teams are comprised mainly of medical scientists. Organizations that offer legal services may tend to value facts and evidence, view emotional behaviors as high risk, and tend to focus on the protection of information and privacy. Automotive companies in Poland and Argentina may have some cultural traits in common, just as fashion retailers in New York and Paris. We might also consider:

- The competitive nature of an industry or sector will also affect an organization's culture. If the external environment is competitive, the organization's culture will internalize that culture;
- If the external environment is emerging and unsettled, it leaves room for the organization to cultivate a culture that takes advantage of that context;
- If the organization is competing in an emerging market, it may be critical to nurturing a creative, innovative, and risk-preferring culture.
- An organization that operates in a highly regulated environment will adopt a cautious, planned, documented, and risk-averse culture to ensure compliance. Conversely, it may create a culture of deception and surreptitious behavior to avoid regulatory requirements;
- If the organization operates in a low competition market where there are few competitors, it may be free to define its own preferred culture;

Business Goals of the Organization (Factor 6)

How might an organization's mission and business goals affect its culture? How an organization establishes its goals and achieves consensus tells us a lot about our culture. Setting and achieving goals means developing a consensus, working together to achieve goals, measuring, and adjusting plans. Goals provided a shared concept and rationale for survival. Culture exists when members share identity, mission, and goals. Goals require group consensus and the development of a shared language and shared assumptions. The mission can be timeliness, but goals must have an endpoint. Your goals will speak directly to your assumptions and beliefs and shape your values and behaviors. Ultimately your business goals will determine whether you have a competitive, entrepreneurial, bureaucratic, or consensual culture.

What are some key questions we might consider to understand how our culture is affected by our business goals? We might ask:

- What can we learn about our culture from our responses to whether we achieve or fail to achieve our goals? How do we change or correct our goals?
- Do we have one set of goals, or are there conflicting business goals? If we have multiple goals, are some dominant and others less important?
- How do we determine the importance of goals? Is there a single mission?
- Who defines the mission? Does the founder define it? Has it changed over time? Does the external market define it?
- Do the individuals across the organization share a mission and demonstrate a shared identity?
- Do individuals associate themselves with the organization, or do they downplay "where they work"?

Our business goals will also determine whether an organization's culture is predominantly competitive, entrepreneurial, bureaucratic, or consensual. In a competitive culture, values relating to demanding goals, competitive advantage, marketing superiority, and profits were emphasized. In the entrepreneurial culture, the emphasis was on innovation, risk-taking, high levels of dynamism, and creativity. In the bureaucratic culture, values like formalization, rules, standard operating procedures, and hierarchical coordination. This culture values predictability, efficiency, and stability. In the consensual culture, elements of tradition, loyalty, personal commitment, extensive socialization, teamwork, self-management, and social influence are essential in the organizational values.

Position of the Organization in the Market (Factor 7)

The market position and brand of your organization will influence its organizational culture. Are you the market leader or a market challenger in your industry? A challenger culture often includes being short-term, execution, results, and action-oriented. A challenger is more agile and pragmatic and will respond quickly to changes in the market and two new customer requirements. The market leader may focus on process efficiencies and effectiveness as a critical cultural competency. This factor will interact with the nature of the business function and the economic sectors.

Internal Structure of the Organization (Factor 8)

An organization's culture also is dependent on its internal structure and the way it organizes itself. This can range from - 'This is how we do things around here!' - to formal procedures. Until the 1980s, most organizations had a strong hierarchically structured administrative structure. The decision-makers were at the top, followed by the functional workers. Next in the hierarchy were the clerical workers and, at the lowest levels, the production and service workers. Organizations have flattened out, and the decision-makers are now at all levels (Grimshaw, 1995). If you have an intense and persistent hierarchical structure, it may be challenging to connect people and to embed a single inclusive organizational culture. The more layers you have in your structure and the more units you have – particularly persistent units that have existed over the years or decades – the easier it will be for subcultures to develop and strengthen. Isolated teams will have their subcultures. The internal structure will affect:

- What the organization chart looks like - how many layers there are in your organization chart;
- Whether your organization is mission or project-focused, product, or service focused.
- How your administrative units are defined. Are units persistently defined from top to bottom, or is there a level below which you have functional teams? Are teams defined dynamically to support projects or missions?
- What the distribution of staff across the organization is. Are most of the staff in units at the lowest levels? Is the majority of staff assigned to core operations in the middle of the organization?
- How communication flows – are decisions made at the top and simply communicated to lo others? Are other levels involved in making decisions?
- Whether decision making is decentralized or centralized, are new strategies made lower down in the organization? Or are strategies only defined by a few at the top and promulgated to others?

The internal structure will also determine whether subcultures develop across and within levels of the organization rather than in an integrated way. In the absence of an integrated culture, subgroups will likely develop.

Management Philosophy and Control Systems (Factor 9)

The management philosophy is a complicated factor. It describes the different ways that an organization might establish control over itself. What are the different facets of this factor, and how might we learn to see them in the organization? This factor reflects and reinforces many of the national factors mentioned earlier, including whether the organization:

- Is process-oriented or results-oriented?
- Is employee or job oriented or people-oriented (i.e., do you focus on investing in your people or on just getting the job done)?
- Is parochial or professional (i.e., does a person's identity derived from the company or profession, or do you see the individual's potential and full intellectual capital assets)?
- Is an open or a closed system (i.e., is it an inclusive culture or an exclusive, secretive, cliquish culture?
- Exerts loose or tight control over people and what they do? Do individuals have the opportunity to be creative and contribute new ideas or do they know they should "do what they are expected to do, and what they are told to do
- Is a normative or a pragmatic organization - do people know they should follow the process, or can they be innovative and focus on the market or customer demands?
- Values individuals and their personal details, or values a strictly work-focused or professional-focused culture?
- Speaks with a common language across the organization or has a more fragmented unit level language?
- Resolves conflicts at the individual level or requires managerial interventions?

Perhaps the most critical aspect of this factor, though, is the control structure and the distribution of power across the organization.

- How are influence, power, and authority allocated? Does everyone have some degree of power or influence, or is there is a significant imbalance?
- How is power determined? Is it "taken" by individuals because a vacuum exists at some levels?
- How are power and influence reified?

- What is the source of power? Who grants it? Can power be earned or assigned? How is power limited?
- What happens when someone challenges power? How are they rewarded or punished?

Control is also defined by the mobility of individuals in an organization. Is an individual's initial position reinforced throughout their career? Can they change roles? Can they advance? There are three dimensions of movement within an organization – lateral movement – from one task to another; (2) vertical movement – from one job class to another; and (3) inclusion within a group to be excluded from the group – favorability or outcast. Generally, the more complex an organization, the more potential there is for movement.

UNIT AND TEAM CULTURE DYNAMIC FACTORS

Organizational cultures are rarely monolithic. From a 50,000 foot view or the outside, an organization's culture may appear holistic and integrated. Upon closer inspection, though, every organizational culture has multiple subcultures. An organization's culture is a composition of all of its subcultures (Martin, 1992; Martin, 2002; Schein, 1996). Martin and Schein suggest that organizational cultures may be (1) cohesive and unitary; (2) integrated, and collections of subcultures; or (3) differentiated. A fragmented culture is ambiguous and open to members' multiple interpretations. (Meyerson and Martin, 1987). Each subculture interacts with others in unique ways (Martin and Siehl, 1983; Bloor and Dawson, 1994; Martin, 2001). We must understand subcultures at an individual level and understand whether and if so, how they contribute to creating a productive, supportive, and "whole organization" culture (Rose, 1988; Sackmann, 1992; Trice and Beyer, 1993). By considering cultural cohesion and strength, we acknowledge that subcultures exist and can develop within strong cultures without weakening the overarching culture.

The most common reason subcultures align with what the organization defines formal units or teams. There are ways to look at the dynamic factors that shape unit or team cultures are (1) factors that are a reflection of and are inherited from the organizational culture; and (2) factors that derive from the composition of the unit or team – what the individuals bring to the unit. These two sets of factors might be view as top-down and bottom-up factors. This is a critical cultural integration level simply because it is where the most generalized and the most individualized cultures meet and blend. This means it is a bit more challenging to develop a cultural profile of the unit. It also means that unit cultures are a starting point for understanding the interaction of cultures across units and the organization.

DYNAMIC FACTORS INHERITED FROM THE ORGANIZATIONAL CULTURE

As noted above, these factors present a top-down view of culture. These factors (Figure 7) are also found at the organization level, and they play an essential role at the unit level – but they may be interpreted differently. The subculture they create may be consistent with or different from the organizational culture. How do the factors that are inherited from the organization change when they reach the unit level? Is there a different cultural effect of each factor, i.e., do the factors interact in different ways? How does the unique composition of the individual cultures or registers affect the inherited factors? How do they affect the cultural composition of the unit? In this section, we walk through each set of factors and suggest ways to see and track these factors to align the unit's culture with the unit's business and information strategies. Inherited factors include:

- Unit leadership style of the unit or group
- Management philosophy or control of the unit or group
- Life cycle stage of the unit within the organization
- The geographic location of the unit or group
- Ethics and rewards practices of the unit or group

Figure 7. Inherited factors at the unit or team level

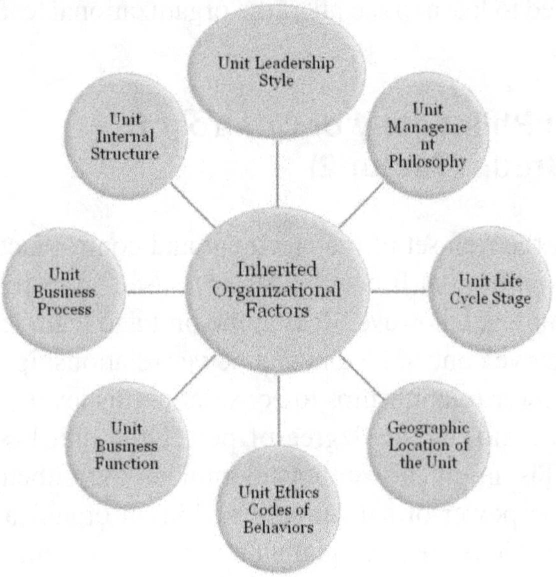

- Business function of the unit or group
- The business process of the unit or group
- The internal structure of the unit.

Unit Leadership Style of the Unit or Group (Factor 1)

How does the unit's leadership style affect the unit's culture? The unit and line managers heavily influence the culture of the unit. Unit managers and leaders are the nearest embodiment of leaders' assumptions and beliefs, values, and behaviors within the unit. The leader or manager of the unit has the most significant opportunity to define and reinforce what factors dominate the unit's culture. Unit managers are also key players in whether the organization's culture is supported or ignored at the unit level. They are also key players in whether and how the strategy is supported.

We need to understand how do unit-level managers think and behave? Do managers have a consistent way of behaving? Can we understand their assumptions, beliefs, and values through their behaviors? Are there artifacts the leaders introduce into their environment that tells us about their preferred culture? Do unit managers' behaviors mirror those of senior managers or the staff in the unit or on the team? How much influence do they have over strategy? We need to learn to see all of the organizational leadership features at the unit level.

Management Philosophy or Control of the Unit or Group (Factor 2)

All units inherit the rich set of management and control factors we defined at the organization level at It may be easier to "see" how this factor affects culture at the unit level, however. It is at the unit and team level that we can most clearly observe control factors and power relationships. There are two dimensions to power relationships to consider at this level.

The first dimension is the degree of power the unit has in the overall organization. This might affect how dominant the subculture is in the organization. The power of subcultures within an organization influences their interactions. Units are not equally powerful - some may enjoy a higher status within the organization and have a degree of control that flows from the centrality in their work of the organization, or the irreplaceability of their expertise or skills (Van Maanen and Barley, 1985; Bloor and Dawson, 1994; Jermier et al., 1991; Kunda, 1992; Stevenson and Bartunek, 1996).

The second dimension is the nature of the power relationships within the unit. Does one individual dominate the culture? Does this person have more influence over how strategy is implemented? At this level, it is essential to understand (1) who has power, (2) what their individual cultures are, and (3) what role they play in designing or implementing strategy.

Life Cycle Stage of the Unit within the Organization (Factor 3)

We described earlier how the life cycle of an organization might affect its culture. At this level, we are interested in understanding the age and maturity of the unit within the broader history of the organization. How new is the function? How well established is the function? How well-entrenched is the function? Consider the effect of a well established monetary unit and their cultural dominance in an organization. Consider the effect an innovation unit might have on an organization's culture – as a young unit, how is it viewed by those who have a historical track record in the organization? Is it viewed as adding value, as disruptive or as a new competitor for resources?

Geographic Location of the Unit or Group (Factor 4)

We described how the geographic location of an organization might translate to the essential traits of individuals and the structure and behavior of the organization. Geography may also affect the unit's culture. For example, we should consider:

- How close the unit is to and how heavily customers influence it;
- Is the unit is distant from central administration – if so, might it develop a culture that more closely resembles the culture of its location?
- How does the function of the unit relate to the country in which the unit is located?
- Does the unit have a highly innovative and creative function, but is located in a country which strong regulations and a hierarchical and heavily bureaucratic tradition?
- How easily do local traditions and conventions influence the function?
- Is local expertise needed to support the unit? If so, does it play a dominant role in defining the culture?

Ethics and Codes of Behavior in the Unit or Group (Factor 5)

At the unit level, it is logical to assume that the leader will set the ethical standards for the unit. He or she has the opportunity to promote strong ethics through their everyday behaviors. The unit manager has the power to reward or punish behavior. However, this influence may be tempered by the general ethical climate of the environment where the unit is located. If the business conventions involve bribes, personal networks, and fealty, the unit manager may not be able to set ethics standards that will be followed. The dominance of the unit's ethics and behaviors will depend upon the pressure exerted by the external environment. Assuming these factors are consistent, though, the unit leader has a significant opportunity to set ethical standards and to reinforce them through rewards and recognition.

Business Function of the Unit or Group (Factor 6)

One of the most substantial types of culture is the culture inherent to a function or subject area.

Perhaps the most significant factor is the functional orientation of the unit. This may be the factor that is easiest for us to see because it is likely the dominant reason the unit exists. Of all aspects of the business function we might define at this level, the two easier to observe might be professional cultures and professional language.

The nature of the work of the unit will often align with a professional culture and all of its inherent assumptions, beliefs, values, behaviors, and artifacts. Professional cultures are often invisible, but their impact is significant. The culture of the unit is a reflection of the education and training, basic assumptions, beliefs, and values of the underlying profession or area of practice. The manufacturing function will hire people who have a team or small workgroup culture. Financial units will draw from the professional cultures of accountants. A marketing function will bring in a different culture – one of independence, creativity, risk-preferring, trial, and error. A communications unit will draw from the cultures of communications and media professionals – they may be detail-oriented, risk-averse, and accustomed to extensive team-reviews and cross-checking. A hospital critical care unit will draw from the cultures of medical professionals – doctors, nurses, specialists - who exhibit strong care assumptions and beliefs, whose behavior is focused on specific individuals, and who tend to be risk-averse. Each of these underlying professions and areas brings their assumptions and beliefs, values and behaviors, and artifacts to the organization.

Also, functional units are likely to adopt and speak in a specialized language and vocabularies in use at the functional level. How we talk to one another and what we talk about is an indication of the unit's culture. These language differences and concentrations may tend to fragment cultures or create barriers to reshaping cultures. It is important to remember the role language might play when we are trying to reshape a unit's culture to support a strategy.

Business Process of the Unit or Group (Factor 7)

This factor can be more clearly observed and defined at the unit or team level – again because it tends to be an organizing factor for administrative units. The organization may have a primary focus – marketing, manufacturing, individualized health care – but in order for the organization to survive, it must have a diverse support structure. This means that a hospital has a supply unit that is focused on ordering supplies and inventorying those supplies. This unit may more closely resemble a retail culture than the broader medical culture.

We should assume that the immediate work process will take precedence in setting the culture, but that it will be influenced by the environment in which that process is carried out.

Internal Structure and Size of the Unit (Factor 8)

The internal structure is a complicated factor at the organization unit, but it takes on a more straightforward and more obvious form and affects at the unit level. It is easier to "see" how this factor affects culture at this level. How does the unit organize it? A team-based culture can exist within a unit and not be an impediment to a command/control culture at the senior leadership level. The cultural tension will be at the boundary of the unit and the organization. The leader will be the mediating factor at this boundary. What cues might we be looking for at the unit level? Does the unit favor individualism or collective behavior? Is it team and collaborative in its behaviors? Are people or results more highly valued? Does the unit demand 200% from every individual, or is it more supportive? Is if recognized as fair, or is cut-throat competition more highly valued?

UNIT AND TEAM COMPOSITION FACTORS

The native cultures of individuals that comprise the unit or team carry equal weight to those factors inherited from the organizational culture. Inherited organizational factors may be commonly defined across organizations – but the cultural registers of individuals that make up a unit give it its unique cultural character. As noted earlier, a unit is defined by the individuals who comprise that unit at any given point in time and their individual cultural registers. The set of compositional factors is a bottom-up description of a unit's culture. They are more dynamic than the inherited factors because they change with the arrival or departure of each individual. The composition of a unit is defined by the people who are assigned to it at any point in time.

Research tends to treat these factors as "demographic differences" (Pelled, 1996). In this text, the authors attempt to break them down and consider how they might play out and how we might shape them to support our strategies. The authors have identified six elements of individuals' cultures whose aggregate composition has an impact on the unit's culture. These six factors include:

- The gender makeup of the unit;

- National culture make up of the unit;
- Generational composition of the unit;
- Size of the group;
- The nature of relationships within the group and its networks to other units;
- The language composition of the unit.

Figure 8. Group composition factors affecting the unit culture

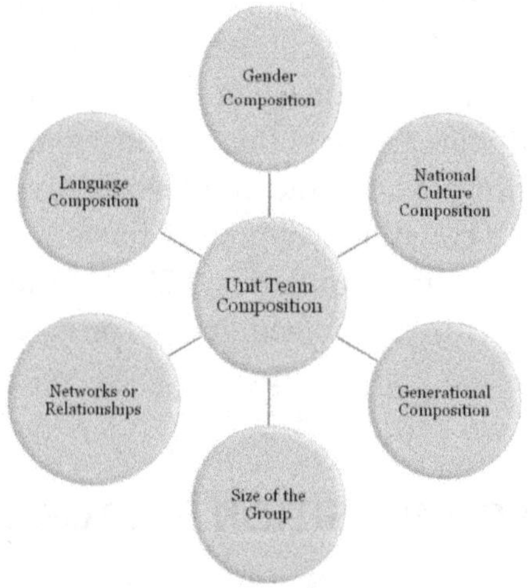

These cultural registers do not exist in a vacuum but shift and shape as they interact with other cultural registers. Individuals share their cultural behaviors and values with others – they influence everyone they come in contact with. The collective culture of a business unit is defined at a given point in time. This makes it more challenging to define and describe. A change in membership or a change in leadership can significantly change the compositional culture. While culture is manifested in the collective, it is lived by each individual. Individuals absorb elements of every culture they are exposed to – it becomes part of his or her fundamental attitudes and behaviors.

Gender Composition of the Group (Factor 1)

What is the gender composition army unit? A group comprised of 19 men and one woman will likely exhibit a more male-oriented culture. A group comprised entirely of women might tend to exhibit a more female-oriented culture (Andreoni and Vsterlund, 2001; Ayman and Korabnik, 2010; Croson and Buchan, 1990; Fischer and Manstead, 2000; Korabnik and Ayman, 2007; Mills, 1988; Shinnar Giacomin and Janssen, 2012). Here we need to be cautious about relying on stereotypes rather than observing how this factor influences culture daily. There are many stereotypes about men and women, but it is essential to review the stereotypes, and the research with a critical eye – culture tends to shape behaviors. Are men likely to be more aggressive in their behaviors and decision-making? Do women tend more towards information-based and risk-balanced decision making? Do women tend to work more independently than men? Are men more likely to form networks and informal relationships with other men? Do women have more open attitudes about asking for and using advice from others?

The gender composition of the group will be an interaction of factors. An individual's gender-related assumptions, beliefs, values, and behaviors are likely to factors. Women of different generations may have different assumptions, behaviors, and values. Women from different national cultures may have different behaviors and norms. Other cultural factors will temper gender. Its function might also influence the gender composition of a unit. If the unit is focused on manufacturing and the culture is engineering-oriented, it may tend toward a male-dominated culture. If the unit is a human resources unit or a critical care nursing unit, it may tend toward a female-dominated culture.

National Culture and Composition (Factor 2)

It is essential to understand the national culture makeup of the unit. We need to understand:

- Whether the unit draws from a single or multiple cultures;
- Whether there is a dominant culture;
- The coherence or variations of these cultures;
- How differences are negotiated and how individuals adapt;
- How the diversity of national cultures aligns with or differs from the organizational culture's espoused assumptions, beliefs, and values;
- Whether the organization is accepting of and encouraging multiple national cultures or demonstrates a preference for one;
- Whether the national culture composition of the unit aligns with the culture of the geographical location of the unit.

Generational Composition of the Group (Factor 3)

Over the past twenty years, we have learned a lot about characteristics that are common to different generations, including the World War II generation, baby boomers, millennials, and generations X, Y, and Z. Generations may differ in how they learn their attitudes toward work, where they place their loyalties, how they interact socially, how they define their career advancement plans, and what reward and recognition structures they value. It is essential to understand whether, and if so, how these differences translate to the unit level. It is essential to understand what differences and similarities mean for defining shared assumptions and beliefs, for identifying and supporting common values and behaviors, and for interpreting a range of artifacts.

The generational composition may also interact with the cultures of business goals and functions. If the organization is a technology company that relies on state of the art technical skills and competencies, it may tend to hire younger staff. This may tend to affect the management philosophy and control focus of the unit. If the unit is focused on accounting, it may tend to recruit more experienced practitioners – from the millennial generation.

Like gender, generational factors are not static. As the World War II generation retires and is replaced by the baby boomer generation, the nature of leadership may change. If the organization skips generations in promoting individuals to leadership positions, it may create a differentiated set of assumptions and beliefs across units. As with gender, the generational composition is not an independent factor.

Size of the Group (Factor 4)

While there is less research on this factor than on the others, researchers have observed that smaller or mid-sized units are more likely than larger units to form cohesive cultures regardless of other influencing factors. Smaller units provide more significant opportunities for the unit members to learn and negotiate relationships, to communicate, to better understand the national culture differences of individuals in the unit. The size of a group also might make it easier for individuals to negotiate differences in age, national culture, language, or functional backgrounds.

Networks or Relationships of the Unit or Group (Factor 5)

Networks and relationships within the group tell us a lot about the values and behaviors of the unit. Networks and relationships help us to understand how cohesive or fragmented the unit culture is. We want to know:

- Is there a single network among all members of the unit?
- Are the relationships within the unit balanced and equal?
- Are there dominant relationships?
- Are some members excluded from networks or "distant" members of networks?
- What are the factors around which networks form?
- Are these factors less related to work than to other cultural characteristics?
- How often are these relationships formed or broken when individuals leave or join the unit?
- Moreover, are these relationships maintained even after individuals leave the group?

Native and Second Languages of the Individuals (Factor 6)

There are many dimensions of language – native spoken language, functional or procedural language, language protocols, and norms. Just as individuals bring their cultural registers to the unit, so do they bring their linguistic registers. If a unit's composition has a dominant spoken language, and a dominant professional language, it may tend to create a more cohesive unit culture. If a unit's composition has multiple spoken languages, the unit may define a "working language," which all members must use. This may present some individuals at an advantage and others at a disadvantage. If a unit has a diverse language composition, but all languages are accepted, there may be a more significant opportunity to develop a shared culture.

INFORMAL SUBCULTURES STRUCTURAL AND DYNAMIC FACTORS

Another dimension of subcultures is whether they are formal or informal. In addition to formally defined and visible subcultures, every organization has many informal subcultures. Formal subcultures may form across levels of the organization – most often with administrative units. Formal cultures are influenced by and affect a rich set of factors. Informal subcultures also will form – these tend to form across or within administrative units. Informal subcultures most often form around individual affinities and dynamic factors or combinations of factors.

The boundaries of informal subcultures are often hard to discover. These subcultures may be defined by factors that cross conventional administrative boundaries. Informal subcultures form around any of those factors we described above. These issues may be transient or persistent (Meyerson and Martin, 1987; Bunderson and Sutcliffe, 2003; Edmondson, 2002). Also, they may form within a single unit or cross-unit boundaries.

Researchers have found that subcultures form around many factors including organizational roles, position and longevity in the organization, and functional or professional identifications, shared understandings of tasks, mission, authority structures, by industry sector (Gregory, 1983; Phillips, 1994; Gregory, 1983; Van Maanen and Barley, 1984, Van Maanen and Barley, 1985; Hofstede, 1998; Schein, 1996; Stevenson and Bartunek, 1996; Riley, 1983; Sackmann, 1992; Jermier et al., 1991).

Figure 9. Subculture boundaries within and across administrative boundaries

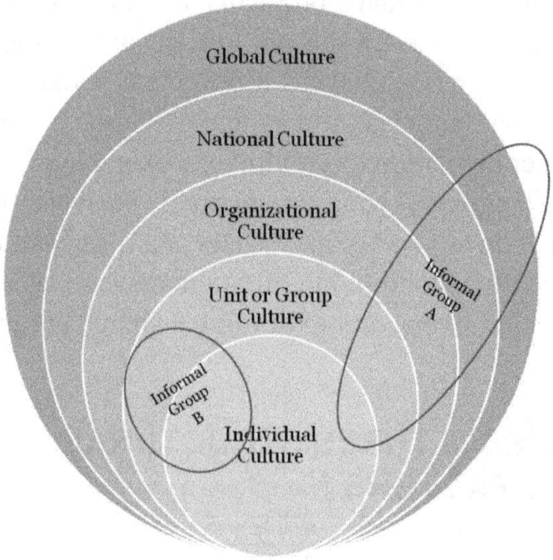

INDIVIDUAL LEVEL DYNAMIC FACTORS

This is not a level that is commonly taken into consideration when we consider how culture affects strategy. Nevertheless, this level of culture is where strategy is translated into actions. Whether tactics are effective will depend on how well their individual cultures align with their individual roles in realizing the strategy. This is where we can more accurately observe how the organization works and behaves. The shaping of culture at this level, though, is the responsibility of the individual. Shaping culture means empowering the individual to shape their cultural register to support the strategy. While the most effective level of alignment, it is also the most difficult to achieve.

The factors that influence this level of culture are consistent with but go beyond those defined for a unit composition. Sociologists describe an individual's cultural profile as a cultural register. A cultural register describes a variation of behavior or language that is used for a particular purpose or in a particular situation.

The cultural factors of interest to us at this level (Figure 10) include an individual's:

- Role and responsibilities in the unit
- Experience and management preferences
- Experiences within the organization
- Nationality
- Skills and competencies
- Levels of expertise
- Gender
- Age
- Personal networks.

Every individual comes to work with multiple cultural registers – meaning they operate within multiple cultures every day – family cultures, national cultures, social cultures, political cultures. What we need to understand here, though, is that these factors may have different levels of influence in each individual. While we might use the same factors to define two individual's cultural registers – the weighting and dominance of any of those factors may be quite different.

Figure 10. Factors that make up an Individual's Cultural Register

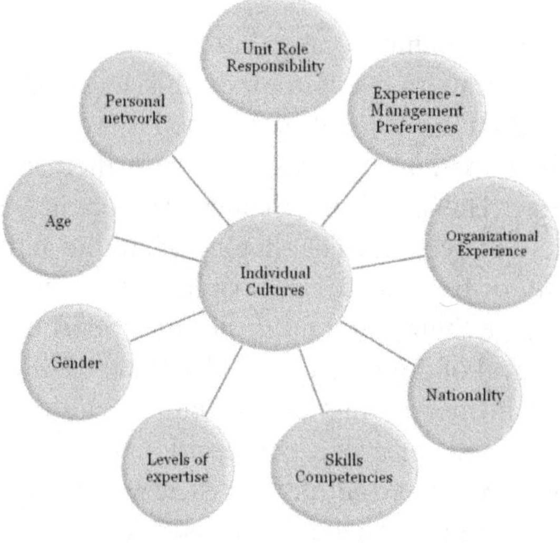

Many of these factors have been discussed in relation to other levels of culture. These factors tell us a lot about the individual's business cultures. They also tell us how an individual is likely to contribute to the nature of a formal or informal subculture. In this section, we will focus on those that have not yet been discussed, including five factors related to the individual:

- Role in the unit
- Management preferences
- Organizational experiences
- Skills and competencies
- Levels of expertise.

Role in the Unit (Factor 1)

An individual's position title and classification relative to others combined may determine how much of an impact their personal cultural attributes have on the unit's culture. For example, an individual with a higher position may mean that their national, gender, and generational attributes have more significant influence than those of others in the unit. Their levels of responsibility may affect the opportunities they have to demonstrate these individual attributes. How long have they been in the unit? An individual with a longer tenure in the unit may have had a more significant effect on the unit's culture than someone who has just joined the unit. Also, every unit has an informal social structure – an individual's position in this informal structure will determine whether their personal communication, learning, work, and other individual styles will have a significant impact on the unit's culture. An individual's promotional history within the unit may also be a signal of the level of influence they have on the unit's culture.

Management Preferences (Factor 2)

At the individual level, management preferences describe an individual's comfort level with working or acting independently. Are they more comfortable with being part of a group? Is the individual comfortable with taking the lead, or do they prefer to follow or be directed by others? These individual cultural attributes might also determine how close the individual is to the unit leadership. What are the individual's cultural preferences for communicating? Are they comfortable speaking their minds? Are they good listeners? What is the individual's decision-making style? Do they tend to make decisions independently, based on personal gains or results? Do they wait for managers to make or signal decisions and then follow those decisions? Do they tend to consider the welfare of the organization, the unit, or other individuals in making decisions? What is the individual's approach to learning, coaching, and mentoring others? How do all of these individual preferences influence the culture of the unit? Furthermore, how do their environments determine these preferences?

Organizational Experiences (Factor 3)

This is an essential dimension of individual culture, which is often overlooked in research. How long has the individual been with the unit? With the organization? The longer their tenure, the more their individual cultures may have been affected by the organization. What is the individual's place in the informal and formal networks across the organization? If an individual has been with the organization for many years, the chances are high that they have many relationships and are an essential part of the organization's formal and informal cultures. If the individual is active in social organizations, their level of influence in informal networks may be significant. How many different positions and roles have the individual held over the years? The broader an individual's exposure to different subcultures, the better they may be at traversing the organization's politics. The number of different positions may also contribute to the individual's status in the organization, and thus to their level of influence on the culture.

The nature of the individual's assignments can also translate to the nature and extent of influence they have on culture. Have they been assigned to troubleshooting roles? Are they rotated across units because of their reliability? Have their roles prepared them to be a steady and calming manager in times of crisis? Have they had multiple leadership roles over time? Have these experiences placed them close to leadership? Have they been influenced by or influenced leaders or managers?

Skills and Competencies (Factor 4)

An individual's skills and competencies are indicators of their formal education, formal training, and their certifications, professional and practical learning preferences. Skills and competencies are not limited to professional training or trades, in any case. They include a wide range of competencies that may tell us something about the individual's cultural preferences for self-growth and development. Does the individual seek out informal external sources of learning? Do they tend to grow their competencies to the fullest extent? Or are they content with minimal level skills?

They may also tell us something about what kinds of informal networks – inside and outside the organization – the individual is likely to form. If an individual is in the legal office with a legal degree – they will tend to form formal and informal networks with other lawyers around the organization, with lawyers from their law schools and in professional legal societies. Each of these individual cultural characteristics plays a role in shaping the unit and the organization's culture.

Levels of Expertise (Factor 5)

The individual's level of expertise may also tell us something about their cultural attributes. There has been considerable research into the values and behaviors of experts – their knowledge sharing behaviors, their communication practices, their networking preferences, and practices. This organization's treatment of experts will affect the individual's cultural attributes. Some organizations tend to reward experts for working independently and for specialized learning. Other organizations will emphasize the importance of experts collaborating with others, mentoring, and coaching to ensure their knowledge flows to others. Individuals may have expertise in some areas, and yet be novices in other areas. Organizations may assign high value to one area of expertise, and that value translates to other behaviors. There could be an adverse cultural effect. How expertise is determined may also have significant cultural impacts for units and individuals. Unless there are formal standards for what defines expertise, the "expert" level may be a signal not of competence or knowledge but cultural dominance of influence. There are examples of individuals who have self-identified as experts but whose expert credentials were not significant. This may be a reflection of the organization's cultural behaviors. It may also reflect an individual's cultural behavior and values.

In addition to the cultural registers that individuals bring to the unit, the organization's culture will shape the individuals' culture. Over time, an individual's cultural register is a composite of all of his/her work experiences and the organizational cultures he/she has experienced (Alderfer and Smith's, 1982)

REFERENCES

Aasi, P., Rusu, L., & Han, S. (2016). The influence of organizational culture on IT governance performance: Case of the IT department in a large Swedish company. In *2016 49th Hawaii International Conference on System Sciences (HICSS)* (pp. 5157-5166). IEEE.

Alderfer, C. P., & Smith, K. K. (1982). Studying intergroup relations embedded in organizations. *Administrative Science Quarterly*, *27*(1), 35–65. doi:10.2307/2392545

Andreoni, J., & Vesterlund, L. (2001). Which is the fair sex? Gender differences in altruism. *The Quarterly Journal of Economics*, *116*(1), 293–312. doi:10.1162/003355301556419

Arnett, J. J. (2002). The psychology of globalization. *The American Psychologist*, *57*(10), 774–783. doi:10.1037/0003-066X.57.10.774 PMID:12369500

Ayman, R., & Korabik, K. (2010). Leadership: Why gender and culture matter. *The American Psychologist*, *65*(3), 157–170. doi:10.1037/a0018806 PMID:20350015

Baumgartner, R. J. (2009). Organizational culture and leadership: Preconditions for the development of a sustainable corporation. *Sustainable Development, 17*(2), 102–113. doi:10.1002d.405

Berson, Y., Erez, M., & Adler, S. (2004). Reflections of organizational identity and national culture on managerial roles in a multinational corporation. In Academy of Management Proceedings (Vol. 2004, No. 1, pp. Q1-Q6). Briarcliff Manor, NY: Academy of Management. doi:10.5465/ambpp.2004.13862566

Bloor, G., & Dawson, P. (1994). Understanding professional culture in organizational context. *Organization Studies, 15*(2), 275–295. doi:10.1177/017084069401500205

Bunderson, J. S., & Sutcliffe, K. M. (2003). Management team learning orientation and business unit performance. *The Journal of Applied Psychology, 88*(3), 552–560. doi:10.1037/0021-9010.88.3.552 PMID:12814303

Croson, R., & Buchan, N. (1999). Gender and culture: International experimental evidence from trust games. *The American Economic Review, 89*(2), 386–391. doi:10.1257/aer.89.2.386

Den Hartog, D. N., House, R. J., Hanges, P. J., Ruiz-Quintanilla, S. A., Dorfman, P. W., Abdalla, I. A., & Akande, B. E. (1999). Culture specific and cross-culturally generalizable implicit leadership theories: Are attributes of charismatic/transformational leadership universally endorsed? *The Leadership Quarterly, 10*(2), 219–256. doi:10.1016/S1048-9843(99)00018-1

Edmondson, A. C. (2002). The local and variegated nature of learning in organizations: A group-level perspective. *Organization Science, 13*(2), 128–146. doi:10.1287/orsc.13.2.128.530

Fischer, A. H., & Manstead, A. S. (2000). The relation between gender and emotions in different cultures. *Gender and Emotion: Social Psychological Perspectives, 1*, 71-94.

Gregory, K. L. (1983). Native-view paradigms: Multiple cultures and culture conflicts in organizations. *Administrative Science Quarterly, 28*(3), 359–376. doi:10.2307/2392247

Grimshaw, A. (Ed.). (1995). *Information culture and business performance*. Hatfield: University of Hertfordshire Press.

Hein, L., & Brinley, J. (2004). *Reasonable men, powerful words: political culture and expertise in twentieth century Japan* (Vol. 16). Univ of California Press.

Hofstede, G. (1980). Culture and organizations. *International Studies of Management & Organization, 10*(4), 15–41. doi:10.1080/00208825.1980.11656300

Hofstede, G. (1983). National cultures in four dimensions: A research-based theory of cultural differences among nations. *International Studies of Management & Organization, 13*(1-2), 46–74. doi:10.1080/00208825.1983.11656358

Hofstede, G. (1984). Cultural dimensions in management and planning. *Asia Pacific Journal of Management, 1*(2), 81–99. doi:10.1007/BF01733682

Hofstede, G. (1998). Attitudes, values and organizational culture: Disentangling the concepts. *Organization Studies, 19*(3), 477–493. doi:10.1177/017084069801900305

House, R. J., and Mansor, N. (1999). *Cultural Influences on Leadership and Organizations: Project Globe* (Vol. 1). Advances in Global Leadership.

Jermier, J. M., Slocum, J. W. Jr, Fry, L. W., & Gaines, J. (1991). Organizational subcultures in a soft bureaucracy: Resistance behind the myth and facade of an official culture. *Organization Science, 2*(2), 170–194. doi:10.1287/orsc.2.2.170

Kunda, G. (1992). Labor and social change. In Engineering culture: Control and commitment in a high-tech corporation. Philadelphia, PA: Temple University Press. http://dx.doi.org/,6,228 doi:10.1287/orsc

Leung, K., Bhagat, R. S., Buchan, N. R., Erez, M., & Gibson, C. B. (2005). Culture and international business: Recent advances and their implications for future research. *Journal of International Business Studies, 36*(4), 357–378. doi:10.1057/palgrave.jibs.8400150

Lewis, R. (2010). *When cultures collide*. Nicholas Brealey Publishing.

Lewis, R. D. (1999). *Cross cultural communication: A visual approach.* Transcreen Publications.

Lewis, R. D. (2003). *The cultural imperative: Global trends in the 21st century*. Intercultural Press.

Martin, J. (1992). *Cultures in organizations: Three perspectives*. Oxford University Press.

Martin, J. (2001). *Organizational culture: Mapping the terrain*. Sage Publications.

Martin, J., & Siehl, C. (1983). Organizational culture and counterculture: An uneasy symbiosis. *Organizational Dynamics*, *12*(2), 52–64. doi:10.1016/0090-2616(83)90033-5

Meyerson, D., & Martin, J. (1987). Cultural change: An integration of three different views. *Journal of Management Studies*, *24*(6), 623–647. doi:10.1111/j.1467-6486.1987.tb00466.x

Mills, A. J. (1988). Organization, gender and culture. *Organization Studies*, *9*(3), 351–369. doi:10.1177/017084068800900304

Moore, I. (2014). Cultural and Creative Industries concept–a historical perpective. *Procedia: Social and Behavioral Sciences*, *110*, 738–746. doi:10.1016/j.sbspro.2013.12.918

Morris, M. W., & Peng, K. (1994). Culture and cause: American and Chinese attributions for social and physical events. *Journal of Personality and Social Psychology*, *67*(6), 949–971. doi:10.1037/0022-3514.67.6.949

Murakami, F., & Singelis, T. M. (2002). Social axioms: The search for universal dimensions of general beliefs about how the world functions. *Journal of Cross-Cultural Psychology*, *33*(3), 286–302. doi:10.1177/0022022102033003005

Naisbitt, J. (1994). *Global Paradox. The Bigger the World Economy, the More Powerful Its Smallest Players*. New York: William Morrow and Company. Inc.

O'Reilly, C. (1989). Corporations, culture, and commitment: Motivation and social control in organizations. *California Management Review*, *31*(4), 9–25. doi:10.2307/41166580

O'Reilly, C. A. III, Chatman, J., & Caldwell, D. F. (1991). People and organizational culture: A profile comparison approach to assessing person-organization fit. *Academy of Management Journal*, *34*(3), 487–516.

Pelled, L. H. (1996). Demographic diversity, conflict, and work group outcomes: An intervening process theory. *Organization Science*, *7*(6), 615–631. doi:10.1287/orsc.7.6.615

Phillips, M. E. (1994). Industry mindsets: Exploring the cultures of two macro-organizational settings. *Organization Science*, *5*(3), 384–402. doi:10.1287/orsc.5.3.384

Riley, P. (1983). A structurationist account of political culture. *Administrative Science Quarterly*, *28*(3), 414–437. doi:10.2307/2392250

Rose, R. A. (1988). Organizations as multiple cultures: A rules theory analysis. *Human Relations*, *41*(2), 139–170. doi:10.1177/001872678804100204

Rousseau, D. M. (1989). Psychological and implied contracts in organizations. *Employee Responsibilities and Rights Journal*, *2*(2), 121–139. doi:10.1007/BF01384942

Rousseau, D. M. (1990). Normative beliefs in fund-raising organizations: Linking culture to organizational performance and individual responses. *Group & Organization Studies*, *15*(4), 448–460. doi:10.1177/105960119001500408

Sackmann, S. A. (1992). Culture and subcultures: An analysis of organizational knowledge. *Administrative Science Quarterly*, *37*(1), 140–161. doi:10.2307/2393536

Schein, E. H. (1992). *Organizational culture and leadership. Jossey-Bass.*

Schein, E. H. (1996). Culture: The missing concept in organization studies. *Administrative Science Quarterly*, *41*(2), 229–240. doi:10.2307/2393715

Schneider, B., Salvaggio, A. N., & Subirats, M. (2002). Climate strength: A new direction for climate research. *The Journal of Applied Psychology*, *87*(2), 220–229. doi:10.1037/0021-9010.87.2.220 PMID:12002951

Schwartz, S. H. (1992). Cultural dimensions of values-Towards an understanding of national differences. *International Journal of Psychology*, *27*(3), 540–540.

Shermont, H., & Krepcio, D. (2006). The impact of culture change on nurse retention. *JONA: The Journal of Nursing Administration*, *36*(9), 407–415. doi:10.1097/00005110-200609000-00007 PMID:16969252

Shinnar, R. S., Giacomin, O., & Janssen, F. (2012). Entrepreneurial perceptions and intentions: The role of gender and culture. *Entrepreneurship Theory and Practice*, *36*(3), 465–493. doi:10.1111/j.1540-6520.2012.00509.x

Smith, P. B., Dugan, S., & Trompenaars, F. (1996). National culture and the values of organizational employees: A dimensional analysis across 43 nations. *Journal of Cross-Cultural Psychology*, *27*(2), 231–264. doi:10.1177/0022022196272006

Smith, P. B., Trompenaars, F., & Dugan, S. (1995). The Rotter locus of control scale in 43 countries: A test of cultural relativity. *International Journal of Psychology*, *30*(3), 377–400. doi:10.1080/00207599508246576

Soares, A. M., Farhangmehr, M., & Shoham, A. (2007). Hofstede's dimensions of culture in international marketing studies. *Journal of Business Research*, *60*(3), 277–284. doi:10.1016/j.jbusres.2006.10.018

Stevenson, W. B., & Bartunek, J. M. (1996). Power, interaction, position, and the generation of cultural agreement in organizations. *Human Relations*, *49*(1), 75–104. doi:10.1177/001872679604900104

Tajfel, H., & Turner, J. (1979). An Integrative Theory of Intergroup conflict. In W. Austin & S. Worchel (Eds.), *Social psychology of intergroup relations* (pp. 33–47). Monterey: Brooks/Cole.

Trice, H. M., & Beyer, J. M. (1993). *The cultures of work organizations*. Prentice-Hall, Inc.

Trompenaars, F. (1996). Resolving international conflict: Culture and business strategy. *Business Strategy Review*, *7*(3), 51–68. doi:10.1111/j.1467-8616.1996.tb00132.x

Van Maanen, J., & Barley, R. S. (1984). Occupational Communities: Culture and Control in Organizations,(w:]. *Research in Organizational Behavior*.

Van Maanen, J., & Barley, S. (1985). *Organizational culture: Fragments of a theory. In Organizational Culture* (pp. 31–53). Beverly Hills: Sage.

ADDITIONAL READING

Aasi, P., Rusu, L., & Han, S. (2016). The influence of organizational culture on IT governance performance: Case of the IT department in a large Swedish company. In *2016 49th Hawaii International Conference on System Sciences (HICSS)* (pp. 5157-5166). IEEE.

Ardichvili, A., Maurer, M., Li, W., Wentling, T., & Stuedemann, R. (2006). Cultural influences on knowledge sharing through online communities of practice. *Journal of Knowledge Management*, *10*(1), 94–107. doi:10.1108/13673270610650139

Balkin, R. S., Schlosser, L. Z., & Levitt, D. H. (2009). Religious identity and cultural diversity: Exploring the relationships between religious identity, sexism, homophobia, and multicultural competence. *Journal of Counseling and Development*, *87*(4), 420–427. doi:10.1002/j.1556-6678.2009.tb00126.x

Boyacigiller, N. A., Kleinberg, J., Phillips, M. E., and Sackmann, S. A. (2004). Conceptualizing culture: Elucidating the streams of research in international cross-cultural management. *Handbook for international management research*, *2*, 99-167.

Chao, G. T., & Moon, H. (2005). The cultural mosaic: A metatheory for understanding the complexity of culture. *The Journal of Applied Psychology*, *90*(6), 1128–1140. doi:10.1037/0021-9010.90.6.1128 PMID:16316269

Cooke, R. A., & Rousseau, D. M. (1988). Behavioral norms and expectations: A quantitative approach to the assessment of organizational culture. *Group & Organization Studies*, *13*(3), 245–273. doi:10.1177/105960118801300302

Cullen, K. L., Palus, C. J., Chrobot-Mason, D., & Appaneal, C. (2012). Getting to "we": Collective leadership development. *Industrial and Organizational Psychology: Perspectives on Science and Practice*, *5*(4), 428–432. doi:10.1111/j.1754-9434.2012.01475.x

Dansereau, F., & Alutto, J. A. (1990). Level-of-analysis issues in climate and culture research. *Organizational climate and culture, 193*(236), 333-349.

Dellheim, C. (1987). The creation of a company culture: Cadburys, 1861-1931. *The American Historical Review*, *92*(1), 13–44. doi:10.2307/1862781 PMID:11612055

Fey, C. F., & Denison, D. R. (2003). Organizational culture and effectiveness: Can American theory be applied in Russia? *Organization Science*, *14*(6), 686–706. doi:10.1287/orsc.14.6.686.24868

Gordon, G. G. (1991). Industry determinants of organizational culture. *Academy of Management Review*, *16*(2), 396–415. doi:10.5465/amr.1991.4278959

Hunt, S. D., Wood, V. R., & Chonko, L. B. (1989). Corporate ethical values and organizational commitment in marketing. *Journal of Marketing, 53*(3), 79–90. doi:10.1177/002224298905300309

Ingersoll, G. L., Kirsch, J. C., Merk, S. E., & Lightfoot, J. (2000). Relationship of organizational culture and readiness for change to employee commitment to the organization. *JONA: The Journal of Nursing Administration, 30*(1), 11–20. doi:10.1097/00005110-200001000-00004 PMID:10650431

Kashima, Y., Yamaguchi, S., Kim, U., Choi, S. C., Gelfand, M. J., & Yuki, M. (1995). Culture, gender, and self: A perspective from individualism-collectivism research. *Journal of Personality and Social Psychology, 69*(5), 925–937. doi:10.1037/0022-3514.69.5.925 PMID:7473038

Kerr, J., & Slocum, J. W. Jr. (1987). Managing corporate culture through reward systems. *The Academy of Management Perspectives, 1*(2), 99–107. doi:10.5465/ame.1987.4275817

Korabik, K., and Ayman, R. (2007). Gender and leadership in the corporate world: A multiperspective model. *Women and leadership: Transforming visions and diverse voices*, 106-124.

Kristof, A. L. (1996). Person-organization fit: An integrative review of its conceptualizations, measurement, and implications. *Personnel Psychology, 49*(1), 1–49. doi:10.1111/j.1744-6570.1996.tb01790.x

Lyons, S. T., Duxbury, L. E., & Higgins, C. A. (2006). A comparison of the values and commitment of private sector, public sector, and parapublic sector employees. *Public Administration Review, 66*(4), 605–618. doi:10.1111/j.1540-6210.2006.00620.x

Marchington, M., Grimshaw, D., Rubery, J., & Willmott, H. (Eds.). (2005). *Fragmenting work: Blurring organizational boundaries and disordering hierarchies*. Oxford University Press on Demand.

Medin, D. L., Ross, N., Atran, S., Burnett, R. C., & Blok, S. V. (2002). Categorization and reasoning in relation to culture and expertise. *Psychology of Learning and Motivation, 41*, 1–41. doi:10.1016/S0079-7421(02)80003-2

Meterko, M., Mohr, D. C., & Young, G. J. (2004). Teamwork culture and patient satisfaction in hospitals. *Medical Care*, 492–498. doi:10.1097/01.mlr.0000124389.58422.b2 PMID:15083111

Miron-Spektor, E., Erez, M., & Naveh, E. (2006). The personal attributes that enhance individual versus team innovation. In *Annual Meeting of the Academy of Management, Atlanta, GA*.

Newman, K. L., & Nollen, S. D. (1996). Culture and congruence: The fit between management practices and national culture. *Journal of International Business Studies*, *27*(4), 753–779. doi:10.1057/palgrave.jibs.8490152

Novinger, S., O'Brien, L., & Sweigman, L. (2005). Challenging the culture of expertise: Moving beyond training the always, already failing early childhood educator. In *Practical transformations and transformational practices: Globalization, postmodernism, and early childhood education* (pp. 217–241). Emerald Group Publishing Limited. doi:10.1016/S0270-4021(05)14010-5

Rashid, Z. A., Sambasivan, M., & Rahman, A. A. (2004). The influence of organizational culture on attitudes toward organizational change. *Leadership and Organization Development Journal*.

VanderVen, K. (1999). You are what you do and become what you've done: The role of activity in development of self. *Journal of Child and Youth Care*, *13*, 133–147.

Weerstra, J. (1994). The Boomer Generation: For Such A Time As This. *International Journal of Frontier Missions*, *11*, 129–132.

Chapter 6
Seeing Information Cultures

ABSTRACT

Information cultures affect an organization's ability to define and implement a practical and effective information strategy. Just as business culture supports or impedes business strategy, so does information culture support or impede information strategy. Organizations typically have many information cultures, some of which may be contradictory. Unmanaged information cultures can present a significant risk in the knowledge economy. Information culture is reflected in the organization's values, norms, and practices concerning the management and use of information. The information science literature provides insufficient treatment to help us understand the day-to-day impacts of information cultures on business. It also fails to provide an inclusive description of the range of cultures extant in the information management profession and practice. Just like business cultures, information cultures exist and may vary by level of the organization. The authors call out and describe dynamic factors that affect information cultures at all five levels.

WHY DO WE CARE ABOUT INFORMATION CULTURES

We care about information cultures because they affect the organization's ability to define and implement a practical and effective information strategy. Just as business culture supports or impedes business strategy, so does information culture support or impede information strategy. The primary reason information management strategies fail is that they fail to consider, align with, or manage the existing information cultures. This is not a trivial

DOI: 10.4018/978-1-7998-4315-3.ch006

challenge. Every organization has one or more information cultures. These information cultures determine whether your strategy will be adopted and supported, or ignored and impeded.

Information cultures have been the focus of both business and information managers. Early, the authors suggest that it is essential to integrate our business and information strategies. It is also essential to ensure that our business and information cultures are also integrated and supportive. The challenge is that in most organizations today, business and information cultures are distinct. Neither are these views integrated or consistently researched in the peer review or gray literature. The business literature focuses on how the business views information and how the information contributes to achieving business effectiveness. The business literature discusses how the use of information improves decision making and business performance. We find treatment of information cultures in the information science literature. Our understanding of information culture comes primarily from the information profession. An organization's information culture in the 20th and the 21st centuries has most often focused on good information management practices. This view of information culture represents the assumptions, beliefs, values, behaviors, and artifacts of the information science and information management communities.

The authors attempt to synthesize the current research and practice from these two domains into a single practical view – the view from within the organization. This means we must draw from the literature of both fields, translate them to Schein's essential model of culture, and interpret them at the national and global level, the organization level, the unit or team level, and the individual level. The authors' goal is to provide managers will a framework and guiding questions that will help them to see the "information culture water" they are swimming in each day. The challenge is that the business and the information science cultures are well developed and well-entrenched. It is unwise for any organization to attempt to change either of these information cultures. It is imperative, though, that we attempt to synthesize and shape them to fit strategies in the business context.

Organizations typically have many information cultures, some of which may be contradictory. Left unaddressed, information cultures create a higher risk in the knowledge economy than they did in the information economy. The risk is that the information culture will deteriorate into information politics. Not only will information politics undermine your information management strategy but your business strategy as well. Information politics can leave your organization vulnerable to wise or strategic actions of competitor organizations in the knowledge economy. Information politics leaves your most essential capital asset – information – vulnerable to attack, theft, subversion, or damage.

Information cultures are essential because they align with and provide the context for making good decisions in the knowledge economy. Information cultures are essential because they bring in the spirit and reification of information as a valuable strategic asset. We care about information cultures because we have double risk and exposure when information culture is ignored. When information culture does not align with the culture, it will be dominated by culture. When information culture does not align with information strategies, the culture will always dominate – this means that information strategies may defer to business cultures. When information culture dominates, information strategies will suffer. In a knowledge economy, there is a second impact – when information cultures are ignored, and information strategies suffer – so do business strategies.

INFORMATION CULTURES – DEFINITION AND CHARACTERIZATION

Information culture is reflected in the organization's values, norms, and practices concerning the management and use of information. Information culture values are deeply held beliefs about the goals and identity of the organization's information assets and how it realizes those goals. These information values are often hard to articulate and even harder to change. They provide the answers to questions such as:

- What does the organization perceive to be the role and contribution of information to organizational effectiveness?
- What values underlie the organizational style of managing its creation and use of information?

How does the organization value information? How we value information - business or information professional – will influence how we behave around the information. What we understand as the useful business life of information – how it supports our immediate business purposes – and what we do with it after that use is gone – tells us about our information values. Do we consider the value of information, or do we only focus on its costs? Do we trust our information? Do we trust others' information? How do we define quality? All of these questions tell us something about our information values.

A culture of information management is one that recognizes the strategic value of information to the institution and promotes and facilitates good information management practice. Organization level information cultures might best be understood as a set of attitudes in which: (1) any information that is available for sharing (and most will be) is well defined and appropriately accessible (allowing for necessary safeguards), (2) the quality of information is fit for purpose (e.g., accuracy, currency, consistency, completeness), and (3) all staff know and exercise their responsibilities toward information. An information management culture would provide a framework for how information is to be shared, captured, stored, modeled, and kept reliable across the organization (Hanson 2011). Information management professionals and practitioners have well-articulated assumptions and beliefs which are frequently found in policy documents at the organization level (Bedford, 2019). For example, information managers believe that:

- information is a tangible capital asset
- information should be managed as a business asset
- information liabilities should be minimized
- information should be used
- information should be valued based on the sum of all its uses
- information should be easy to find, access and use
- its full life span determines the value of information
- information is manageable
- the information has a business context
- information costs and liabilities should be managed
- information management is a core business process
- managing information is everyone's responsibility
- information is managed according to best practices across its life cycle
- There is a single view of the information life cycle across areas of practice

Information norms derive from information values but have a more direct influence on information behaviors. Norms are rules or socially accepted standards that define what is normal or to be expected in the creation, use, management, and valuation of information in the organization. Norms give people a way to gauge what is 'normal' in handling and using the information in a given context and at a specific time. They tell us what the acceptable information standards and codes of behavior (Chatman, 1999) are. Norms or rules may be informal or formal. Informal norms and attitudes influence the creation, flow, and use of information in individuals and groups. Formal rules, routines, and policies may exist to plan, guide, and control information as an organizational asset. Each area of practice in information science has a set of values, norms, guiding principles, and standards that reflect the history and thinking of that entire profession. While these are not difficult to discover, they are not inherently consistent across areas of practice, and they are not related to the business value of information.

Behaviors are repeated patterns of action that involve organizational roles, structures, and forms of interactions. Each business function, business process, and every information management area of practice has a very well established and entrenched set of practices and procedures. Values and norms together mold the information *practices* of people and groups in an organization. Information practices are the observable, stable patterns of working and interrelating that link people, information, and technology in the social performance of organizational work. Insofar as information practices are enacted by a social structure of roles, rules, and warrants, they are a manifestation of cultural norms and values. What values and behaviors extend from our assumptions and beliefs about information? In an information culture, we might value it. These are built into performance standards, into industry standards, and also designed into information technologies. They describe how people find, organize, use, and share information as part of their standard work patterns. Some of these behaviors, practices, and policies may either incentivize or impede the effective use of information in a business context. Common information behaviors might focus on:

- information integrity
- formal validated information over informal and invalidated information
- information is used to manage and monitor capabilities and processes
- information is used in decision making
- information is used to manage and assess the performance
- information is transparent – it describes errors and failures as well as successes
- information is shared internally, and information sharing is rewarded
- information is used for sense-making, enlightenment, and learning
- information is used to develop a better understanding of a problem
- information is used to help individuals know what and how to do something

- information is factual
- information is conformational – it is used to verify other information
- information is projective and predictive of future events
- information is motivational and is used to initiate or sustain personal involvement
- information is personal and political
- information is proactive and is used to promote innovation in products and services

INFORMATION CULTURE – PEER-REVIEWED AND GRAY LITERATURE

While the information science literature references the essential elements of culture, the peer-reviewed and gray literature provide insufficient treatment to help us understand the day to day impacts of information cultures on business. It also fails to provide an inclusive description of the range of cultures extant in the information management profession and practice. The existing literature is useful in helping information science professionals, and practitioners understand how the business treats information. However, it does not provide an in-depth research foundation for understanding the essential nature of information cultures that exist in organizations today.

The authors provide a high-level review of the current thinking and research on this topic – as a foundation upon which to build. The earliest discussion and description of information culture come from the business world and three researchers in particular – Tom Davenport, Larry Prusak, and. James McGee. How can we leverage and build upon their work? Tom Davenport (Davenport Eccles and Prusak, 1998) was among the earliest to introduce the idea of an information environment and ecology. Davenport called out information behaviors and culture as one of the six components of an organization's information ecology. He defines information behaviors to include information sharing and use (making information available), handling information overload (making information engaging so that the right people recognize and use the right information); and dealing with multiple meanings (creating a shared understanding of concepts and terms used in an organization).

Additionally, Davenport calls out information politics – information behaviors that derive from the power and governance methods designed by management. This definition of information culture focuses on selective stages of the information life cycle, specifically Stage 2 Creation and Capture, Stage 4 Organization and Description, and Stage 6 Availability and Use. Today, we understand that information culture pertains to all stages of the life cycle, to all levels of the organization, and all roles.

Davenport later teamed up with Prusak (1997) to provide a combined business and information perspective on information culture. They define information culture as a pattern of behaviors and attitudes that describe the organization's orientation toward information. They provide examples of behaviors and attitudes, including an organization's preference for facts or rumors, the incentives to share or hoard information, preferences for exchange and delivery channels – face to face email, or social medial. They also highlight the existence of levels and variants of information culture across the organization.

Prusak continued this work in collaboration with James McGee (1993). These authors expanded upon the earlier work of Davenport by calling out five models of information behaviors. We align these five models with the values and norms dimension of information culture. The five models include technocracy, utopianism, anarchy, feudalism, monarchy, and federalism. Technocratic Utopianism is a profoundly technical approach to information management that stresses the categorization and modeling of an organization's full information assets, with heavy reliance on emerging technologies. Anarchy is the absence of any overall information management policy, which leaves individuals to obtain and manage their information. Feudalism is the management of information by individual business units or functions, which define their own information needs and report only limited information to the overall corporation. Monarchy defines a management approach in which the leaders' information characterizations and behaviors are not shared across the organization. This approach also tends toward information hiding and hoarding. Finally, feudalism is an approach to information management that is based on consensus and negotiations of the critical information elements and reporting structures for the organization.

There are also references to an information culture in the information science literature, specifically the work of Travica (1995a; 1995b) and Choo (2002; 2005; 2013). While these are essential sources, they reinforce the ideas of information use and sharing discussed by Davenport, Prusak, and McGee.

LEARNING TO SEE INFORMATION CULTURES ACROSS THE ORGANIZATION

Just like business cultures, information cultures exist and may vary by level of the organization. There are five levels of information culture – just as there are five levels of business culture. Two levels – national and global – are external to the organization. Three levels are internal to the organization. There are three levels of culture in any organization. The highest level in the organization. The next level is the unit or group level – the level at which we see the culture in action. This is the critical level for ensuring your information culture is understood, embraced, and built into reward and recognition systems. If the information culture that is understood and lived at this level does not support your information management strategy, your strategy will fail. Finally, culture is lived at the individual level. This level also is essential for your information culture because individuals collectively shape culture. It speaks to how individuals behave towards and treat the information daily. To illustrate levels, we focus our examples on the norms and behaviors aspect of information culture.

We need to understand the factors that affect information cultures because tees are the points of leverage for aligning culture and strategy. The same factors apply here as apply to business cultures. To understand information cultures, we need to review these factors and consider how they play out at each level of the organization.

DYNAMIC FACTORS – GLOBAL AND NATIONAL LEVEL INFORMATION CULTURES

What is the organization's world view, and how does its inherent national or global culture tell us what kinds of information are essential and which are not important? Worldview is a collective perception by members of a culture world regarding those things which are regarding what is essential to business success. Today we see some organizations focusing heavily on structured data at the expense of personal knowledge and experience. Other organizations value customer feedback and information over structured data analytics. An organization's worldview provides a collective approach to assess the importance of information.

How does a nation's culture affect an organization's information orientation? How does the interaction of people, information, and technology affect business performance (Marchand, Kettinger, and Rollins)? Business Views at the National Level can also help us to learn whether national business associations or industries have information policies and standards. Information Views at the National Level national-level information policies and standards from information management professional associations.

Where an organization's headquarters is located will affect these world views, business views, and information views. Moreover, where the organization's subsidiaries or field offices are located may also affect the coherence of that information culture.

National cultures also affect national information infrastructures. The more extensive and accessible a national infrastructure, the more likely a population is to develop strong information management assumptions, beliefs, values, behaviors, and artifacts. The existence and extent of a national information infrastructure can also affect the rate and propensity of information technology adoption. It may also affect an individual's and organization's acceptance of emerging information technologies.

DYNAMIC FACTORS – ORGANIZATION LEVEL INFORMATION CULTURES

The organizational level culture is the official culture – it is the culture that is officially sanctioned, presented to the external business environment, and promoted internally. Organizational culture is comprised of the culture of leaders and top-level managers and aggregation of all of the lower level cultures. This is an essential point of leverage for developing an information culture. After an extensive exploration of the peer review and gray literature, the authors identified nine factors that may affect information culture at the organization level. These factors include:

- Use of Information Technology (Factor 1)
- Information Management Policies and Standards (Factor 2)
- Information Creation and Use (Factor3)
- Information-Based Interactions and Communications (Factor 4)
- Leaders Behaviors and Decision Making Styles (Factor 5)
- External Business Environment (Factor 6)

- Life Cycle Stage of the Organization (Factor 7)
- Internal Structure of the Organization (Factor 8)
- Management Philosophy and Controls (Factor 9)

Use of Information Technology (Factor 1)

Information cultures leverage and enable information strategies through the use of technology (Deal and Kennedy, 1999; Orlikowski, 1996; Orlikowski and Gash, 1994; Earl 1994). Deal and Kennedy (1999), prominent researchers of organizational culture, suggest that technology influences information cultures in multiple ways. There are both desirable and undesirable effects of technology on information cultures.

Undesirable effects might include:

- Intensive use of technology which results in diminished social interaction with one's peers and a sterile interface with a computer rather than a supervisor" (Deal and Kennedy, 1999)
- Diminished face-to-face communication in favor of impersonal electronic exchange
- Mechanized rituals at the expense of personal relationships and rituals
- The replacement of personal networks and contacts with new digital cultures and mediated life experiences
- Increased isolation of individuals and the increased distance between members of an organization

Desirable effects might include:

- Used the term "technological frames" to refer to the way organization members make sense of and assign meaning to organizational artifacts and assumptions (Orlikowski and Gash, 1994)
- Ability to express information and knowledge symbolically through language, visual images, metaphors, and stories. (Kunda, 1992; Martin, 1992).
- Opportunity to reshape a dysfunctional information culture in the course of implementing new technologies (Sarker and Lee, 2000)
- An increase in the level of trust, efficiency and information infrastructure and the tendency to equalize access to information across the organization;

- An increase in inter-departmental communication and coordination as a result of increased technology infrastructures (Baskerville and Myers, 2004; Klein and Myers, 1999; Deal and Kennedy, 1999; Hanseth et al., 2001; Markus, 1983; Orlikowski, 1992, 1996; Orlikowski and Gash 1994; Orlikowski and Yates, 1994; Sarker and Lee, 2000; Zuboff, 1984).
- Increased support for access to and use of information in decision making and business processes across the organization;

Information Management Policies and Standards (Factor 2)

Information management policies and standards have considerable influence over the information culture of an organization. At a minimum, their existence tells us that the organization is aware of information as an asset, and has some underlying assumptions and beliefs about its value. Information management practices, including the capability to manage information effectively over the life cycle of information use, including sensing, collecting, organizing, processing and maintaining information tells us that the organization is aware of essential behaviors and norms. Additionally, how well these policies and standards are operationalized throughout the organization tells us whether individuals believe in and trust the organization's information culture. Acceptance of these policies and standards at the business unit level is a crucial indicator of a healthy or an unhealthy information culture. They can also tell us whether we have gaps in information culture between those developing and managing information policies and systems, and those who are implementing and using them. Do unit-level information policies and standards align with or contradict those at the organization level?

Information Creation and Use (Factor 3)

The primary question here is whether the organization's information culture promotes the creation and use of information. Are there explicit references to information creation and use? To information sharing? Are there explicit references in policies to information exchange, information quality control and evaluation, and information integration across administrative boundaries? What indications do we have that an organization's most prominent information culture instills and promotes everyday behaviors that reward the effective use of information?

In addition to looking for explicit references to these essential norms and behaviors, we also want to observe senior managers' information behaviors. Where senior managers live these information practices, they will be trusted and mimicked across the organization. Where they demonstrate an aversion to information creation and use, information policies and strategies will fail.

Information-Based Interactions and Communications (Factor 4)

Organization level information cultures enable information interactions among individuals and discourage information hoarding, hiding, appropriation, and theft (Dougherty 1992; Purser Pasmore and Tenkasi, 1992; Nonaka 1994; Henderson 1994; Brown 1991). Open communication, across all levels and all administrative boundaries are a sign of a healthy information culture. Most organizations have a good understanding of their communication behaviors. In many cases, these can be expanded to include an analysis of information interactions and exchange.

Leaders Behaviors and Decision Making Styles (Factor 5)

Earlier in the text, the authors suggested that leaders and leader's behaviors are an important signal and determinant of an organization's culture. This holds for their business- and information-related actions. In terms of cultural elements, perhaps the most critical focus is values and behaviors. Do leaders 'eat their own dog food' or do they simply serve it to others? Do they practice what they preach or have a separate code of behavior? Where leaders connect espoused and actual values and realize those values in their day to day decisions, rewards, choices, and how they allocate resources – they will strengthen the culture. This may be easier to accomplish for business behaviors than for information behaviors because senior leaders may not have a good grounding in information practices. They have information experiences and training that have served them well throughout their careers. Nevertheless, these experiences may not be sufficient to establish a healthy information culture for an organization in the knowledge economy. There are noteworthy exceptions to this characterization – including some highly productive and successful leaders who have understood the power of information and the importance of information cultures. Our goal and our challenge are to make these cases the norm rather than the exception.

External Environment (Factor 6)

At the organization level, the external environment is more likely to affect the business culture directly and the information culture indirectly. This is simply because information culture is often an internal phenomenon today – a reflection of the way the business behaves in this external environment and the way it responds to that environment. The effects are likely to be information protection and securitization or information access and disclosure. We can expect to see changes in the internal information culture, though, if the external environment changes. If the external markets suddenly shrink due to tariffs or reduced trading opportunities, information cultures might shift from openness to protection. If espionage increases in a highly competitive market, organizations may adopt more secure practices for their critical business information.

Life Cycle Stage of the Organization (Factor 7)

This factor can help us to understand and forecast how an organization might value its information. When an organization is young and emerging, it may be more focused on information creation, discovery, organization, and use. As the organization matures and becomes more established in the market, it may realize the increased value of its information assets and tend to focus more on securitization, classification, internal reuse, and preservation. As an organization matures or exits the market, information values and practices may decline simply because the value of that information to business has not decreased.

Internal Structure of the Organization (Factor 8)

The internal structure of the organization will influence the flows of information. Here we look for indications of networks of individuals, of interactions among individuals in the organization's networks, and with individuals beyond the organization. We also look for indications of the kinds of information that are flowing across these networks – these flows and messages tell us what is essential to the business unit. What happens to these networks and relationships when the organization relies on project or mission-based teams? Do information behaviors and values help to create a coherent information culture across the organization, or do they lead to increased fragmentation of the emergence of multiple information subcultures?

Another aspect of this factor that has been observed to affect an organization's information culture is the presence or absence of sanctioned and supported cross-administrative informal subcultures. Where sanctioned and supported, the existence and support of these informal subcultures can contribute to information flows and behaviors. Where suppressed or discouraged, they can contribute to unhealthy and competing information cultures.

Management Philosophy and Controls (Factor 9)

Business managers are accustomed to observing and managing power and control relationships across the organization. In most cases, senior managers handle these relationships and behaviors to benefit the organization and its business performance. Business managers may be less tuned in to the way that information is used to exert power across the organization than to functional and process behaviors. The power and control, though, that information can exert at the organization level are significant. These power relationships derive from the value the organization places on information assets and the way that information is communicated and leveraged every day. They also derive from knowledge of and experience with information management practices. Information management professionals may tend to be less visible than business managers in an organization, but the power they exert over business information is significant. A healthy information culture will ensure that the power relationships between business managers and information professionals be managed. Moreover, those information professionals are engaged in business decisions and processes across the organizations.

UNIT LEVEL INFORMATION CULTURES

Business units are hubs and communities of information in every organization. The information cultures of these divisions, functional areas, professional communities, project teams, and issue-based communities will determine whether your information strategy succeeds or fails (Boland and Tenkasi 1995). The information culture of a business unit is defined by the manager and the individuals that comprise it. The daily actions and behaviors of business units are where your information management goals will be adopted or ignored. Just as we noted for business cultures, there are both inherited organizational factors and compositional factors that define a business unit's information culture. Seeing your unit level information cultures involves looking for both the inherited factors and the compositional factors. What assumptions, beliefs, values, and behaviors do business units inherit from the organization? What information culture attributes to individuals bring to the unit?

INFORMATION CULTURE FACTORS INHERITED FROM THE ORGANIZATION

The authors conducted an extensive exploration of the peer review and gray literature on information culture in both the business and information science fields. The authors synthesized all of the factors into thirteen high-level factors. In a given context, any or all of the inherited organizational factors described below might define a business unit's information culture.

- Information Behavior of the Unit Leaders (Factor 1)
- Life Cycle Stage of the Unit (Factor 2)
- Geographical Location of the Unit (Factor 3)
- Unit Level Ethics and Rewards (Factor 4)
- Unit Focused Business Environment (Factor 5)
- Unit Level Areas of Practice (Factor 6)
- Type of Decision Making and Processes (Factor 7)
- Internal Structure of the Unit (Factor 8)
- Communication Preferences and Practices (Factor (9)
- Cross-Organization Partnerships (Factor (10)
- Information Security and Confidentiality (Factor 11)
- Management Philosophy of the Unit (Factor 12)
- Information Sharing and Exchange Behaviors (Factor 13)

Information Behavior of Unit Leaders (Factor 1)

Unit managers will play a key role in defining the unit's information culture. Through their actions, choices, communications, and decisions, they telegraph the role and value of information, what they believe about the role of information in the unit's business. Unit level managers' perceptions of and behaviors related to information are a defining factor in the real information culture of an organization. To develop an effective information culture, you need to understand how unit-level managers think about information. Unit level managers may understand the information in terms of information packaging, as information flow, as a source of new knowledge and insights, as a factor in shaping judgments and decisions, and as an asset, they can use to influence others. Alternatively, they may see information as a transformative force that shapes judgments, influence others, and is an integral aspect of the organization's business goals and strategies. What do unit managers in your organization do to build a robust information culture? What do they do to undermine an information culture?

Life Cycle of the Unit (Factor 2)

A business unit's life cycle can tell us whether the information practices and behaviors are well established, mature, rigid or emerging, adaptive, and flexible. A younger business unit – newly formed or emerging – is more likely to establish shared values and behavioral norms within the new group. An older unit is likely to have established behaviors and information management norms. Additionally, a younger unit will have less historical information to protect, and fewer established behaviors to safeguard.

The life cycle stage can also tell us something about the number of connections the unit has throughout the organization. Mature or aging units might have more extensive connections and a more established reputation information recognition and exchange throughout the organization. Younger units may be open to sharing because they are in the process of establishing those relationships. Additionally, younger business units are more likely to be drawing information from other sources – the emphasis on behavior may be on information discovery and exploration. Older business units may have a more extended history of internal information production, so they may tend to focus on internal unit information storage and organization, reuse, and preservation. The age of a business unit might also tell us something about how the unit's information is regarded and valued throughout the organization. Newer units may be in the process of establishing a reputation and business value of their information, whereas the reputation and value may be well known for information in more established units.

Geographical Location of the Unit (Factor 3)

There are two dimensions to this factor. The first dimension is the geographical or national context in which the business unit exists – and the effect of that context's information culture on the business unit. In a highly competitive and risk-averse geographical context, a business unit's members may exhibit information protective and hoarding behaviors. They may hesitate to share information and tend to take a "need to know" approach to using others' information. In contrast, a business unit located in a geographical location that is dominated by cross-industry collaboration and knowledge society principles may tend towards sharing their own and using others' information.

The second dimension is the geographical proximity of the unit to the organization's headquarters. The higher the geographical distance of a business unit from central administrative offices, the more the unit may tend to establish a unique information culture. The unit might adopt the espoused organization information culture, but establish its own information culture in its daily activities and behaviors.

Ethics and Rewards of the Unit (Factor 4)

This factor speaks to the existence of unit or subculture standards and valuations of information. The literature tells us that it is often the case that information values and appreciation often reflects the dominant professional culture of the unit. If the unit is focused on financial management, there will be a set of principles and standards related to financial information. There will be professional ethics for working with financial information – privacy issues, legal constraints, regulatory concerns. Moreover, there will be established adjudication and punishment systems when those norms and standards are violated. Other information professional associations may also establish ethics and rewards. For example, data management associations, archives associations, health information management associations have all addressed these topics.

Unit Focused Business Environment (Factor 5)

The business environment affects both the business and the information culture of the unit. If the business unit's business is highly regulated, its information culture will adopt these norms and behaviors. If the unit faces significant external foreign competition, it may tend to adopt more protective or security-focused internal behaviors. It may tend to view with suspicion external sources of information. There are business intelligence case studies that describe information theft and appropriation behaviors of some units operating in high competition markets. Dumpster diving for information, information espionage – all are information behaviors in high competition markets. These same behaviors may also be detectable in markets where there is a high rate of change. However, some organizations develop extreme collaborative information cultures as a way of coping with highly unstable or emerging markets.

Unit Level Area of Practice (Factor 6)

The alignment of unit information cultures with professional areas of practice was mentioned earlier in connection with ethics and standards. This factor focuses on the broader nature of the practices. On the business side of the organization, the area of practice will tell us a lot about the information culture. This is because the practice likely has an external supporting professional, union, or community that defines the role and value of information. In those units, we will be able to see these alignments and better understand those information cultures.

The business side of the organization may tend to see information management as a single area of practice, but in fact, there are at least nine practices. Each practice has its assumptions and beliefs, its information education and training curricula, historical values, established and certifiable behaviors, professional norms and standards, and artifacts. While there are some common elements, each area of practice has a distinct information culture. Table 1 provides a high-level description of the information culture of each area of information practice. It is essential for business managers to understand these variations because these variations can create information culture tensions. They can also create variant information cultures for business unit managers.

Table 1. Information cultures of information management areas of practice

Area of Practice	Nature of Information Culture
Publishing	The dominant information culture is profit or product oriented. Publishing technologies are designed for editors, proofreaders, and agents, and include editing applications, publications management, formatting systems, and peer review systems that handle feedback and versions/revisions. Also here speak to the book culture
Library Management	The information culture of this practice is service-oriented and heavily influenced by the dominant social culture of the geographical location. Legal requirements tend to focus on the availability of and access to services for stakeholders. Financial requirements focus on accountability to stakeholders. Historically, libraries have been supported by dedicated or generalized integrated library systems. In recent years, though, more generalized technologies have been brought into the library workflow.
Archives Management	Archives Management Profession and Practice Because of the preservation aspect of this practice, the information culture tends to be conservative, traditional, protectionist, and exclusionary. Archives management technologies tend to focus on digital archive repositories and physical archives tracking and management. The culture is protectionist but not exclusionary. Records managers may tend to affiliate with user groups supported by technology vendors and to develop their communities around vendor conferences. Technologies that support records management tend to be functional modules of document or content management systems
Knowledge Management	The dominant information culture is one of consulting and trade shows. Individual and large corporate consulting firms have dominated the area of practice. Knowledge technologies tend to focus on collaboration, semantic and text analytics, and social media
Data Management	The dominant information culture is business-oriented, quality control-oriente, and regulatory-oriented. It tends to be cautionary and risk-averse. This area of practice has the most extensive experience with supporting technologies, including data warehouses, translational data management systems, metadata and met information management, business process management, business rules repositories and business rules engines
Information Architecture	collaborative, integrating, design-focused, the balance of art and engineering cultures, focuses on the use of information rather than the information itself
Content Management	The dominant information culture is entrepreneurial and community-based. It is characterized by intense development and learning among community members.
Digital Asset Management	The information culture is dominated by large media companies, are revenue and intellectual property protection driven. Digital asset management systems may be coupled with content management systems

Type of Decision Making and Process (Factor 7)

Decision making and business processes are the primary uses of information. Every business process and function is based on information. It has information inputs, it transforms information in the process, and it embeds that information in its products and services. Every business process generates information as a management tool. Decision making is grounded on information. Looking at whether or not business units leverage information every day – tells us much of what we need to know about its information culture. Are business processes, by definition, independent or team-based? Team-based processes require information sharing and exchange, whereas those which are focused on a single expert or research may have fewer incentives to share information. In fact, many business units likely have a wealth of information artifacts that are strong indicators of information culture. These might include business and competitive information models and methods, procedural manuals, procedural know-how, business process certifications, and standard reporting practices.

Internal Structure of the Unit (Factor 8)

The internal structure of a business unit reveals much about its information culture. Is there an atmosphere of trust among the members of the unit? Do they openly share information? Do they trust each other's knowledge and information? Is there a cooperative or a competitive working environment? In a cooperative environment, information is likely to flow freely throughout the day. In a competitive environment, information exchange may be more infrequent. Information culture researchers have also noted that a unit's morale might influence its information culture – a unit with positive and reinforcing morale is more likely to have open communication and information flows. A unit with lower morale may have more closed communication patterns and fewer paths and channels to support information and knowledge flows.

How autonomous is the unit? How much leeway does the unit have to establish its own information culture? Is the unit rule or creative in its orientation? Rule orientations might tend to encourage a culture of compliance and sharing but on a limited scale. Flexible and creative units might tend to encourage extensive use and production of information.

Are the unit's decision-makers more cautious and risk-averse in their decisions? Do they tend to use more information and information of quality and integrity? Do they tend toward careful and precise decisions? Or, do they prefer to make decisions based mainly on personal experience and "gut responses"?

Unit Level Communications (Factor 9)

This factor interacts with others but has a primary effect on shaping unit information cultures (Curry and Moore 2003). Communication is the way information flows throughout and beyond the unit. Vertical communication structures tell us that information is communicated downward from senior leaders to employees. Horizontal communication structures tell us how information flows within and across departments, teams, and communities. Are there feedback mechanisms in the unit? Can employees voice their ideas or share information? Is communication oral or written? Davenport and Prusak (1997) tell us that the choice of communication channels is a dimension of the unit's information culture. Do the members tend to use face-to-face communications, or do they prefer the more impersonal digital channel based cultures? Is communication within the unit designed to increase understanding and knowledge, or is it intended to "get things right" (Handy, 1993)? Is communication implicit and infrequent, or is it explicit and frequent?

Cross Organization Partnerships (Factor 10)

What kind of partnerships does the business unit have within the organization? Does it have a vibrant partnership network, or is there a lack of horizontal relationships? Is there a willingness to be open in working and sharing information with other units? With what other units does the unit have working relationships? Is there a strict set of hierarchical relationships or a networked structure? Are there strict unit boundaries, or are there hybrid structures? Does the organization create ad hoc or issue-based teams from across the organization? Do these partnerships lead to cross-function information and data sharing? Do they lead to cross-function information quality reviews and management? What kinds of partnerships does the unit have with external distributors and suppliers? With its distributors? With its customers? How does it leverage partner and customer information? Are they part of its information culture?

Information culture researchers also remind us that a business unit's relationship with information management and technology units can have a strong influence on its information culture. The stronger this relationship, the more likely the unit is to have a supportive and proactive information culture.

Information Security and Confidentiality (Factor 11)

The Information security and confidentiality requirements of a business unit will have a significant impact on its information culture. Military, legal, or national security business units must have substantial barriers in place to protect their information assets. These will impose barriers to information exchange. Units that require confidentiality will also have inherent barriers to information sharing. The information culture here will be predisposed to resist sharing and towards suspicion and caution. Business units that deal with personal information – personal and financial – will also tend to guard the individual's privacy and to request permission before sharing. This factor also interacts with geographical location factors, and possibly with age demographics.

Management Philosophy of the Unit (Factor 12)

As we noted earlier for business cultures, power, and control are among the most significant factors affecting a culture. This is equally true of information cultures as it is for business cultures. The power of information and knowledge is perhaps less visible than political or financial power. However, it is just as powerful. Consider how much of the power of the members of a unit or group derives from the control they have over organizational information. Every organization has information "haves" and "have nots." Information based power is generally concentrated among those who have been at the organization longest, those who are politically favored or more highly placed. In some organization's control over certain types of information is an indication of power. For example, knowledge of and information about the organization's operations and management, as well as its past, can make an individual valuable to new managers. Such information might be hoarded or monopolized to maintain power. Information "haves" may attempt to protect their knowledge and their power base. Others can be excluded from power by denying access to information. Consider how a lack of access to work manuals or simple descriptions of procedures and technical standards might compromise an individual's performance.

Ideally, a business unit will tend to discourage these types of information power and control behaviors. Such internal unit information behaviors tend more towards politics and self-interest and fail to benefit the unit or organization. Units might also discourage information monopolies based on past performance. Ideally, business units will encourage and incentivize information sharing and the even distribution of information power.

Information Sharing and Exchange Behaviors (Factor 13)

The authors have spoken to this factor indirectly – as an effect of other factors. However, it takes a primary role in defining a unit's information culture. The literature on information sharing and exchange is significant - the authors attempt to touch on only a few points to illustrate the importance of the factor. The nature of information sharing and exchange tell us about the members' underlying information assumptions and beliefs. Are the members of the unit united around shared meaning and thought (Janis, 1982; Lewin, 1948; Boisot, 1987; Ouchi, 1979, 1980)? Do we observe instances of information hoarding and hiding? Do the members have an aversion to documenting their knowledge and information? A refusal to document information may signal an unhealthy information culture. Do the members act out of self-preservation in refusing to document or share the knowledge that would lead to others' gains? Do members of the unit leak information to others outside the unit in an attempt to harm the unit or managers (Boisot, 1987; Boisot, 1998)? Does information share encompass both direct person-to-person sharing and codification for broader sharing over distance and time? Codification increases the scope of information diffusion, whereas limited and direct communication may tend to favor retaining information with the center of power in the unit.

UNIT COMPOSITIONAL FACTORS

In addition to the factors inherited from the organization level, individuals that make up a business unit contribute to its information culture. Compositional Factors at the unit level include:

- Gender composition
- Diversity composition
- Generation/age composition;
- Size of unit
- Networks and relationships.

Gender Composition of the Unit (Factor 14)

We have two kinds of business units in every organization. There are business units – units, communities, and teams that support the core business organizations of the organization. Furthermore, there are business units that enable those units by providing support services. Often these supporting units are focused on information management practices. It makes good sense for organizations to concentrate the expertise of these individuals in units where they can support the whole organization rather than be built into and dedicated to a few operations. Business operations focused units may tend to have a gender mix. Units focused on information management will tend to be comprised of women. This is because, over the past 75 years, the information profession has been dominated mainly by women. The chances are that the information cultures of most business units will be gender-neutral. We cannot say categorically that women tend to be better information managers than men. Much depends on the cultural environment and the roles that women have been able to play in business over the years. Where they are new to the business world, they may tend towards more information custodial or stewardship roles than active information creators and users. One area where we cannot and should not accept stereotyped behaviors is in information sharing and use behaviors. Detailed and definitive research that suggests women or men tend to share or use information more effectively is lacking.

Diversity Composition of the Unit (Factor 15)

The diversity composition of the unit can be an incentive or an impediment to developing a healthy information culture. Consider how diversity might contribute to the development of robust information-sharing culture – where the business culture encourages individuals to interact and increase their knowledge of other national cultures. Such business cultures can encourage individuals to develop good listening and communication skills, to include more diverse individuals in their own personal and professional networks, and to see information from new and multiple perspectives. On the other hand, consider business cultures may exacerbate and emphasize differences, and impede a health information culture. Information sharing across cultures requires effective and open communications, patience, and openness to seeing things from different perspectives.

Size of the Unit (Factor 16)

Research does suggest that the size of the unit is a significant factor in whether the unit will develop a cohesive business culture. The size of the unit can mean shorter distances between individuals and shorter information distribution times. Smaller groups mean closer proximity of members – and broader dispersion of and access to information. Surveys of information sharing and awareness in major organizations have demonstrated that small to medium size units have more cohesive and productive information cultures. Members of smaller groups have greater opportunities to blend their assumptions and beliefs, to shape their values and develop common information behaviors.

Networks and Relationships (Factor 17)

We know that networks and relationships are essential factors inherited from the organization. However, it is also essential to see how the networks and relationships of the individual members of the unit can shape the information culture. If a unit is comprised of at least one information management professional or individuals with information management training, the information networks of that unit will be more extensive than the networks of other units. This means that the chances of integrating information assumptions, beliefs, values, and behaviors into the everyday operations of the unit are increased.

INFORMATION CULTURES OF INFORMAL GROUPS

The information cultures of informal groups are essential to organizations. They tend to strengthen the general network cohesiveness and richness of relationships across the organization. These information subcultures can fill gaps in formal information structures and cultures. They are particularly important during times of crisis or conflict when the flow of information may tend to be constrained or controlled for business purposes. What is an example of an informal group information culture? Consider the subculture that forms around individuals who frequent the organization's gym every day over the lunch hour. These informal groups are often critical information channels. Consider a ski club or a beekeeping community in a large academic institution where individuals typically only interact with others in their immediate department. Consider how the information sharing and interaction practices of these communities can augment the behavior of their home departments and units.

Informal subgroups are critical sources of cultural cohesion. They can form within or across administrative units. They can form along the lines of any of the factors identified at the organization, the unit, or the individual level. The authors' experience suggests that the value of these informal group information cultures is significant, mainly when supported and acknowledged by the organization.

INFORMATION CULTURES OF INDIVIDUALS

This level of information culture is critical to ensuring that your information strategy is embraced and is operationalized. It tells us how the organization behaves every day at the individual employee level. This also is the most challenging level to understand and affect culture because we understand individuals and their assumptions and beliefs about information. We have already discussed all the factors that might determine an individual's information assumptions and beliefs – their national cultures, their demographic attributes, their business training and education, their professional experiences. Rather than review those attributes again, let us consider some common information cultural artifacts that might help to expose these assumptions and beliefs. If we can learn to see an individual's information artifacts, we have a starting point for understanding their innate information cultures. These artifacts are important because they can be trusted. Most individuals will tell us they value information highly because they know it is an exposed organization or unit value. Actual values, though, may be clearer just from looking at the environment or observing behaviors. Consider the following "artifacts" of information culture:

- A *unit manager's office* has no visible examples of information assets. Information is not viewed as an asset the manager uses to manage his business or to make decisions
- A staff office is filled with *boxes of print folders, and lose files* tells us that there is little value assigned to organizing and describing information. It is highly likely that the condition of documents will deteriorate or be damaged. These records are not accessible to anyone other than the staff member.
- Search *system reports and visualizations* tell us search is heavily used and effective. These artifacts reinforce the importance of information and the investments that have been made in support of access and discovery.
- Meetings are held with *no agendas, no minutes, and no formal record of decisions*. There is a subtle message that information is not an essential input to the meeting, that discussions are not to be shared outside the meeting, and that a record of decisions to be made is not a valued behavior.
- Research data are stored on *personal laptops and network drives*. Research data is a personal asset or is not valued as an asset used in any future process, project, or decision. Preservation of research data is unimportant.
- Managers make decisions and communicate these decisions in *conversations in the hallway*. The use of the organization's information is less important than the manager's experience and gut feelings. Managers are not accountable for poor decisions.
- The lobby of an organization has an *LCD that plays messages* from all of the critical information managers. Knowledge of information managers is treated as a critical information asset. Recordings communicate the importance of beliefs and values throughout the organization.
- Chief Architect has a set of *information and data architecture principles* on the wall in his office. Core values about information are on display for everyone to see. The Chief Architect refers to them throughout the day and reinforces them.
- The cafeteria has *table tents* that remind individuals of the information management support and training services. Value of information is reinforced through only low-cost artifacts displayed where individuals are socializing and relaxing.
- The organization's *library is an open area* adjacent to the cafeteria – with few walls. The library is seen as a social as well as a research and

study area. Open walls make it easy for anyone to drop in and watch the information sources that are being streamed throughout the day.

- The organization's library is always filled with *individuals visibly working with information*. This implicit artifact reinforces an critical behavior and norm – information use is a typical behavior that is acceptable to management.
- There is a *visible virtual/physical shop* where external stakeholders can purchase the organization's information. There are two artifacts here – the physical or virtual store, and the digital or physical products. The fact that the organization packages its information for internal and external consumption is a significant cultural artifact.
- *Online self-study options* for learning how to fulfill individual information management responsibilities. This virtual artifact tells us that management values information management and makes this career option available to anyone interested. It also tells us that information is a professional practice rather than an informal off the cuff process.
- Every staff job description has *information culture and information management responsibilities*. This is a tangible artifact that reinforces the belief that information assets are essential to the organization, and the norm that managing these assets is everyone's responsibility.
- *Information management roles* are evaluated according to defined indicators and metrics. This intangible artifact reinforces the belief that information has value, and the norm that information behaviors have consequences.
- There are *visible award systems* for individuals who have high information management activities. This visible and tangible artifact reinforces the belief that information is a business asset, and that using information for business purposes is an important social norm.
- Senior and unit managers value the *awards for information management* they receive and post them on their office walls just as staff does. These implicit artifacts reinforce an essential social norm – everyone is responsible for information management. It is a high level of responsibility.
- The *organization's intranet has daily stories* about the importance of information – all stories have embedded links to the organization's information assets. This explicit artifact reinforces the importance of information production and consumption. It also highlights the use of official information in business decisions and processes.

- *Town halls* of vice-presidents are live-streamed and preserved as information assets. The leader actively shares and uses information in these town halls. The leader understands that his/her *communications* are also official information and ensures that the full town hall exchange is captured and preserved as a multimedia object.
- *Information value statements* can be found on signage throughout the organization – in business and support units. This explicit artifact posted in the lobby reinforces the organization's underlying assumptions and beliefs about information. The staff understands that good information management practices are essential to the business.

What can we learn about the innate information cultures of each of these individuals? What would you infer about their information behaviors? How might these behaviors translate to support for or impediments to information strategies? How would you use this information to better shape the information culture?

CONCLUSION

After reading this chapter, you should be able to:

- Describe the elements of information cultures
- Explain the current peer-reviewed and gray literature on information cultures
- Explain how to discover information cultures across the organization
- Interpret the organization level dynamic factors for your organization
- Interpret the unit and team level dynamic factors for your organization
- Interpret the dynamic factors for your informal groups
- Interpret the individual level dynamic factors for your organization

REFERENCES

Baskerville, R., & Myers, M. D. (2004). Special issue on action research in information systems: Making IS research relevant to practice: Foreword. *Management Information Systems Quarterly*, *28*(3), 329–335. doi:10.2307/25148642

Bedford, D. A. D. (2019). Strategic Management of Business-Critical Information Assets. In *Advances in Information Quality and Management*. Hershey, PA: IGI Global.

Boisot, M. (1987). *Information and organizations: The manager as anthropologist*. Fontana Press.

Boisot, M. H. (1998). *Knowledge assets: Securing competitive advantage in the information economy*. OUP Oxford.

Boland, R. J. Jr, & Tenkasi, R. V. (1995). Perspective making and perspective taking in communities of knowing. *Organization Science*, *6*(4), 350–372. doi:10.1287/orsc.6.4.350

Brown, M. E. (1991). A General Model of Information-Seeking Behavior. In *Proceedings of the ASIS Annual Meeting* (*Vol. 28*, pp. 9-14). Academic Press.

Chatman, E. A. (1999). A theory of life in the round. *Journal of the American Society for Information Science*, *50*(3), 207–217. doi:10.1002/(SICI)1097-4571(1999)50:3<207::AID-ASI3>3.0.CO;2-8

Choo, C. W. (2002). *Information management for the intelligent organization: the art of scanning the environment*. Information Today, Inc.

Choo, C. W. (2005). Information failures and organizational disasters. *MIT Sloan Management Review*, *46*(3), 8.

Choo, C. W. (2013). Information culture and organizational effectiveness. *International Journal of Information Management*, *33*(5), 775–779. doi:10.1016/j.ijinfomgt.2013.05.009

Choo, C. W., Bergeron, P., Detlor, B., & Heaton, L. (2008). Information culture and information use: An exploratory study of three organizations. *Journal of the American Society for Information Science and Technology*, *59*(5), 792–804. doi:10.1002/asi.20797

Choo, C. W., Furness, C., Paquette, S., Van Den Berg, H., Detlor, B., Bergeron, P., & Heaton, L. (2006). Working with information: Information management and culture in a professional services organization. *Journal of Information Science*, *32*(6), 491–510. doi:10.1177/0165551506068159

Curry, A., & Moore, C. (2003). Assessing information culture—An exploratory model. *International Journal of Information Management*, *23*(2), 91–110. doi:10.1016/S0268-4012(02)00102-0

Curry, A., & Moore, C. (2003). Assessing information culture—An exploratory model. *International Journal of Information Management*, *23*(2), 91–110. doi:10.1016/S0268-4012(02)00102-0

Davenport, T. H., Eccles, R. G., & Prusak, L. (1998). Information politics. *The strategic management of intellectual capital*, 101-120.

Deal, T., & Kennedy, A. (1999). *The New Corporate Cultures: Revitalizing the Workplace after Downsizing, Mergers, and Reengineering*. Cambridge, MA: Perseus.

Dougherty, D. (1992). Interpretive barriers to successful product innovation in large firms. *Organization Science*, *3*(2), 179–202. doi:10.1287/orsc.3.2.179

Earl, M. J. (1994). The new and the old of business process redesign. *The Journal of Strategic Information Systems*, *3*(1), 5–22. doi:10.1016/0963-8687(94)90003-5

Handy, C. (2011). *The empty raincoat: Making sense of the future*. Random House.

Hanseth, O., Ciborra, C. U., & Braa, K. (2001). The control devolution: ERP and the side effects of globalization. *ACM SIGMIS Database: the DATABASE for Advances in Information Systems*, *32*(4), 34–46. doi:10.1145/506139.506144

Hanson, T. (2011). Developing an information strategy. *EDUCAUSE Review*, *46*(6), 82–84.

Harper, G. R., & Utley, D. R. (2001). Organizational culture and successful information technology implementation. *Engineering Management Journal*, *13*(2), 11–15. doi:10.1080/10429247.2001.11415111

Henderson, R. (1994). Managing innovation in the information age. *Harvard Business Review*.

Janis, I. L. (1982). *Groupthink: Psychological studies of policy decisions and fiascoes* (2nd ed.). Boston, MA: Cengage Learning.

Klein, H. K., & Myers, M. D. (1999). A set of principles for conducting and evaluating interpretive field studies in information systems. *Management Information Systems Quarterly*, *23*(1), 67–93. doi:10.2307/249410

Kunda, G. (1992). *Labor and social change. Engineering culture: Control and commitment in a high-tech corporation.* Philadelphia, PA: Temple University Press.

Leidner, D. E. (1998). *Understanding information culture: Integrating knowledge management systems into organizations.* INSEAD.

Leidner, D. E., & Kayworth, T. (2006). A review of culture in information systems research: Toward a theory of information technology culture conflict. *Management Information Systems Quarterly*, *30*(2), 357–399. doi:10.2307/25148735

Lewin, K. (1948). Resolving social conflicts; selected papers on group dynamics. Harper & Brothers.

Markus, M. L. (1983). Power, politics, and MIS implementation. *Communications of the ACM*, *26*(6), 430–444. doi:10.1145/358141.358148

Martin, J. (1992). *Cultures in organizations: Three perspectives.* Oxford University Press.

McGee, J. V., Prusak, L., & Pyburn, P. J. (1993). *Managing information strategically: Increase your company's competitiveness and efficiency by using information as a strategic tool* (Vol. 1). John Wiley & Sons.

Myers, M. D., & Tan, F. B. (2002). Beyond models of national culture in information systems research. In *Human factors in information systems* (pp. 1–19). IGI Global. doi:10.4018/978-1-931777-10-0.ch001

Nonaka, I. (1994). A dynamic theory of organizational knowledge creation. *Organization Science*, *5*(1), 14–37. doi:10.1287/orsc.5.1.14

Orlikowski, W. J. (1992). The duality of technology: Rethinking the concept of technology in organizations. *Organization Science*, *3*(3), 398–427. doi:10.1287/orsc.3.3.398

Orlikowski, W. J. (1996). Improvising organizational transformation over time: A situated change perspective. *Information Systems Research, 7*(1), 63–92. doi:10.1287/isre.7.1.63

Orlikowski, W. J., & Gash, D. C. (1994). Technological frames: Making sense of information technology in organizations. *ACM Transactions on Information Systems, 12*(2), 174–207. doi:10.1145/196734.196745

Orlikowski, W. J., & Yates, J. (1994). *Genre repertoire: Norms and forms for work and interaction*. Academic Press.

Ouchi, W. G. (1979). A conceptual framework for the design of organizational control mechanisms. *Management Science, 25*(9), 833–848. doi:10.1287/mnsc.25.9.833

Ouchi, W. G. (1980). Markets, bureaucracies, and clans. *Administrative Science Quarterly, 25*(1), 129–141. doi:10.2307/2392231

Prusak, L. (1997). *Knowledge in Organizations Resources for the Knowledge-Based Economy* (1st ed.). Newton, MA: Butterworth-Heinemann.

Prusak, L. (1998). *Presentation to the conference board*. In Conference on Knowledge Management and Organizational Learning, Chicago, IL.

Purser, R. E., Pasmore, W. A., & Tenkasi, R. V. (1992). The influence of deliberations on learning in new product development teams. *Journal of Engineering and Technology Management, 9*(1), 1–28. doi:10.1016/0923-4748(92)90009-T

Sarker, S., & Lee, A. S. (2003). Using a case study to test the role of three key social enablers in ERP implementation. *Information & Management, 40*(8), 813–829. doi:10.1016/S0378-7206(02)00103-9

Travica, B. (2005). Information Politics and Information Culture: A Case Study. *Informing Science, 8*, 8. doi:10.28945/496

Travica, B. (2005). Information view of organization. *Journal of International Technology and Information Management, 14*(3), 1.

Vance, A., Elie-Dit-Cosaque, C., & Straub, D. W. (2008). Examining trust in information technology artifacts: The effects of system quality and culture. *Journal of Management Information Systems, 24*(4), 73–100. doi:10.2753/MIS0742-1222240403

Zuboff, S. (1989). *In the age of the smart machine: Thefuture of work and power. Reprint edition.* New York, NY: Basic Books.

ADDITIONAL READING

Chen, D. Q., Mocker, M., Preston, D. S., & Teubner, A. (2010). Information systems strategy: Reconceptualization, measurement, and implications. *Management Information Systems Quarterly, 34*(2), 233–259. doi:10.2307/20721426

Collins, C. D. (2010). *Knowledge and information sharing: A multiple-case study of the information culture of the British Columbia salmon fishery.* Indiana University.

De Long, D. (1997). Building the knowledge-based organization: How culture drives knowledge behaviors. *Ernst and Young Center for Business Innovation, Working Paper, Boston.*

De Long, D. W., & Fahey, L. (2000). Diagnosing cultural barriers to knowledge management. *The Academy of Management Perspectives, 14*(4), 113–127. doi:10.5465/ame.2000.3979820

Gendina, N. (2017). Information Culture and Information Literacy as a Scientific Direction and a Field of Educational Activities in Russia. In *Pathways Into Information Literacy and Communities of Practice* (pp. 167–202). Chandos Publishing. doi:10.1016/B978-0-08-100673-3.00007-1

Griffith, D. A., Myers, M. B., & Harvey, M. G. (2006). An investigation of national culture's influence on relationship and knowledge resources in interorganizational relationships between Japan and the United States. *Journal of International Marketing, 14*(3), 1–32. doi:10.1509/jimk.14.3.1

Hansen, P., & Widén, G. (2017). The embeddedness of collaborative information seeking in information culture. *Journal of Information Science, 43*(4), 554–566. doi:10.1177/0165551516651544

Iivari, N. (2005). The role of organizational culture in organizational change-identifying a realistic position for prospective IS research.

Jarvenpaa, S. L., & Staples, D. S. (2000). The use of collaborative electronic media for information sharing: An exploratory study of determinants. *The Journal of Strategic Information Systems*, *9*(2-3), 129–154. doi:10.1016/S0963-8687(00)00042-1

Kaarst-Brown, M. L., Nicholson, S., Von Dran, G. M., and Stanton, J. M. (2004). Organizational cultures of libraries as a strategic resource.

Lederer, A. L., & Sethi, V. (1988). The implementation of strategic information systems planning methodologies. *Management Information Systems Quarterly*, *12*(3), 445–461. doi:10.2307/249212

Lopez-Nicolas, C., and Meroño-Cerdán, Á. L. (2009). The impact of organizational culture on the use of ICT for knowledge management.

Loshin, D. (2010). *Master data management*. Morgan Kaufmann.

Lubar, S. (1999). Information culture and the archival record. *The American Archivist*, *62*(1), 10–22. doi:10.17723/aarc.62.1.30x5657gu1w44630

Riyaz, A., & Smith, K. (2012). Chapter 8 Information Culture in the Maldives. In Library and information science trends and research: Asia-Oceania (pp. 173-208). Emerald Group Publishing Limited.

Söllner, M., Pavlou, P. A., and Leimeister, J. M. (2013). Understanding trust in IT Artifacts–a new conceptual approach. *Available at SSRN 2475382*.

Sundqvist, A., & Svärd, P. (2016). Information culture and records management: A suitable match? Conceptualizations of information culture and their application on records management. *International Journal of Information Management*, *36*(1), 9–15. doi:10.1016/j.ijinfomgt.2015.08.004

Tsouvalis, J., Seymour, S., & Watkins, C. (2000). Exploring knowledge-cultures: Precision farming, yield mapping, and the expert–farmer interface. *Environment & Planning A*, *32*(5), 909–924. doi:10.1068/a32138

Widén, G., & Karim, M. (2017, September). Role of Information Culture in Workplace Information Literacy: A Literature Review. In *European Conference on Information Literacy* (pp. 21-29). Springer, Cham.

Winter, A. F., Ammenwerth, E., Bott, O. J., Brigl, B., Buchauer, A., Gräber, S., ... Heinrich, A. (2001). Strategic information management plans: The basis for systematic information management in hospitals. *International Journal of Medical Informatics*, *64*(2-3), 99–109. doi:10.1016/S1386-5056(01)00219-2 PMID:11734379

Section 4

Documenting Strategies and Cultures

Chapter 7
Balancing Organization Strategies and Cultures

ABSTRACT

The goal of this chapter is to identify and manage risks related to information strategies and the businesses' use of information in the knowledge economy. Business and information managers must find a fit that grows our information and business cultures and supports our business and information strategies. There is no single tool or rule that you can follow to address the risk. The risk always derives from the business context. It is different for each organization, and it is dynamic even within that organization over time. The authors provide a framework the reader can work with to think through and develop a fit that works by any business context. The authors also provide a seven-step methodology that considers strategy and culture and guides the organization through designing and achieving a balance.

WHY DO WE CARE ABOUT ALIGNING ORGANIZATIONAL STRATEGIES AND CULTURES?

The goal of this chapter is to identify methods for reducing the risk of strategic failures at the organization level. In particular, we are interested in managing those risks that relate to information strategies and the business' use of information in the knowledge economy. As we noted in Chapter 1, we know that risk exists whenever our cultures are at odds with our strategies. In the

DOI: 10.4018/978-1-7998-4315-3.ch007

knowledge economy, this risk increases when our information strategies are out of synch with our business strategies and our business cultures.

The assessment process helps us to mitigate risk by identifying pain points (i.e., in our business and information strategies) and looking for and leveraging cultural attributes to alleviate those pain points. Every pain point is unique to a context – to a business and information strategy. Every point of cultural leverage is unique to a context – a specific strategic challenge. Ignoring our pain points is a high-risk strategy in the knowledge economy because they will only increase over time. Ignoring our culture as an attribute and a comparative advantage is a lost opportunity. Wholesale changes to culture can introduce new risks with the potential to do far more significant damage. We can only reduce or mitigate risk by learning how to shape our culture to support our strategies at the point of development and implementation.

While we know which approach will help us to manage risk, we acknowledge that there is no general rule that a manager can follow to achieve this result. Every organization, every business unit, team, or community, presents unique challenges and unique opportunities. Moreover, that unique culture is dynamic over time. It is dynamic because we learn and make progress or because the context changes. Strategies change because business environments – internal and external – change. Cultures change because people join the organization, and others leave. Our goal as business and information managers is to find a fit that grows our information and business cultures and supports our business and information strategies. There is no single tool or rule that you can follow to address the risk. There is, though, a framework you can work with to think through and develop a fit that works for you today, in the situation. We incline to think we can solve the problem by focusing on organization-level strategies and cultures. However, it is not sufficient that we apply the framework and manage the fit at the organization level. We must design a fit at the organization level, but that will fail if strategies and cultures are not aligned in divisions and teams across the organization. Let us begin at the organization level. We explain how to apply the framework at the organization level – and to establish a methodology that can be used at the unit and individual level.

What is the framework? The framework (Figure 1) is comprised of three elements, including (1) harmonized business and information *strategies*; (2) harmonized business and information *cultures;* and (3) achieving a balance by calibrating culture to support the strategy in any business context.

Figure 1. Framework for aligning business and information strategies and cultures

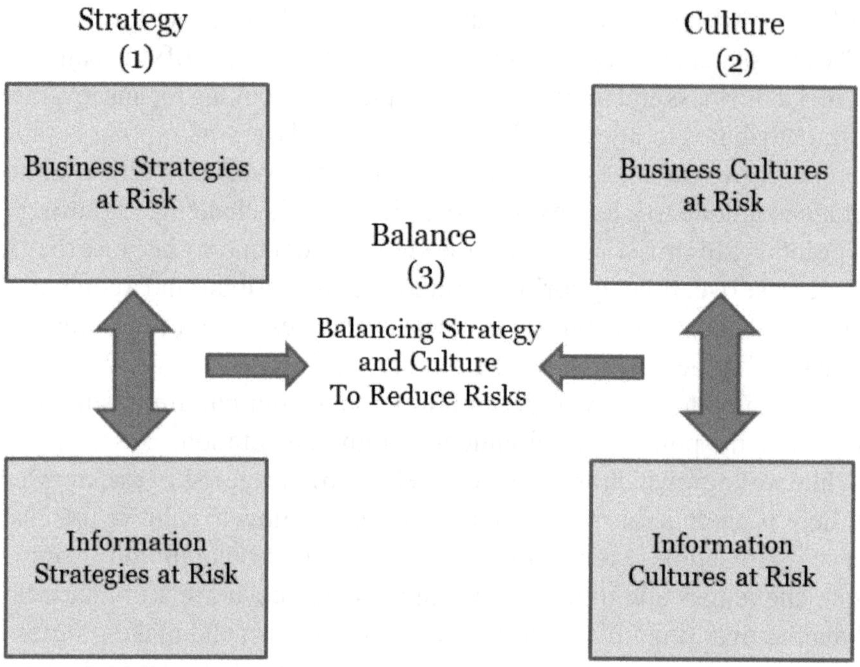

The authors define a seven-step methodology to align strategies and culture in any context. The seven steps include:

Table 1. Seven-step methodology

Step 1. Assess the Current Risks (Pain Points) in our Business Strategies
Step 2. Assess the Current Risks (Pain Points) in our Information Strategies
Step 3. Identify Common Risks (Pain Points) in Business and Information Strategies
Step 4. Assess the Current State of Business Cultures (Leverage Points)
Step 5. Assess the Current State of Information Cultures (Leverage Points)
Step 6. Identify Common Cultural Leverage Points for Strategies at Risk
Step 7. Align The Cultural Points of Leverage With Strategic Risks and Pain Points

Remember that we do not want to change or reshape culture for the general purpose of improving the work culture. We do not want to tackle the whole culture. This will be a costly exercise, and it is unlikely to be successful. Individuals are willing to adapt their cultures to serve a current business goal, but they are not willing to change their whole inherent personal culture. We apply the framework and shape the culture only at strategic points in the organization.

Moreover, we should put the process in the hands of those who are responsible for achieving the strategic goals and objectives. Then each leader, each division, each unit – designs a fit to support the current business need. Over time this approach gradually creates a new business methodology. It shifts the nature of strategic planning always to include culture shaping. Shaping our culture becomes part of the way we work.

Alignment and fitting cultures and strategies are most effective by levels of the organization because there are different factors and impacts. We begin with the organization level because this is the level where we can set the tone, establish an institutional process, and account for progress. In the sections below, we walk through each of these seven steps. Chapter 7 focuses on organization-level strategies and cultures. Chapter 8 focuses on division, unit, and team level strategies and cultures. Finally, Chapter 9 focuses on individual strategies and cultures. While the framework remains the same, the factors vary, and who conducts the assessment also varies.

STEP 1: ASSESS THE CURRENT RISKS (PAIN POINTS) IN OUR BUSINESS STRATEGIES

What is the Objective of This Step?

In Chapter 1, we walked through four possible options for dealing with strategies and cultures. The authors recommended focusing on Option 4 – which involves integrating culture analysis and shaping into each strategic development and management function. This means we must start from the point of a healthy strategy to develop a process – we should focus on strategies and fix what we can before we begin to consider reshaping culture to support those strategies. A healthy business strategy is an essential starting point.

The goal of this step is to develop a working description of the organization's most strategic and organization-wide strategies. This description serves as a foundation for considering organization level risks, and as a foundation for the full multilevel description of the organization. Remember that this is the foundation for aligning the business and the information strategies – we do not expect to link this result directly to cultures – though a manager could do that if they were not focused on information strategies.

How Do We Find Current Organization Level Strategies?

First, focus on finding those strategies that are explicit and published. We can do this by searching the organization's information repositories, intranets, and external websites. We are looking for strategies that have been formulated by the senior leadership of the organization – those strategies that are designed to support the organization's mission directly, goals, and performance. Focus your search on the strategic units of the organization – for the last two to three years – because you want to find strategies that have had sufficient time to be implemented. How do we search for them? We look for anything labeled strategy, policy, or a plan of any sort.

After you have exhausted this approach, identify a sample set of individuals who are responsible for formulating these strategies. The goal of these interviews – which could be completed either in person or via an electronic survey – is to identify other strategies you were unable to find in your first pass search. These interviews will help to discover all those hidden strategies, shared strategies, false strategies we described in Chapter 3. We are also looking for strategies that are embedded in planning documents, strategies which may have been described in communications and strategies which take the form of policy statements. Once you have a representative set of both explicit and implicit strategies, you can move to the next step, which is describing the content of these strategies.

How Do We Describe the Strategies we Find?

The objective of this task is to characterize those strategies in terms of their content. What is the nature of the strategy – does it have all of the components we would expect to find in a complete strategy? This task takes the form of a focused review of the strategies we have found. This is best performed by an individual working with a structured framework. The output of this task is essentially a metadata description of each strategy – a high-level record that we can then use to assess health. What does this part of the framework look like?

Table 2. Framework for describing the content of business strategies

What is the nature of the business strategy? Is the strategy:
• Explicit Realized Strategy
• Hidden Strategy
• Shared Strategy
• False Strategy
• Learned Strategy
What are the essential elements we find in the strategy? Do we find:
• A statement of a business vision
• A description of business mission and goals
• The organization's business principles
• References to business tactics
How was the Strategy Developed? Who contributed to the strategy?
Who is aware of the strategy?
How is the strategy currently managed?
o By an individual responsible and accountable for the strategy?
o Trough Active Progress Reports?
o Through Periodic review and adjustment of the strategy
Does the business strategy address information assets?
How does the business strategy treat information assets?
• Strategy references information assets as having business value
• Strategy references information as a critical business asset
• Strategy References the Business Transformation of Information
• The strategy refers to unit or team level strategies and goals

How Do We Assess The Current Health Of Each Strategy?

The objective of this task is to characterize the strengths and weaknesses of the strategies we have found. In this task, we focus on the health of the strategy. What constitutes a healthy strategy? What are the characteristics of a poor or failing business strategy? A primary characteristic of success in our view is whether it references and acknowledges the business value and role of information. If it does, we take this as a vital sign of good health. However, beyond that, we need to know: We can consider the strengths of those strategies that are in good health – to see what we can learn about cultural alignment, support, and connections to the business strategy. We can focus on those that are moderately healthy or in poor health – these are the ones we want to look at in terms of cultural alignment. Moreover, we can look for weaknesses in all of these strategies. What does this part of the framework look like?

Table 3. Framework for assessing the health of a business strategy

Has the strategy been successfully implemented?
• The strategy was successfully implemented
• The strategy was partially successful
• Strategy was not successful
Did the strategy produce the intended business value?
What aspects of the strategy were successful? What aspects failed?
Why was the strategy successful? Why was the strategy not successful?

This task involves talking to or collecting information from the individuals who are responsible for implementing the strategy. A structured survey or interview guide would not be effective because we do not know all of the possible answers to these questions. The most effective approach would be to ask open-ended questions and to analyze the results then. In this task, we are looking for reasons the strategy did or did not succeed that might be related to the business use and management of information.

Assume that at the end of this task, we will have an extended description of each strategy. We will be able to identify those strategies that may carry a risk we are unable to tolerate. That level of risk must be determined by each organization, at a given point in time and for a given business context.

Which Strategies Pose A Risk And What Is The Level Of That Risk?

This task should produce a list of the strategies we found that are at risk – perhaps organized by the administrative area that produced them. The list of strategies is prioritized in terms of the degree and nature of the risk. Which has the most significant business impact or value? Which have risks that can be addressed by filling in gaps in the strategies? Which have significant business risks based on a history of failure or partial success? Which strategies have low risks?

At the end of this task, we are not prepared to take up the assessment of the information strategies. We have a business foundation for understanding which of our business strategies are at risk and why.

STEP 2: ASSESS THE CURRENT RISKS (PAIN POINTS) IN OUR INFORMATION STRATEGIES

What is the Objective of this Step?

The objective of this task is to develop a picture of information strategies at the organization level that will serve as a foundation for creating a whole organization integrated strategy. We are assessing information strategies in the context of the business. We use the same process for identifying, describing, assessing the degree of health, and risk of each information strategy. However, risk and health are defined in the context of how well the information strategy supports the business – we are looking at information assets as strategic business assets. We are not assessing information strategies in terms of how well they align with information cultures but in terms of how well they fit business strategies.

Overview of the General Methodology

This task helps us to build out the second part of the left side of the framework (Figure 2). Our goal is to update our target list of at-risk business strategies with our list of at-risk information strategies. Our search will turn up healthy information strategies, information strategies that need targeted improvements, and information strategies that have failed or have performed at low levels in the past.

How Do We Find Current Organization Level Information Strategies?

The first step is to find the organization level information strategies. We are looking for those strategies that have been formulated by the senior leadership of the organization – those strategies that are designed to support the organization's mission directly, goals and performance or those strategies formulated by enabling units such as information management units and division – but whose intended audience is the whole organization. Focus first on finding those information strategies that are explicit and published. We can do this by a search for the organization's information repositories, intranets, and external websites.

Just as we suggested for business strategies, information strategies may not be labeled explicitly as "strategies" – instead, they may be published as policies or procedures. Remember that we are looking for strategies that may focus on process and forms of information. It is not sufficient to simply search for and ask about "information strategies" per se – we need to be a bit more focused on our search. Consider those life cycle strategies discussed in Chapter 4 as possible examples of information strategies at this level. As was the case for business strategies, information strategies may be labeled strategy, policy, or plan.

Having exhausted the search for explicit and documented information strategies, talk to individuals who are responsible for formulating these strategies. For information strategies, the key individuals to start with are those senior leaders who have responsibility for information and data management. Look at your organization chart. Determine where information roles and responsibilities are assigned. Focus on those individuals who have responsibility for information technology since some of these strategies might be embedded in those strategies. The purpose of these interviews – which could be completed either in person or via an electronic survey – is to identify other strategies you were unable to find in your first pass search – all those hidden strategies shared strategies, or false strategies, strategies which are embedded in planning documents, in communications, or which take the form of policy statements.

How Do We Describe the Strategies we Find?

Once you have a representative set of both explicit and implicit strategies, you can move to the next step, which is describing the content of these strategies. This task takes the form of a focused review of the strategies you have collected. This is best performed by an individual working with a structured framework. The output of this task is essentially a metadata description of each strategy – a high-level record that we can then use to assess health. What does the framework look like for this step?

How Do We Assess The Current Health Of Each Strategy?

In this task, we focus on the health of the information strategy. What constitutes a healthy information strategy? A healthy information strategy is one that recognizes the business value of information and speaks to the role that information management plays in supporting the organization's business visions and missions. Where this is missing from an information strategy, we have a pre-existing condition. This condition must be satisfied if we hope the information strategy to succeed. It is not sufficient for information strategies to be formulated and managed by information managers – they must be owned and lived by business managers. Realistically, though, this is likely to be a pre-existing condition of any information strategy we discover. A primary characteristic of success in our view is whether it references and acknowledges the business value and role of information. If it does, we take this as a vital sign of good health.

What are the characteristics of a poor or failing business strategy? We need to know whether the information strategy was successfully implemented. If not, what were the points of concern? Did it generate the expected results – regardless of whether they were linked to business value? Furthermore, why was the strategy successful? Why was it not successful?

As was the case for business strategies, this task involves talking to or collecting information from the individuals who are responsible for implementing the strategy. As for business strategies, we do not know all of the possible answers to these questions, so the best approach is an open-ended set of questions and a thoughtful analysis of the results. Upon completion of this task, you will have in hand an extended description of each strategy.

Table 4. Framework for describing the content of business strategies

What is the nature of the business strategy? Is the strategy:
• Explicit Realized Strategy
• Hidden Strategy
• Shared Strategy
• False Strategy
• Learned Strategy
What are the essential elements we find in the strategy? Do we find:
• A statement of a business vision
• A description of business mission and goals
• The organization's business principles
• References to business tactics
How was the Information Strategy Developed? Who contributed to the strategy?
Who is aware of the information strategy?
How is the information strategy currently managed?
o Does business or an information unit manage it?
o By an individual responsible and accountable for the strategy?
o Trough Active Progress Reports?
o Through Periodic review and adjustment of the strategy
Does the business strategy address information assets?
Does the information strategy relate to and support the business, or is it focused on information management?
• Are there references to current business strategies?
• Does the strategy align with the organization's vision and goals?
• Does the strategy refer to business products and services?
• How much of the strategy is focused on an area of information practice?
• How much of the strategy focuses on a stage of the information life cycle?

Table 5. Framework for assessing the health of a business strategy

Has the strategy been successfully implemented?
• Strategy was successfully implemented
• Strategy was partially successful
• Strategy was not successful
Did the strategy produce the intended results?
What aspects of the strategy were successful? What aspects failed?
Why was the strategy successful? Why was the strategy not successful?

Which Information Strategies Pose A Risk And What Is The Level Of That Risk?

The product of this task is an updated list of strategies with business risks. The updated list highlights additional areas where new risks were identified. This shifts from potential risk and failure to focus on the business value of information. The list is prioritized - with the highest risk strategies at the top. Strategies of most significant risk are those with both a business and an information risk. In the next priority are strategies where there is at least a partial alignment. Finally, the lowest priority are those strategies where there is either a business or an information risk. Again this list is prioritized according to the business value of the owning unit. Having completed the prioritization and identified high-risk strategies, we can now focus on assessing the information strategies. We have a business foundation for understanding which of our business strategies are at risk and why.

STEP 3. IDENTIFY COMMON RISKS (PAIN POINTS) IN BUSINESS AND INFORMATION STRATEGIES

What is the Objective of This Step?

The objective of this step is to identify our areas most significant strategic risk. An understanding of how the business thinks about risk is essential to this step. Also, critical is an understanding of the organization's level of tolerance for risk. This step must involve business managers who can make these calls.

How do We Identify the Areas of the Most Significant Strategic Risk?

At this point, we have what we need to create a reasonable picture of strategies at the organization level. We have a reasonable understanding of where our business strategies are healthy and successful and where they are in questionable or poor health. We need to look at this from a functional or organizational perspective. Areas of most significant risk are those without a business or an information strategy – obvious gap areas. Area of risk also includes those functions or units where the alignment suggests that there is both a sub-optimized business strategy that is (1) missing an information strategy; (2) has a partially formed information strategy; or (3) an information strategy that is focused only on information management. At this point in the process, we are identifying potential target areas – areas where we can improve the business strategy by aligning and improving the information strategy. The output or outcome of this task is a list of potential target areas that we can use to align with our analysis of cultures. This target list also describes the nature of the risk and our thoughts on how to address the risks.

STEP 4: ASSESS THE CURRENT STATE OF BUSINESS CULTURES (LEVERAGE POINTS)

What is the Objective of This Step?

This is the first of three steps to describe the business and the information culture of the organization. Furthermore, remember that we are not assessing the culture generally but only the cultures where our strategies are at risk. We want to make sure that culture is not a risk factor in those cases. Our first step is to identify those functional units of interest – we take as a starting point those units that are on the target list of at-risk strategies produced in Step 3. Also, remember that we are not after a whole scale realignment or change of the culture – we are attempting to shape the business culture so that it more directly aligns with and supports our business and information strategies.

How do we do this? We do this by creating a cultural profile of the unit that has the strategic risk. The cultural profile helps us to understand what factors are points of leverage we might use to support the strategy.

What Does a Cultural Profile Look Like at this Level?

However, to understand what shapes our cultures, we have to look at different factors – we need to develop an understanding of our cultures, and these factors provide insights. Not all of the existing methods and tools will tell us what we need to know about these factors, so you should be prepared to create your view. In some cases, there might be a tool that can give you a partial picture – but no single tool will tell you everything you need to know. In chapter x, we identified the factors we expect to influence our culture at the organization level. In this step, we want to know which aspects of culture these factors affect. Our assessment is of factors and their impact on specific elements. We conduct this assessment also for those units or functions that are assigned to the strategic levels of the organization because we need to apply what we learn about culture with the kinds of strategies that we find at the organization level.

Developing a National Culture Profile of the Unit that Produced the Strategy

Developing a profile is not a trivial task. Developing a description of any one of these factors requires the use of cultural assessment tools or the advice and guidance of a cultural analyst. These are not tasks that a business manager can take on without expert guidance. In order to develop this profile, then we must look at the tools that are available to us and fit the tools to the factor.

There is a wide range of cultural analysis and assessment methods. The authors have identified five high-level categories of methods to help you navigate this emerging field, including:

- Cultural profiling and inventory methods ((Rosinski, 2010; Gallego-Toledo, 2015; Seufert, 2002; Mannion Konteh and Davies, 2009; Fowler and Mumford, 1999)
- Culture intelligence scales (Ang and Van Dyne, 2015; Van Dyne, Ang and Koh, 2015; Van Dyne, Ang and Koh, 2009)

- Cultural competency surveys and quizzes (Crandall et al., 2003; Lie et al., 2011; Thom et al., 2006)
- Cultural network and behavior analysis (Glenn, 1988; Lamal, 1997; Norton, 1995)
- Cultural performance metrics (Kendra and Taplin, 2004; O'Reilly et al., 2014; Goves and Feyerherm, 2011)

The authors' general observation from conducting this research is that most of these tools are aimed at either the country, the organization as a whole or an industry. Few of the methods have advanced to the point of application and testing at the unit, team, or individual level. Each method takes a different approach and produces a particular result. Some are intended to be applied to organizations or groups, and others are targeted at individuals (Betancourt et al., 2016; Bhui et al., 2007; Brislin Worthley and Macnab, 2006; Bu-Quammaz Bikmen and Birgonul, 2006; Campinha-Bacote, 2002; de la Garza Carranza and Egri, 2010; Peterson, 2011; Sue and Torino, 2005). Some provide simple descriptions for a set of cultural variables or factors, whereas others might evaluate the strength or weakness of cultural interactions (Cross, 1988; Gelfand Imai and Fehr, 2008; Imai and Gelfand, 2010; Jang and Barnett, 1994; Janssen and Brett, 2006; Johnson Lenartowicz and Apud, 2006; Mueller and Veinott, 2008; Mueller Sieck and Veinott, 2007). Some of these methods have been developed into practical instruments that can be applied to any organization (Cooke and Szumal, 2000; Rasmussen, Sieck, and Osland, Sashkin, and Rosenbach, 1990). Others represent new theories and research methods but have not had sufficient rigorous testing to be used as "off the shelf" tools(Ang and Inkpen, 2008; Ang and Van Dyne, 2015; Ang, Van Dyne and Koh, 2006; Ang et al. 2007; Earley and Mosakowski, 2002; Earley Murnieks and Mosakowski, 2007; Emirbayer and Goodwin, 1994; Livermore and Soon, 2015; Livermore, Van Dyne and Ang, 2012; MacNab, Brislin and Worthley, 2012; Morosini, Shane, and Singh, 1998; Mosakowski Calic and Earley, 2013; Ng, Van Dyne and Ang, 2009; Ng, Van Dyne and Ang, 2009; Colders, Chernyshenko and Stark, 2008; Rasmussen, Sieck, and Osland, 2012; Rockstuhl et al., 2011; Sieck, Rasmussen and Smart, 2010; Thomas, 2006; Thomas, 2015; Thomas et al., 2008). Others represent one-off research projects – which have a good foundation you might be able to adapt to suit your purpose (Apud, Lenartowicz and Johnson, 2003: Brouthers and Brouthers, 2001; Elenkov and Manev, 2005; Koh, Joseph, and Ang, 2009; Mtolo, 2017; Rockstuhl et al., 2012). The majority of work remains in the theory and research space, which presents changes for managers seeking practical solutions. The authors offer step by step methods and "thinking processes" we hope will help you to leverage and adapt what you find in the published literature to meet your business needs.

These tools will give you a good and reliable sense of what your organization's culture looks like. This information can be beneficial, but it will not answer the questions we are posing about the influence of that culture on how we do business or on how culture affects how we leverage or manage information.

This level of interpretation is left to the organization. The authors recommend that you engage with a cultural expert or analyst to help you administer the cultural assessments, and to interpret the results in terms of their implications for business and information strategies. For example, once you have the results of a cultural analysis of the strategic functions of the organization, you should be able to leverage them to answer the questions in the national culture framework (Figure 6) and the organizational culture framework (Figure 7).

Table 6. National culture factors of interest

• Does our organization have a predominant national culture?
• How does national culture affect the way we do business?
• What influence does our geographic location have on the way we do business?
• How does our national culture influence our approach to work?
• Are we People or Process Oriented?
• Are we Competition or Collaboration Oriented?
• Are we Risk Takers or Risk Avoiders?
• Do we prefer Financial or Social Rewards?
• How do we design our meetings and events?
• What Leadership Characteristics do we value?
• How do we view the role of Managers and Workers?
• What is our attitude toward Engagement and Social Behavior?
• What is our Attitude toward Discussions and Debates?
• What is our Attitude toward learning?

Table 7. Organization culture factors of interest

• What is the Leadership style of the organization, and how does it affect the business strategy?
• What is the Life cycle stage of the organization, and how does it affect the business strategy?
• How does the Geographic location of the organization affect the business strategy?
• How do our Ethics and standards affect our business strategies?
• How does the Business sector focus of the organization affect our business strategy?
• How do the organization's Business goals affect the business strategy?
• How does the Position of the organization in the market affect our strategy?
• How does the internal structure of the organization affect the strategy?
• How does the Management control and philosophy of the organization affect the strategy?

STEP 5. ASSESS THE CURRENT STATE OF INFORMATION CULTURES

With this step, we are attempting to understand how the information culture aligns with or differs from the information culture. We are looking for synergies or areas of tension with the intent of reconciling these. The goal of this step is to create a picture of the organization's business and information cultures at the organization level. After we have that picture, then we can compare culture and strategy. For each leadership or strategic role, we would assess the impacts of these different factors on the essential elements of an information culture.

Table 8. Factors affecting assumptions and beliefs about information

• Attitudes toward Information as an asset
• Attitudes toward the value of Information
• Information use and transformation practices
• Support for Information access, availability and use
• Support for Information sharing and exchange
• Attitude toward Information integrity
• Use of Information in decision making
• Use of Information in business processes
• Use of Information in forecasting and planning
• General Leadership attitudes toward information
• Leaders communication about information
• Leaders rewards and recognition of information
• Leaders hiring of individuals who respect information
• Leaders resource allocation for information management

STEP 6. IDENTIFY COMMON CULTURAL LEVERAGE POINTS FOR STRATEGIES AT RISK

This step produces an integrated and harmonized set of cultural attributes at the strategy level. This is a joint effort – one that is negotiated between business and information managers. The business team brings an understanding of the business culture to the discussion, and the information professionals bring an interpretation of information management values and behaviors. The harmonized result is a powerful management tool for the organization. It leverages information behaviors to bolster the business culture, and it translates information management values to practical business behaviors.

STEP 7. ALIGN THE CULTURAL POINTS OF LEVERAGE WITH STRATEGIC RISKS AND PAIN POINTS

At this point, you should have in hand (1) a target list of organization-level business strategies whose health is at risk; and (2) a sense of the business and information cultures of the units responsible for and likely to implement these strategies. Your task is now to determine how to leverage the cultural attributes available to you in order to bolster the strategy when it is being developed. These cultural attributes are also essential management factors that can be called upon to ensure the success of a strategy as it plays out.

The challenge for the owners of the strategies is to determine what those factors are – which are the most important in their situation – and how best to design them into the strategy development and planning process. What changes should managers make to the strategy development and management process in order to reduce the risk of strategic failure? What kind of business risk does the strategy present? What is the business value of that risk? How much of that risk is the organization willing to accept? What is the direct cost of building cultural analysis into the early stages of strategy development? What are the indirect costs? Is the function or unit leader capable of taking on this new task? Do you need to build institutional capacity to support the organization? What level of cost are you willing to pay to lower the cultural risk? What will it take actually to make the cultural adjustments? Will the risk remain constant or increase if you do nothing?

INTEGRATING AND DOCUMENTING STRATEGIES AND CULTURES ACROSS THE ORGANIZATION

At every level of the organization, the task must be taken up by the owner of the strategies. There is, though, a need to bring all of these efforts back into an organization level methodology and an integrated organizational picture of business and information strategies. What is a practical approach to achieve this result? The most effective approach may be to select a few high profiles 'at risk' strategies, adapt the process to include cultural shaping, and use these examples to both demonstrate the value and to develop a repeatable methodology. Remember that the goal is not to change the organization's culture for the sake of change or to achieve some ideal organizational profile. The goal is to improve and shape culture at the level of strategy to ensure our strategies succeed.

SCENARIOS DRAWN FROM REAL WORLD EXPERIENCES

While there is much in the text to which a reader might relate, the authors thought it might be useful to provide some scenarios drawn from their real-world experiences. The intent is to illustrate the challenges we have faced when strategies and cultures have different strengths. Each experience is represented as a scenario. Each scenario represents a different level of strength or weakness of the culture or the strategy. In a concise narrative, we consider the effect on the business environment of a realignment and balancing of culture and strategy. While the scenarios are grounded in the authors' real experiences, no single scenario is an accurate representation of any event, any organization, unit, or individual. Each scenario has been edited and changed to illustrate the point. We present nine scenarios – ranging from scenarios with well-aligned and balanced cultures and strategies to scenarios with disconnected cultures and strategies. These scenarios are all focused on the organization level.

Figure 2. Matrix of scenarios at the organization level

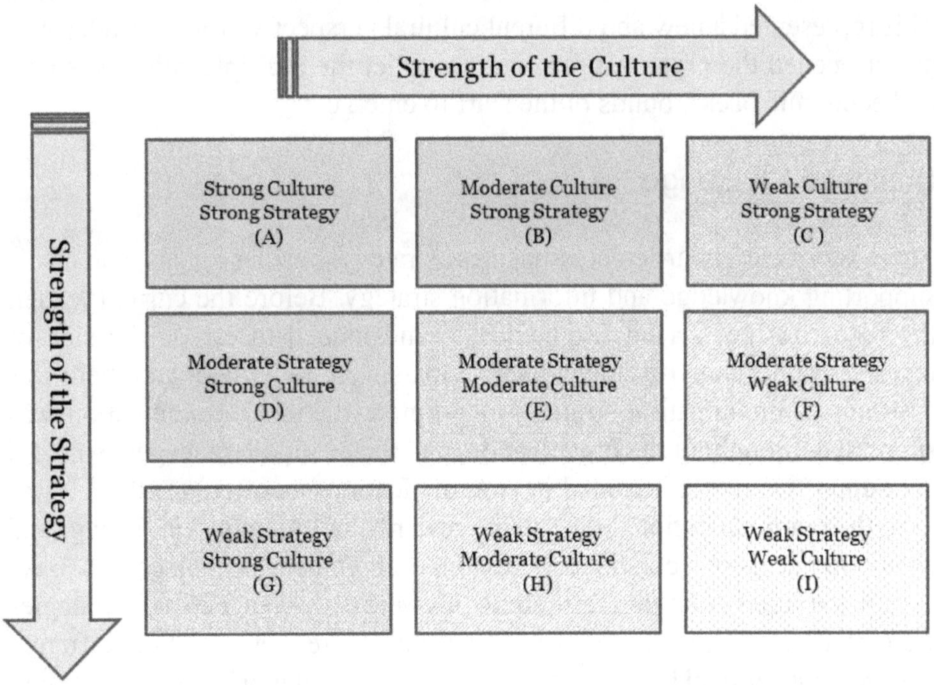

Scenario A. Strong Strategy Strong Culture

Organizational Context

International organization, multicultural, representing many different business sectors, multiple languages, many different economic and social class backgrounds, every generation from WWII to the youngest generation, and a highly mixed gender composition of staff. In a mature stage of its life cycle – with concerns emerging around the future of the organization in a changing economic and business environment. The organization has had a split culture over the years – representing the culture of banking, the culture of policy development, and a culture of service to and support for under-resourced communities. In the past, most presidents had been drawn from the banking culture and one national culture – American culture. The newly appointed President represented both the banking culture and also the economic development cultures. Additionally, the new president had grown up in a very diverse national culture – one with roots in Europe and Asia. This represented a new and different cultural perspective for the leadership, and it opened the organizational culture to let the multiple cultures, social and economic backgrounds of the staff to emerge.

Business Challenge

There was a clearly articulated business strategy, business goals, and also a supporting knowledge and information strategy. Before the current leader, the focus has been a bit fragmented – and tended to err on the side of investors rather than on stakeholders. Goals were redefined, and there was a strong communication strategy to promote them. Communication was supported throughout the organization, and those middle managers who did not support were not included in communications as often as others. Over time the communication strategy, the rewards and recognition, hiring, and promotion decisions convinced individuals and business managers to make the shift. Hidden strategies, false strategies were called out. Learned strategies were realigned. This was significant because there were so many different cultures, educational backgrounds, and views on collaboration, competition, engagement – the dominant new culture of the organization seemed to go to the core assumptions of each individual – why are you here? Why do you want to be here? Some variant cultures reflected the economic sector of focus – for example, transportation, private sector business, industry, and agriculture tended to retain their traditional cultures.

In contrast, gender, health, education, and civil society tended to adapt to new cultures more readily. The leadership leveraged these early adopters of the new goals and culture and promoted them with budgets. For those groups that would not adapt or whose "learned cultures" were dominant – leadership used disruptive methods – such as creating parallel organization units that created competition. An internal competition was apparent, and who was being rewarded was clear. Eventually, most staff in the "old units" adopted new goals and strategies. Those business managers who did not adapt were often moved into other positions or offered exit or retirement packages.

The Result

As a result of these efforts, the fundamental culture of the organization shifted dramatically. The fundamental change lasted ten years after the departure of the organization's president. Moreover, it protected the organization through two subsequent leadership teams.

Scenario B. Strong Strategy Moderate Culture

Organizational Context

Religious institutions dedicated to education and representing a particular community within the religion. The organization is over 200 years old with solid traditions in teaching, research, ethics, and community engagement. Recently, the average faculty age has been trending downward to ensure that there is a reliable and vibrant new research base. Education and teaching, though, are the core capabilities of the university. As a result, it is one of the top undergraduate universities in the nation. University has an international student body and faculty – while multiple faiths are represented the dominant faith of students and faculty is aligned with the organization's religious affiliation.

The Business Challenge

President has adopted an active and open communication strategy with all faculty and students. All communications are positive, even when addressing a concern or danger. They are reassuring and calming, designed to build confidence and strengthen the community. Recently, an issue arose which challenged some of the fundamental beliefs of the organization – related to the institution's early history. The organization could have ignored the issues and simply stated that "that was then, and we are different now." While this would have been an easier and more comfortable strategy, the leadership chose to tackle the issue head-on and create opportunities for students and faculty to engage in deciding how they wanted to handle the issue. Community engagement focused on the culture at the business unit and individual levels – and tested the culture to determine how it would withstand this shock. By leveraging the existing culture – and testing it – a strategy that was acceptable and effective emerged. The university supported the "middle-level strategy" that emerged and let it grow over several years. Ultimately, the university adopted the strategy – and made it an integral part of the university's policies and action plans.

The Result

It was a brilliant approach to leveraging culture to design a strategy. This organization is unusual in terms of organizations of this age. What allowed it to succeed with this approach was the fundamental and shared culture – assumptions and beliefs – that was at the heart of the moral crisis that arose.

Scenario C. Strong Strategy Weak Culture

The Organizational Context

This scenario describes a young organization, focused on a single industry, early business goals but heavily tied to the philosophy of the founders and not necessarily adhered to by investors and stakeholders, gender-focused and concentrated – male engineers, represents primarily wealthier and more highly educated staff, concentrated in a unique part of the country where that industry is concentrated. Early on, there were a lot of shared strategies and a few hidden strategies – over time, the hidden strategies tended to build coalitions and strengthen. The organization's culture was intentionally developed and communicated – but as the founders retired or their presence in the work environment declined – the hidden strategies and financial goals of the staff tended to strengthen. There were robust business strategies in place – and given the "flatness" and openness of the environment – these strategies were well aligned across all levels. There were simply no "pockets" where other strategies could develop.

The Business Challenge

The business challenge that shifted the strategy was increased competition from other organizations – particularly those in Asia which offered lower-cost labor to produce. The primary revenue that came from production began to decline, which put the innovation strategies at risk. There was a need to refocus the manufacturing and production part of the business in order to maintain market share. At this point, the "hidden strategies" and other cultures that had been growing in the financial and accounting offices gained ground. When investors recruited for a new CEO, they recruited a high-profile woman with a financial and marketing background. This was an unfortunate choice because her essential strategies, and her fundamental culture was at odds with the organization. There were clashes – and some famous ones – with the Board, with the manager, and with investors.

The Result

As a result of her radical and dramatic attempts to change strategy from the top, the engineering and innovation culture pushed back. Many of the critical innovators left and went to competitors. The internal disruption had severe financial impacts – which caused the board to terminate the CEO – in a very public way. The public airing of challenges damaged not only the organization's strategy and culture but its reputation.

Scenario D. Moderate Strategy Strong Culture

The Organizational Context

This is a mid-life organization whose leadership has changed significantly over its life. The business strategy has remained consistent – to sell healthy and sustainable food to a select market of consumers. The strategy has been to keep the scale of the operation small and to develop a loyal customer base. The company makes its money, not through the volume but the quality of products and quality of service. The company has developed a customer base whose loyalty rivals that of Apple. There are direct personal contacts between staff and customers, and the environment is dense on social interactions and individualized service. The company attracts a particular type of individual – with a social attitude and a robust belief system in the products. The company offers career paths for some employees, but it is expected that many staff will be hired for shorter periods. This means the culture needs to be cohesive and integrating – given the direct connections with customers, and new workers must adapt to the culture on their first day. The nature of the close team and cross-communication flows – it means that new workers will succeed or fail based on how well they can work with others. Culture builds from the bottom up. There are only two levels of staff at each store – managers and team workers. Corporate leadership is off-site and, in some cases, on another continent. There is routine communication with corporate and semi-annual site visits – listening visits – but in general, stores are left to connect to the local community. There is a moderate strategy in place – but each location has the flexibility to determine how to achieve that strategy for the local community. Because stores are located all over the country, there are several regional cultures represented. This flexibility is critical to ensure that local community requirements and cultures are supported.

The Business Challenge

Local manager out of synch with culture – disruptive and insensitive. The new manager came into a new store in a prime location, and the business of the location increased dramatically. As a result, the store became one of the top producing locations across the country. Rather than continue to support a balanced strategy/culture, the new manager focused on increasing business strategy – to grow profits – at the expense of the culture. He began hiring staff who were less interested in a team environment and customer interaction and more interested in shorter hours. He reduced pay and hours, increased profits, but also increased tensions. Additionally, because of the financial focus, the manager let some of his core assumptions and prejudices show through to offend the teams.

The Result

The teams complained to corporate, and after a series of consultations, the manager was removed. New management was brought in, but not before key staff left and relocated to other stores across the country. The staffing situation has not yet stabilized five years later because of the reputation the store gained across the internal network. The reputation is slowly being rebuilt, due to the actions of new managers and support from corporate leadership.

Scenario E. Moderate Strategy Moderate Culture

The Organizational Context

Young organization in the early stages of development. We might say it is just defining itself, its business goals, and strategies. The early years of the organization were defined by a small number of individuals who had an idea but no real business strategy. The strength of the business concept, though, encouraged a leader with business and personal skills to step in and define a strategy that moved the organization through an initial development phase. The strategy was built around the initial idea, so retained the original commitment of those supporting the organization and the customers and community it served. While there was a high-level business strategy, it had not yet been translated to the everyday work environment, nor had it been translated to strategies that the community or partners could buy into. The new CEO brought in individuals with expertise in different areas of the work and empowered them to develop strategies. As these individual strategies developed, the leader began to build a strategy that would support individuals – at the employee level. Having this structure in place – and allowing it to grow – has allowed a business strategy to emerging. It is still growing and will continue to evolve as the organization continues to grow. The culture has been built from the bottom up – with oversight but not pressure from leadership. In this case, the culture is focused on individuals and their capacity to learn and grow with the business. Most of the staff have not had successful experiences in other organizations and are learning both social and business skills while working at the organization. Culture is evolving that supports individuals and the connections between these individuals and the local community. All managers and individuals work in one facility, though there is growing outreach to other business sectors and communities beyond the immediate neighborhood.

The Business Challenge

The organization experiences a growth spurt that challenges both the strategy and the culture by bringing new exposure to individuals and the business.

The Result

This scenario is likely to have a good result because there is awareness of the importance of culture and the expectation that the expanded business strategy will not change the organization's core business goals. The culture will have to be managed carefully, though, to ensure that increased notoriety and publicity do not threaten the reflective and learning culture of individuals.

Scenario F. Moderate strategy weak culture

The Organizational Context

This organization represents a policy level governance organization. The policy is focused on and draws from a historical and critical profession – education. Because it is in a mature phase of its life cycle, there are many strong traditions and practices which are firmly entrenched. Because the organization is tied to a profession, this means many stakeholders in other organizations will have an influence over policy – specifically colleges and universities. The strategy is characterized as moderate here because there are multiple levels and facets. Mostly, the strategy aligns with a profession – teaching in primary and secondary schools. However, these schools represent different business goals and different business environments. For example, the profession represents teachers in religious schools, in public sector schools, in military schools, in prison environments. The profession includes teachers with different specializations, different roles – administrators and counselors, and curriculum developers. While each school may have a common strategy, when you look at strategy at the state or national level – the common elements of the strategy are fewer in comparison to the variant elements. The real impact to strategy, though, comes from a weak cross-profession culture. In the aggregate, the culture is seen as weak, though the cultures within each of these different areas of practice, levels, environments, and regions are firm.

The Business Challenge

There is significant disruption in the educational environment due to new technologies, new business models, and the need for a new vision for education. Additionally, the efforts of particular subcultures to establish standards for others to abide by are further weakening the culture and bringing the fundamental strategy into question. As a result, the national strategy, which was once strong, is weakens. There are attempts to work through professional associations to develop new visions, policies, and strategies, but there is little consensus across cultures. Ultimately, the culture appeared to hit a low point and resulted in disruptive actions across principal subcultures. These subcultures have begun to coalesce through networks, and are developing new strategies and activities to move towards a new vision.

The Result

The bottom-up movement, while gaining ground, is not yet sure of success. This is a case where a stronger strategy and culture would help to advance the new movement. However, no leader has yet stepped in to create that new and revitalized culture. In this case, a strong leader is needed. The outcome is uncertain. In the meantime, individual communities will attempt to move their strategies forward. The active community or sector culture will dominate until a strong professional leadership emerges.

Scenario G. Weak Strategy Strong Culture

The Organizational Context

In this scenario, the organization is a sizeable national-level structure that has been in place for 275 years. There is a core strategy of service to the public, research and development, education, and financial support. The organization has many distinct components, each focused on and reflecting on a different economic sector. Strategies often take the form of policies and procedures rather than well-formed strategies – simply because the strategy is expected to change every few years. Moreover, the changing strategy reflects the interest of the new administration. Depending on the duration of the new leadership, the strategy may or may not have enough time to percolate down through the organization. It is likely it impacts only the top leadership and has little or no buy-in from or impact to individuals, business units, or teams. As a result, the environment has a fragmented strategy from top to bottom, as well as across different organizational units. The heritage of the organization and the core assumptions and beliefs of service create an influential culture. In particular, there is a strong sense of purpose, commitment, and ethics among the staff. Furthermore, this culture is developed and lived throughout a full career life. The culture is not one of financial rewards and recognition, but dedication to service and the organization.

The Business Challenge

Top leadership has always respected the core purpose of the organization. Regardless of the variations in strategy, the culture has consistently supported the current strategy. It has never been the case that the core culture of the organization has been challenged, so we have never had a rigorous test of what happens to strategy when the culture is not aligned. In its most recent change in top leadership, though, the new administration has brought it a new culture – which is focused on total loyalty and support for the leader. New leaders have been brought in mainly from the private sector – and shifted the culture from one of service and financial responsibility to personal profit and benefit. The new leadership has articulated no clear strategy beyond personal profit and benefit, so the connections across levels of the organization have broken. This means that individual and business unit strategies are still in place, supported by traditional cultures, but top-level managers and their strategies have been brought into question. This would be manageable if new strategies were promoted, but there are no new strategies to follow or enact. The top-level managers find the new leadership strategies of personal profit and benefit in sharp contrast with their cultures – precisely values, ethics, and behaviors. The result is that this level of the organization is rapidly disintegrating.

The Result

The shift of strategy is beyond the control of career professionals. All of the support functions and institutions are being systematically attacked. There are signs that the fundamental culture is strong enough to withstand this new variant. However, if the variation in culture and strategy continues, the outcome is uncertain. The culture may be strong enough to reassert itself, or it may breakdown and result in the fragmentation of lower levels of the organization. If the variant is short term, it will be possible to rebuild the strategy and to reinforce strategy, and to continue to evolve the culture.

Scenario H. Weak Strategy Moderate Culture

The Organizational Context

The organization is a non-profit associated with an academic institution, specifically a medical school and teaching hospital. The business goal of the non-profit is to translate the research results of the medical school and to teach hospital to practical guidance for practitioners in low-resource communities around the world. The organization is focused on women's and infant health in particular. The staff at the headquarters location reflects the national culture of its location primarily, but the widely distributed network represents many different cultures. Additionally, the staff and clients of the distributed network represent many different levels of social, economic, and educational status. While the primary business goal is to improve the lives of women and children in these communities, a critical internal business strategy focuses on communication. They are learning how to translate and communicate research results and lessons learned to local environments and learning how to listen to the staff across the network. To achieve the core business strategy, the headquarters strategy must be sufficiently adaptable and flexible to support the local strategies. What is an effective strategy in Kenya may not be an effective strategy in the mountains of Chile or a large urban area of South Asia. The organization's culture must be flexible, supportive, adaptable, and tolerant of many views and perspectives. For the past ten years, the administration of the parent organization – the university – was highly conservative and supportive of a particular religious viewpoint regarding women's health. This constrained the staff at headquarters from listening, and focused most of the communication on broadcasting and "talking to" practitioners. Additionally, the political climate gave rise to the hiring of a CEO who reflected these views. The culture shifted to one of inclusivity, internal competition, and away from collaboration. As a result, many subcultures have formed within a relatively small organization.

The Business Challenge

The restricted strategy has resulted in lowered performance and lower impacts on the community of women and infants served by the organization. These impacts stand in stark contrast to the advances of the medical school and teaching hospital. The non-profit decides that the problem is that the information is simply not easily accessible to practitioners and decides that a new technology platform and new information architecture is needed to remedy the problem. Practitioners in the network are not consulted for input. Selected individuals within the organization with technical expertise are given prominent roles in the project. A significant amount of financial resources are expended to implement the new solution. In the end, though, the new solution is not adopted by the network, and local strategies continue to dominate. Communication does not improve. The translation of research results does not improve, and impacts on women's and infant's health improve only where local practitioners and strategies are found to be effective.

The Result

The parent organization determines that the problem is the CEO they put in place and encourages that individual to take early retirement. A new CEO is brought in, one who understands the need to rebuild the culture and to refocus the culture on the practitioner network. This is an effective business strategy, but the challenge for the new CEO is the amount of time and resources she must now devote to rebuilding the culture. Her overall resources have not increased. She has a system that is designed to "talk to" rather than "listen to" practitioners. She will need to redefine the business strategy while she is rebuilding the business culture. This is a tall order.

Scenario I. Weak Strategy Weak Culture

The Organizational Context

The scenario is a sequel to Scenario A. The organization is as it was described in Scenario A with one notable exception. The previous President retired and took a position with an investment bank outside of the development world. The new President was appointed to carry out a business strategy and new business goals that were in substantial alignment with the national culture from which he came. Whereas the previous president had brought in an international and multicultural perspective and opened the culture, the new president strongly represented one national culture – and a small portion of that culture. The business strategy that the new president was charged to implement was one of developing economic markets for the benefit of the country he represented. The core business goal of improving the lives of the world's poor was put aside in favor of the development of resources in those developing countries. The focus shifted from the welfare of individuals to the identification and development for the export of natural resources in the organization's client countries. Of notable interest for those investments were countries that had energy and mining-related resources.

The Business Challenge

The new president brought in an entirely new management team to implement his new business strategy. He also brought the communication strategy and hiring practices that were common in his previous organization. The initial error was in isolating himself and his team from the business strategies of the individual divisions. His attempt to radically change the culture by changing the communication strategy brought significant results. The shift from open communications and speaking one's mind, to closed and cautious communications, began to raise the level of distrust between senior leadership and business units. Because the culture of business units was influential, the staff were shielded from the impacts of management decisions. However, hiring and dismissal decisions soon made it clear that the way to advance one's strategy was to become a member of the President's trusted network. Staff in one division, in particular, noticed the new behavior of their top management, and noted the traditional protective behaviors of documenting, avoiding contacts, and merely following the new President's directives. When these directives began to violate the organization's ethics and legal codes of behavior and governance, managers had to find new ways to publicize what was occurring inside the organization. Whereas the previous administration had openly communicated with stakeholders and the media, there was little or no communication coming from the new administration. Instead, communications went to and from the national government almost exclusively. In the end, the culture of the organization pushed back to support the organization's business strategy, specifically its hiring and promotion policies. It could only accomplish this, though, by going outside the organization to lodge complaints with those other national agencies that were complicit in the activities. Additionally, low-level staff broke ethical codes by releasing internal strategy documents to demonstrate the shift in strategy and the unethical behavior of top-level management.

The Result

While the short-term impact was to remove the new President and the team he brought into the organization, the long-term impact was more significant. The organization's strong culture was sufficient to ensure its strategy would prevail. Moreover, those managers who had led through behavior and by demonstrating their values were recognized as internal heroes. However, the organization's strategy was in disarray – the top-level strategy needed to be reformulated and re-annunciated. Business unit level strategies and individual strategies remained strong, where original managers remained in place. Where they were removed or replaced by the new President, though, those strategies also began to fail. The organization's attempts to bring in new leadership and reinforce the strategy were mostly unsuccessful and lead to the beginning of a decline for the organization. The new President had an economic policy background and private sector connections. He was not respected by the banking elements of the organization, nor by the economic development elements. He continued to try to promote the resource-focused development strategy. Unfortunately, his background represented a single national view of that strategy, and rather than positioning the organization to take a new role in economic development; he placed the organization in direct competition with other consulting and private investment groups. Ultimately, this was not an environment in which the organization could compete. The strategy failed and created disastrous consequences for several emerging economies. The organization has continued to struggle with the balancing of culture and strategy and has continued to decline in its sector. Additionally, the expertise, which was the competitive advantage of the organization, has largely abandoned the organization and moved to national governance roles or development consulting firms. In this case, the drastic shift in both culture and strategy significantly unbalanced the organization and made a recovery difficult.

BALANCING AND ALIGNING STRATEGY AND CULTURE

What can we learn from these scenarios? In each scenario, we can see the interplay of culture and strategy. We learn that understanding the factors that shape each organization's culture is essential to understanding what you have to work with and how we can leverage critical factors to achieve a positive outcome. What is also clear is how dependent both strategy and culture are on the fortunes of any organization. What is clear is how much influence the factors we outlined have on that interplay. Perhaps the most apparent conclusion though – whether reading a scenario or being a player in any of these scenarios – is how transitory these outcomes are – because both strategy and culture are heavily dependent on individuals and groups of individuals – whenever the cast of players change – both the strategy and the culture will change. This is perhaps most clear when we look at strategy and culture from the perspective of leaders. What we are beginning to learn and to study is the long-term effect those leaders have on the organization as a whole – and how long it takes for change to take hold at lower levels. What happens once the change at lower levels occurs? Does this stabilize strategy and culture? Does it strengthen the organization? Does it make it more resilient? What can we teach leaders about balancing culture and strategy? What can leaders learn from these scenarios? These are answers we do not yet have.

CONCLUSION

After reading this chapter, you should be able to:

- Explain why we need to align our organization strategies and cultures
- Describe the seven-step methodology for aligning strategies and cultures
- Applying the seven-step methodology for aligning strategies and cultures in your organization
- Explain how to document the status of your strategies and cultures
- Explain how to identify the gaps and pain points across the organization
- What does this mean for organizational leaders?

REFERENCES

Ang, S., & Inkpen, A. C. (2008). Cultural intelligence and offshore outsourcing success: A framework of firm-level intercultural capability. *Decision Sciences, 39*(3), 337–358. doi:10.1111/j.1540-5915.2008.00195.x

Ang, S., & Van Dyne, L. (2015). *Handbook of cultural intelligence: Theory, measurement, and applications*. Routledge. doi:10.4324/9781315703855

Ang, S., Van Dyne, L., & Koh, C. (2006). Personality correlates of the four-factor model of cultural intelligence. *Group & Organization Management, 31*(1), 100–123. doi:10.1177/1059601105275267

Ang, S., Van Dyne, L., Koh, C., Ng, K. Y., Templer, K. J., Tay, C., & Chandrasekar, N. A. (2007). Cultural intelligence: Its measurement and effects on cultural judgment and decision making, cultural adaptation and task performance. *Management and Organization Review, 3*(3), 335–371. doi:10.1111/j.1740-8784.2007.00082.x

Apud, S., Lenartowicz, T., & Johnson, J. P. (2003). Intercultural competence: what do practitioners really know? *Proceedings, Academy of International Business South-East Region Conference.*

Betancourt, J. R., Green, A. R., Carrillo, J. E., & Owusu Ananeh-Firempong, I. I. (2016). Defining cultural competence: A practical framework for addressing racial/ethnic disparities in health and health care. *Public Health Reports.* PMID:12815076

Bhui, K., Warfa, N., Edonya, P., McKenzie, K., & Bhugra, D. (2007). Cultural competence in mental health care: A review of model evaluations. *BMC Health Services Research, 7*(1), 15. doi:10.1186/1472-6963-7-15 PMID:17266765

Brislin, R., Worthley, R., & Macnab, B. (2006). Cultural intelligence: Understanding behaviors that serve people's goals. *Group & Organization Management, 31*(1), 40–55. doi:10.1177/1059601105275262

Brouthers, K. D., & Brouthers, L. E. (2001). Explaining the national cultural distance paradox. *Journal of International Business Studies, 32*(1), 177–189. doi:10.1057/palgrave.jibs.8490944

Campinha-Bacote, J. (2002). The process of cultural competence in the delivery of healthcare services: A model of care. *Journal of Transcultural Nursing, 13*(3), 181–184. doi:10.1177/10459602013003003 PMID:12113146

Cooke, R. A., & Szumal, J. L. (2000). Using the Organizational Culture Inventory to understand the operating cultures of organizations. Handbook of Organizational Culture and Climate, 4, 1032-1045.

Crandall, S. J., George, G., Marion, G. S., & Davis, S. (2003). Applying theory to the design of cultural competency training for medical students: A case study. *Academic Medicine*, *78*(6), 588–594. doi:10.1097/00001888-200306000-00007 PMID:12805037

Cross, T. (1988). *Cultural competence continuum*. Academic Press.

de la Garza Carranza, M. T., & Egri, C. P. (2010). Managerial cultural intelligence and small business in Canada. *Management Revue*, 353-371.

Earley, P. C., & Mosakowski, E. (2002). Linking culture and behavior in organizations: Suggestions for theory development and research methodology. In *The many faces of multi-level issues* (pp. 297–319). Emerald Group Publishing Limited. doi:10.1016/S1475-9144(02)01038-X

Earley, P. C., Murnieks, C., & Mosakowski, E. (2007). Cultural intelligence and the global mindset. In *The global mindset* (pp. 75–103). Emerald Group Publishing Limited. doi:10.1016/S1571-5027(07)19004-5

Elenkov, D. S., & Manev, I. M. (2005). Social Culture Intelligence, Top-Level Leadership And Innovation Influence: An International Study. In Academy of Management Proceedings (Vol. 2005, No. 1, pp. F1-F6). Briarcliff Manor, NY: Academy of Management.

Elenkov, D. S., & Manev, I. M. (2009). Senior expatriate leadership's effects on innovation and the role of cultural intelligence. *Journal of World Business*, *44*(4), 357–369. doi:10.1016/j.jwb.2008.11.001

Emirbayer, M., & Goodwin, J. (1994). Network analysis, culture, and the problem of agency. *American Journal of Sociology*, *99*(6), 1411–1454. doi:10.1086/230450

Fowler, S. M., & Mumford, M. G. (1999). *Intercultural Sourcebook: Cross-Cultural Training Methods* (Vol. 2). Yarmouth, ME: Intercultural Press, Inc.

Gallego-Toledo, J. M. (2015). Cultural profiling and a Chinese experience. *Journal of Chinese Human Resource Management*, *6*(2), 120–132. doi:10.1108/JCHRM-09-2015-0014

Gelfand, M. J., Imai, L., & Fehr, R. (2008). Thinking intelligently about cultural intelligence. *Handbook on cultural intelligence: Theory, measurement and applications*, 375-388.

Glenn, S. S. (1988). Contingencies and metacontingencies: Toward a synthesis of behavior analysis and cultural materialism. *The Behavior Analyst, 11*(2), 161–179. doi:10.1007/BF03392470 PMID:22478011

Hofstede, G. (1980). Culture and organizations. *International Studies of Management & Organization, 10*(4), 15–41. doi:10.1080/00208825.1980.11656300

Hofstede, G. (1984). *Culture's consequences: International differences in work-related values.* Beverly Hills, CA: Sage.

Hofstede, G. (2001). *Culture's consequences: Comparing values, behaviors, institutions and organizations across nations.* Thousand Oaks, CA: Sage.

Hofstede, G., Hofstede, G. J., & Minkov, M. (2010). *Cultures and organizations: Software of the mind (revised and expanded).* New York, NY: McGraw-Hill.

Imai, L., & Gelfand, M. J. (2010). The culturally intelligent negotiator: The impact of cultural intelligence (CQ) on negotiation sequences and outcomes. *Organizational Behavior and Human Decision Processes, 112*(2), 83–98. doi:10.1016/j.obhdp.2010.02.001

Jang, H. Y., & Barnett, G. A. (1994). Cultural differences in organizational communication: A semantic network analysis 1. *Bulletin of Sociological Methodology. Bulletin de Methodologie Sociologique, 44*(1), 31–59. doi:10.1177/075910639404400104

Johnson, J. P., Lenartowicz, T., & Apud, S. (2006). Cross-cultural competence in international business: Toward a definition and a model. *Journal of International Business Studies, 37*(4), 525–543. doi:10.1057/palgrave.jibs.8400205

Kendra, K., & Taplin, L. J. (2004). Project success: A cultural framework. *Project Management Journal, 35*(1), 30–45. doi:10.1177/875697280403500104

King, T., & Byers, J. F. (2007). A review of organizational culture instruments for nurse executives. *JONA: The Journal of Nursing Administration, 37*(1), 21–31. doi:10.1097/00005110-200701000-00005 PMID:17172969

Koh, C., Joseph, D., & Ang, S. (2009, February). Cultural intelligence and collaborative work: intercultural competencies in global technology work teams. In *Proceedings of the 2009 international workshop on Intercultural collaboration* (pp. 261-264). ACM. 10.1145/1499224.1499271

Lamal, P. A. (Ed.). (1997). *Cultural contingencies: Behavior analytic perspectives on cultural practices*. Greenwood Publishing Group.

Lie, D. A., Lee-Rey, E., Gomez, A., Bereknyei, S., & Braddock, C. H. III. (2011). Does cultural competency training of health professionals improve patient outcomes? A systematic review and proposed algorithm for future research. *Journal of General Internal Medicine*, *26*(3), 317–325. doi:10.100711606-010-1529-0 PMID:20953728

Livermore, D., & Soon, A. N. G. (2015). *Leading with cultural intelligence: The real secret to success*. Amacom.

Livermore, D., Van Dyne, L., & Ang, S. (2012). Cultural intelligence: Why every leader needs it. *Intercultural Management Quarterly*, *13*(2), 18–21.

MacNab, B., Brislin, R., & Worthley, R. (2012). Experiential cultural intelligence development: Context and individual attributes. *International Journal of Human Resource Management*, *23*(7), 1320–1341. doi:10.1080/09585192.2011.581636

MacNab, B., Brislin, R., Worthley, R., Galperin, B. L., Jenner, S., Lituchy, T. R., ... Bess, D. (2007). Culture and ethics management: Whistle-blowing and internal reporting within a NAFTA country context. *International Journal of Cross Cultural Management*, *7*(1), 5–28. doi:10.1177/1470595807075167

Mannion, R., Konteh, F. H., & Davies, H. T. O. (2009). Assessing organisational culture for quality and safety improvement: A national survey of tools and tool use. *BMJ Quality & Safety*, *18*(2), 153–156. doi:10.1136/qshc.2007.024075 PMID:19342532

Maznevski, M. (2008). Cultural intelligence: Domain and assessment. *International Journal of Cross Cultural Management*, *8*(2), 123–143. doi:10.1177/1470595808091787

Morosini, P., Shane, S., & Singh, H. (1998). National cultural distance and cross-border acquisition performance. *Journal of International Business Studies*, *29*(1), 137–158. doi:10.1057/palgrave.jibs.8490029

Mosakowski, E., Calic, G., & Earley, P. C. (2013). Cultures as learning laboratories: What makes some more effective than others? *Academy of Management Learning & Education*, *12*(3), 512–526. doi:10.5465/amle.2013.0149

Mtolo, S. G. (2017). *The Influence of Cultural Intelligence on the relationship between Social Capital and Entrepreneurial Performance: A study of foreign traders in Johannesburg's informal economy* (Doctoral dissertation).

Mueller, S. T., Sieck, W. R., & Veinott, E. (2007). *Cultural metrics: A finite mixture models approach* (Technical Report DAAD19-01-2-0009). Fairborn, OH: Klein Associates Division of ARA.

Mueller, S. T., & Veinott, E. S. (2008). Cultural mixture modeling: Identifying cultural consensus (and disagreement) using finite mixture modeling. *Proceedings of the Cognitive Science Society*.

Ng, K. Y., Van Dyne, L., & Ang, S. (2009). From experience to experiential learning: Cultural intelligence as a learning capability for global leader development. *Academy of Management Learning & Education*, *8*(4), 511–526. doi:10.5465/amle.8.4.zqr511

Ng, R. (2013). Cultural intelligence. *The encyclopedia of cross-cultural psychology*, 310-313.

Norton, W. (1995). Behavior Analysis and the Cultural Geographic Study of Place. *Journal of Cultural Geography*, *15*(2), 1–15. doi:10.1080/08873639509478351

Peterson, B. (2011). *Cultural intelligence: A guide to working with people from other cultures*. Nicholas Brealey.

Purnell, L. (2002). The Purnell model for cultural competence. *Journal of Transcultural Nursing*, *13*(3), 193–196. doi:10.1177/10459602013003006 PMID:12113149

Rasmussen, L. J., Sieck, W. R., & Osland, J. (2010). *Using cultural models of decision making to develop and assess cultural sensemaking competence. In Advances in Cross-Cultural Decision Making*. Boca Raton, FL: CRC Press, Taylor and Francis Group.

Rockstuhl, T., Dulebohn, J. H., Ang, S., & Shore, L. M. (2012). Leader–member exchange (LMX) and culture: A meta-analysis of correlates of LMX across 23 countries. *The Journal of Applied Psychology*, *97*(6), 1097–1130. doi:10.1037/a0029978 PMID:22985117

Rockstuhl, T., Seiler, S., Ang, S., Van Dyne, L., & Annen, H. (2011). Beyond general intelligence (IQ) and emotional intelligence (EQ): The role of cultural intelligence (CQ) on cross-border leadership effectiveness in a globalized world. *The Journal of Social Issues*, *67*(4), 825–840. doi:10.1111/j.1540-4560.2011.01730.x

Rosinski, P. (2010). *Coaching Across Cultures: New Tools for Leveraging National*. Hachette UK.

Sashkin, M., & Rosenbach, W. E. (1990). *Organizational culture assessment questionnaire*. Academic Press.

Seufert, S. (2002). Cultural perspectives. In *Handbook on information technologies for education and training* (pp. 411–421). Berlin: Springer. doi:10.1007/978-3-662-07682-8_26

Sieck, W. R., Rasmussen, L. J., & Smart, P. (2010). Cultural network analysis: A cognitive approach to cultural modeling. In *Network science for military coalition operations: Information exchange and interaction* (pp. 237–255). IGI Global. doi:10.4018/978-1-61520-855-5.ch011

Sue, D. W. (2001). Multidimensional facets of cultural competence. *The Counseling Psychologist*, *29*(6), 790–821. doi:10.1177/0011000001296002

Sue, D. W., & Torino, G. C. (2005). Racial-cultural competence: Awareness, knowledge, and skills. Handbook of racial-cultural psychology and counseling: Training and practice, 2, 3-18.

Thom, D. H., Tirado, M. D., Woon, T. L., & McBride, M. R. (2006). Development and evaluation of a cultural competency training curriculum. *BMC Medical Education*, *6*(1), 38. doi:10.1186/1472-6920-6-38 PMID:16872504

Thomas, D. C. (2006). Domain and development of cultural intelligence: The importance of mindfulness. *Group & Organization Management*, *31*(1), 78–99. doi:10.1177/1059601105275266

Thomas, D. C. (2015). Cultural intelligence. Wiley Encyclopedia of Management, 1-3.

Thomas, D. C., Elron, E., Stahl, G., Ekelund, B. Z., Ravlin, E. C., Cerdin, J. L., ... Brislin, R. (2012). Development of the cultural intelligence assessment. In *Advances in global leadership* (pp. 155–178). Emerald Group Publishing Limited. doi:10.1108/S1535-1203(2012)0000007011

Van Dyne, L., Ang, S., & Koh, C. (2015). Development and validation of the CQS: The cultural intelligence scale. In *Handbook of cultural intelligence* (pp. 34–56). Routledge.

Van Dyne, L., Ang, S., Ng, K. Y., Rockstuhl, T., Tan, M. L., & Koh, C. (2012). Sub-dimensions of the four factor model of cultural intelligence: Expanding the conceptualization and measurement of cultural intelligence. *Social and Personality Psychology Compass*, *6*(4), 295–313. doi:10.1111/j.1751-9004.2012.00429.x

ADDITIONAL READING

Bellot, J. (2011). Defining and assessing organizational culture. *Nursing Forum*, *46*(1), 29–37. doi:10.1111/j.1744-6198.2010.00207.x PMID:21306393

Bu-Qammaz, A., Dikmen, I., and Birgonul, M. T. (2006). Cultural risk assessment in construction projects. *CCIM2006 Sustainable Development through Culture and Innovation.*

Glisson, C. (2007). Assessing and changing organizational culture and climate for effective services. *Research on Social Work Practice*, *17*(6), 736–747. doi:10.1177/1049731507301659

Groves, K. S., & Feyerherm, A. E. (2011). Leader cultural intelligence in context: Testing the moderating effects of team cultural diversity on leader and team performance. *Group & Organization Management*, *36*(5), 535–566. doi:10.1177/1059601111415664

Janssens, M., & Brett, J. M. (2006). Cultural intelligence in global teams: A fusion model of collaboration. *Group & Organization Management*, *31*(1), 124–153. doi:10.1177/1059601105275268

Kirmayer, L. J. (2012). Rethinking cultural competence. *Transcultural Psychiatry*, *49*(2), 149–164. doi:10.1177/1363461512444673 PMID:22508634

Koutroumanis, D. A., and Alexakis, G. (2009). Organizational Culture In The Restaurant Industry: Implications For Change. *Journal of Organizational Culture, Communications and Conflict, 13*(2).

Kumas-Tan, Z., Beagan, B., Loppie, C., MacLeod, A., & Frank, B. (2007). Measures of cultural competence: Examining hidden assumptions. *Academic Medicine*, *82*(6), 548–557. doi:10.1097/ACM.0b013e3180555a2d PMID:17525538

O'Reilly, C. A. III, Caldwell, D. F., Chatman, J. A., & Doerr, B. (2014). The promise and problems of organizational culture: CEO personality, culture, and firm performance. *Group & Organization Management*, *39*(6), 595–625. doi:10.1177/1059601114550713

Oolders, T., Chernyshenko, O. S., & Stark, S. (2008). Cultural intelligence as a mediator of relationships between openness to experience and adaptive performance. Handbook of cultural intelligence: Theory, measurement, and applications, 145-158

Pavlidis, G., Koutsoudis, A., Arnaoutoglou, F., Tsioukas, V., & Chamzas, C. (2007). Methods for 3D digitization of cultural heritage. *Journal of Cultural Heritage*, *8*(1), 93–98. doi:10.1016/j.culher.2006.10.007

Pieraccini, M., Guidi, G., & Atzeni, C. (2001). 3D digitizing of cultural heritage. *Journal of Cultural Heritage*, *2*(1), 63–70. doi:10.1016/S1296-2074(01)01108-6

Shenkar, O. (2001). Cultural distance revisited: Towards a more rigorous conceptualization and measurement of cultural differences. *Journal of International Business Studies*, *32*(3), 519–535. doi:10.1057/palgrave.jibs.8490982

Sousa, C. M., & Bradley, F. (2006). Cultural distance and psychic distance: Two peas in a pod? *Journal of International Marketing*, *14*(1), 49–70. doi:10.1509/jimk.14.1.49

Stanco, F., Battiato, S., & Gallo, G. (Eds.). (2011). *Digital imaging for cultural heritage preservation: Analysis, restoration, and reconstruction of ancient artworks*. CRC Press.

Tarique, I., & Takeuchi, R. (2008). Developing cultural intelligence: The roles of international nonwork experiences. Handbook of cultural intelligence: Theory, measurement, and applications, 56-70.

Triandis, H. C. (2006). Cultural intelligence in organizations. *Group & Organization Management*, *31*(1), 20–26. doi:10.1177/1059601105275253

Triandis, H. C. (2008). Cultural intelligence. Handbook of cultural intelligence.

Wagner, W., & Yamori, K. (1999). Can culture be a variable? Dispositional explanation and cultural metrics. *Progress in Asian social psychology, 2*.

Chapter 8
Balancing Unit and Team Level Strategies and Cultures

ABSTRACT

The goal of this chapter is to identify methods for reducing the risk of strategic failures at the division, the unit, the community, or the team level. In particular, the authors are interested in managing those risks that relate to information strategies and the businesses' use of information in the day-to-day work and operations of any organization. The framework and methodology they follow to identify misalignments, to develop target lists of strategies at risk are the same at these lower levels. What is different is the breadth and depth of business strategies they have to work with, the nature of the impact of lacking or sub-optimized information strategies at the operational level, and the cultural factors they need to see and shape. They establish a general methodology around the framework at the organization level and promote that methodology throughout the organization. The authors walk through the seven-step methodology, noting that line managers and team members must take ownership of and be engaged in the assessment process.

WHY DO WE CARE ABOUT ALIGNING UNIT AND TEAM LEVEL STRATEGIES AND CULTURES?

The goal of this chapter is to identify methods for reducing the risk of strategic failures at the division, the unit, the community, or the team level. In particular, we are interested in managing those risks that relate to information strategies

DOI: 10.4018/978-1-7998-4315-3.ch008

and the business' use of information in the day to day work and operations of any organization.

All of the arguments and justifications we laid out in Chapter 7 are valid at the operational levels. The risks we encounter at these levels when strategies and cultures are not aligned may have more significant business costs because they impact our products and services – what we do. We will not repeat those arguments and justifications in this chapter, but we do remind the reader that they apply to these levels as well.

The framework and methodology we follow to identify misalignments, to develop target lists of strategies at risk are the same at these lower levels. What is different is the breadth and depth of business strategies we have to work with, the nature of the impact of lacking or sub-optimized information strategies at the operational level, and the cultural factors we need to see and shape.

What is different is who is responsible and accountable for applying the framework, and for shaping culture to support strategy. Ideally, we establish a general methodology around the framework at the organization level and promote that methodology throughout the organization. We apply the framework and shape the culture only at strategic points in the organization. Moreover, we must put the process in the hands of those who are responsible for achieving the strategic goals and objectives. Managers who are responsible for developing strategies should now be responsible for integrating cultural analysis into the strategy development and management process. Then each leader, each division, each unit – designs a fit to support the current business need. Over time this approach gradually creates a new business methodology. It shifts the nature of strategic planning always to include culture shaping. Shaping our culture becomes part of the way we work.

ADAPTING THE FRAMEWORK TO UNIT AND TEAM LEVELS

How do we adapt to the framework? Of the seven steps, which steps change, and which remain the same? For those that change, what changes?

Table 1. Adapting the seven-step methodology

Step 1. Assess the Current Risks (Pain Points) in our Business Strategies
· *Managers of individual strategies will create their target lists of risks*
Step 2. Assess the Current Risks (Pain Points) in our Information Strategies
· *Managers will work with information professionals to understand risks and pain points*
Step 3. Identify Common Risks (Pain Points) in Business and Information Strategies
· *Business and information managers will negotiate and integrate risks and prioritize risks to identify the most significant threats*
Step 4. Assess the Current State of Business Cultures (Leverage Points)
· *Managers will work with cultural experts to define points of leverage and gain support from their support teams*
Step 5. Assess the Current State of Information Cultures (Leverage Points)
· *Managers and information professionals work with cultural experts to identify points of leverage between business and information cultures*
Step 6. Identify Common Cultural Leverage Points for Strategies at Risk
· *Managers work in consultation with units to define the most powerful points of leverage*
Step 7. Align The Cultural Points of Leverage With Strategic Risks and Pain Points
· *Managers and staff integrate cultural analysis into strategic planning processes and adopt it as a standard business process*

STEP 1. ASSESS THE CURRENT RISKS (PAIN POINTS) IN OUR BUSINESS STRATEGIES

The objective of this step is comparable to that at the organization level. An additional challenge is that we expect there will be more strategies at this level, and we will need to have a reliable and representative list of what exists. We look in all of the same places, but we must also extend where we look to include unit-level files, network drives, and personal collections.

How do we find current unit level strategies? The strategies we are looking for will pertain to the work of the unit or the team. Those who do the work of the unit or the team know what strategies to look for and where to look. We can describe these strategies by answering the same questions we asked at the organization level. We should, though, allow some flexibility for unit staff and managers to expand that list.

Similarly, we can assess the health of the strategy using the same questions we posed at the organization level. Determining the health of the strategy, though, means talking to or collecting information from the individuals who are responsible for implementing the strategy. These individuals are the best explanations for why the strategy did or did not succeed

This task should produce a list of the strategies we found that are at risk – perhaps organized by the administrative area that produced them. The list of strategies is prioritized in terms of the degree and nature of the risk.

STEP 2. ASSESS THE CURRENT RISKS (PAIN POINTS) IN OUR INFORMATION STRATEGIES

What is different at this level for this step is the need for unit and team managers to work closely with information professionals to identify information strategy gaps or sub-optimized information strategies. The challenge is that business managers and unit staff may not realize where there are gaps and how to fill them. This realization may only result from a cross business-information partnership and collaboration. There may be less effort devoted to the discovery of information strategies than to the formulation, drafting, or adaptation of information strategies that support the unit or the team.

STEP 3. IDENTIFY COMMON RISKS (PAIN POINTS) IN BUSINESS AND INFORMATION STRATEGIES

This step also follows the framework and methodology established at the organization level, but its success is entirely dependent on a close working relationship among unit-level business managers, staff, and information professionals.

STEP 4. ASSESS THE CURRENT STATE OF BUSINESS CULTURES (LEVERAGE POINTS)

This step is more challenging at this level than it is at the organization level. It is challenging for two reasons. The first reason is that we have a different set of cultural factors to consider (Table 2). The second reason is that there are fewer cultural analysis tools to apply to this level, and there is little reliable research upon which to build.

Table 2. Organization-inherited level culture factors of interest

· What is the Leadership style of the unit, and how does it affect the business strategy?
· What is the Life cycle stage of the unit, and how does it affect the business strategy?
· How does the geographic location of the unit affect the business strategy?
· How do our ethics and standards affect our unit business strategies?
· How does the business sector focus of the organization affect our business strategy?
· How do the organization's business goals affect the business strategy?
· How does the position of the unit in the organization affect our strategy?
· How does the internal structure of the unit affect the strategy?
· How does the management control of the unit affect the strategy?

Table 3. Unit compositional culture factors of interest

· What is the gender makeup of the unit?
· What is the national culture made up of the unit?
· What is the generational composition of the unit?
· What is the size of the group?
· What are the relationships within the group and with other units?
· What is the language composition of the unit?

STEP 5. ASSESSING IDENTIFY COMMON CULTURAL LEVERAGE POINTS FOR STRATEGIES AT RISK

The factors for assessing the information culture of the unit or team are consistent with those of the organization. The challenge is that we must have a broader team of business managers, staff, information professionals, and cultural analysis experts to conduct the assessment. We also have less cultural research to rely on to support this task.

STEP 6. IDENTIFY COMMON CULTURAL LEVERAGE POINTS FOR STRATEGIES AT RISK

Just as at the organization level, this is a joint effort at the unit level. This step is negotiated between business and information managers. The harmonized result leverages information behaviors to bolster the business culture, and it translates information management values to practical business behaviors.

STEP 7. ALIGN THE CULTURAL POINTS OF LEVERAGE WITH STRATEGIC RISKS AND PAIN POINTS

At this point, you should have in hand (1) a target list of unit-level business strategies whose health is at risk; and (2) a sense of the business and information cultures of the units responsible for and likely to implement these strategies. The unit's task is now to determine what changes to the strategy development and management process that might reduce the risk of strategic failure for each of these functions or units. What kind of business risk does the strategy present? What is the business value of that risk? How much of that risk is the organization willing to accept? What is the direct cost of building cultural analysis into the early stages of strategy development? What are the indirect costs? Is the function or unit leader capable of taking on this new task? Do you need to build institutional capacity to support the organization? What level of cost are you willing to pay to lower the cultural risk? What will it take to make the cultural adjustments? Will the risk remain constant or increase if you do nothing?

DOCUMENTING THE RESULTS OF THE ASSESSMENT

The challenge here is far greater than what we described at the organization level because of the sheer scale of this effort. Consider that this process will play out in every unit of the organization. At the organization level, there is an added challenge of ensuring that all of these new processes and 'fits' also connect to the organization level.

SCENARIOS DRAWN FROM REAL WORLD EXPERIENCES

While there is much in the text to which a reader might relate, the authors thought it might be useful to provide some scenarios drawn from their real-world experiences. The intent is to illustrate the challenges we have faced when strategies and cultures have different strengths. Each experience is represented as a scenario in which the strategy or the culture is at a different level of strength. In a concise narrative, we consider the effect on the business environment of a realignment and balancing of culture and strategy. While the scenarios are grounded in the authors' real experiences, no single scenario is an accurate representation of any event, any organization, unit, or individual. Each scenario has been edited and changed to illustrate the point. We present nine scenarios – ranging from scenarios with well-aligned and balanced active cultures and strong strategies to scenarios with disconnected weak cultures and weak strategies. These scenarios are all focused on the unit or team level.

Figure 1. Matrix of scenarios at the unit or team level

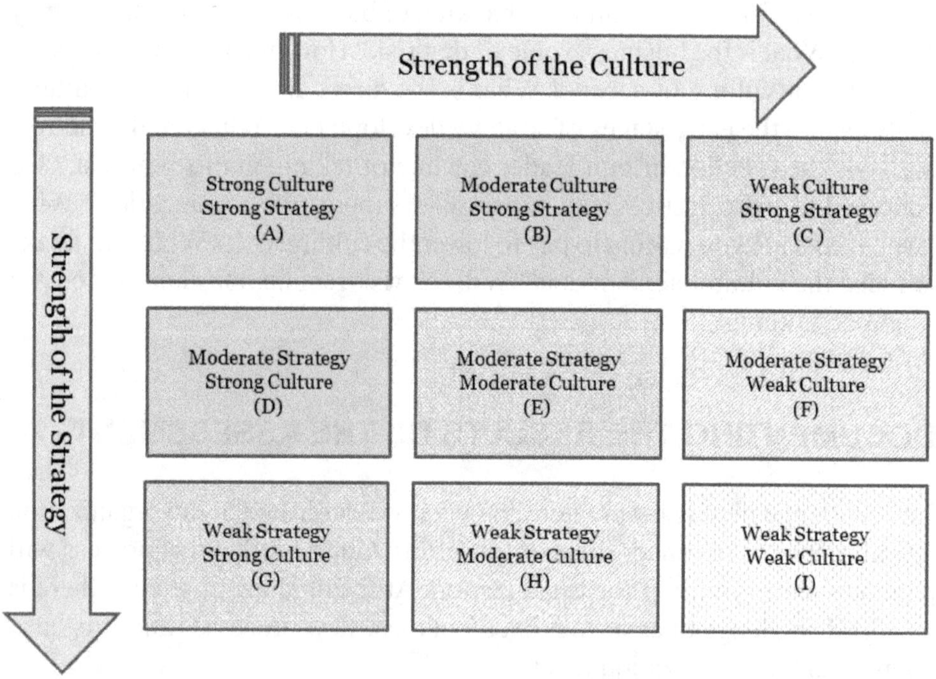

Scenario A. Strong Strategy Strong Culture

Organizational Context

This scenario represents a technology unit within a multicultural organization. The unit manager develops a strong business vision that had room to integrate existing strategies and also to advance each of those strategies. Because the manager is a visionary rather than a strategist, she brings in and empowers other individuals to build out strategies. Because of the inclusive culture she adopts, everyone in the division feels valued and welcome in the division. They can see that their work is supported and implemented. As a result, the manager can define a bottom consolidated strategy because the full staff supports that. By definition, the consolidated strategy often includes multiple approaches to the same problem – with the one that worked the best was the advanced one – but there was room for every strategy that worked. Additionally, everyone had an opportunity to grow and develop in the culture professionally. Additionally, the strategy was well aligned with and negotiated with top leadership. Individual strategies of the units were "managed" – every individual was rewarded in some way. The culture was one of consensus – convince, find the point of leverage, work it out before the formal meeting. In general, the unit culture was low key – at its core, respectful, and reflective. The individual national cultures were promoted and celebrated. The unit management philosophy heavily influenced by national culture, social culture, and gender – it erred on the side of listening, engagement, and empowerment. The Unit was at the early maturing stage of life – there were about 20 different practices around the organization that had to be consolidated and reformed into a new strategy – one that aligned with the cutting edge innovation of the external business market. The age composition was mature individuals drawn from information management and information technology – many experts. This expertise reflected practices in different countries – all had to be realigned to support the organization's new information strategy. The size of the group was large – but broken into different functional areas each could grow at its own pace – some were traditional, some were cutting edge. The language of the unit was also diver, with some subcultures and subgroups forming around traditional national practices. Different functional areas had different gender dominance. Some function groups had extremely strong networks that developed around national hiring practices and management control philosophies – at the group or subunit level, whereas others were more open and consultative. Every individual had their strategy and business goals based on their prior roles and responsibilities.

The Business Challenge

Strong new CIO with a dominant network and national culture but with little expertise in the area. This creates a new challenge to the internal culture and also to strategy because the top leadership is coming from a profession with a more traditional "no risk-taking" culture to guide the culture of "reasonable risk-takers" and "cutting edge technologies." The overall business goals for this unit were – invent new approaches to support the team's work in the field. This was a challenging field environment – where each distributed field office location had an entirely different work infrastructure. This variation creates tension among the top-level managers within the division. Fortunately, the culture within this particular business unit and the personal business strategy of this particular manager has a strong positive effect on the division leadership. Without being intrusive, the manager can help guide and support the division leader to his benefit and the benefit of her staff.

The Result

The result was a success for the business unit and, in general, for the division – due to the management culture of this dominant manager. However, the stress of managing multiple national cultures in a large division both "up" (e.g., in terms of the division leadership) and "down" was stressful for the manager. She retired for health reasons after a few years. In the end, the culture did not survive the departure of the unit manager and the division leadership. An additional factor was the age of the professional staff and experts within the unit – and waves of retirements after their departure. Changes in the top leadership of the organization further undermined the overall culture by reducing the stature and role of the division within the organization – from one of critical support and innovation to commercial solutions. The business strategy became dominant over culture, and a new imbalance was created that has not yet been corrected.

Scenario B. Strong Strategy Moderate Culture

The Organizational Context

In general, this scenario addresses how strategy and culture might play out in a rapid growth business environment whose culture is strongly influenced by the local business sector and community. The parent institution has existed for close to a century but has not been on the national radar as a top tier institution. The sudden growth of the local industry, and the strong connections between that industry and the institution, fuel new internal pressures for growth. The need for new business strategies touches every business unit of the organization. The leader of this particular unit has established a collegial but unobtrusive culture across the organization. Individuals with a long history at the organization continue to feel comfortable and to feel a part of the culture. Because of the changing external business environment – and the focus of the parent organization, which is cutting edge science and engineering education – there is a need to change the traditional strategy. The renewed strategy is fueled by an influx of new investment and resources. In order to handle the new internal business (e.g., research) demands of faculty and researchers – and the new affiliated institutions developed on the campus – this unit brings in new staff at senior and middle management levels. Each new manager is given the resources to hire in their immediate management teams. All new managers draw heavily from the local populations, but the managers coming in represent other regional cultures. They are all from the same national culture but represent very different cultural, social, and economic environments. They all represent the same professional focus – which is a small national community. Affiliation with the new organization elevates several the reputation and stature of several of the managers within the profession. The open, collaborative, and nourishing culture established by the Director enables each of these new managers the latitude they need to grow.

The Business Challenge

The heavy external business pressures coming from parts of the parent organization called for an expansion of the business strategy – both in terms of scale and scope. While there are some essential guidelines and policies formulated by leadership, each management area develops its business strategy. Each new manager builds its internal networks and focuses their strategies on the promotion of their professional areas of focus. While this elevates the stature of the organization, it creates internal tensions with the traditional networks – particularly those where the staff has long histories with the institution.

The Result

While the strategies of individual business areas were strong and gained national prominence for their managers and teams, the lack of a core culture allowed the personal strategies of individual managers to become dominant. As a result, the moderate culture resulted in ethical and social boundaries being tested and pushed in ways that strained the organization. Over a decade, each of the new managers was involved in an internal scandal. Each was "promoted out" of the organization to avoid negative publicity. In the end, the next level of managers was able to stabilize the culture and establish a more collaborative cross-organization network and culture that allowed the internal unit to survive management upheaval within the parent organization. It was sufficient to sustain the unit through these new challenges.

Scenario C. Strong Strategy Weak Culture

The Organizational Context

Very traditional manufacturing business whose strategy and culture have reflected not only a single national approach to business but also a strong regional culture within that country. The business area is one where there are a few top competitors, and reputation and safety, reliability and trust of the customer base is essential. This affects the internal culture of the organization. Because of increasing competition from lower labor costs in other production environments, the organization is incentivized to expand its locations to be closer to international markets. Additionally, the organization had acquired and absorbed several other national companies in Europe, South America, and Asia. The rapid expansion in location and management cultures has had an impact on both strategy and culture at headquarters. The approach to the integration of the new acquisitions has been one of absorption. However, it has also meant increased exposure of the traditional national cultures and business attitudes at headquarters to different approaches. Top leadership has been vital in success or failure over the past thirty years during this expansion. Strong leadership, which focuses on inclusion and adaptation of culture to support strategy, has been critical. The external pressures, though, from shareholders from product quality to business profits, has had a substantial impact on both strategy and culture. The strategy has been strengthened at the expense of culture. Whereas pockets of innovation continue to flourish, in general, the culture outside of headquarters has continued to fragment.

The Business Challenge

Headquarters staff and experts have been retiring at a high rate – reflecting the age composition of the organization. In contrast, the age concentration of new locations around the world is much younger. As headquarters location hires in new talent, they are increasingly from outside the national culture, and increasingly multi-disciplinary. This increases the need to support learning across the organization – to build a new knowledge base across the organization. These new needs – along with the social and management behaviors of younger generations – have shifted communication structures from the traditional top-down – to more horizontal. There is a new push to share information and knowledge across the organization to improve business products, to satisfy new learning and behavior expectations has had an impact on both strategy and culture. Unit level managers have been able to exert a significant amount of influence over the culture, though their impact on strategy has been weaker. There are pockets of new cultures emerging, though a consistent cross-organization culture is still lacking.

The Result

The organization will continue to be dominated by the local and international business market and by the strong internal engineering and financial business focus needed to survive in that market. Local cultures will continue to develop within business units, and the ultimate role of culture will depend on the fortunes of the new learning culture across the organization. At present, the learning culture is only touching the research and development areas of the organization. It has not yet had an impact on the manufacturing or production operations of the organization. Culture that only refects the elite or higher classified levels of the organization is unlikely to be effective in supporting strategy. A supportive culture must reflect all business areas of the organization.

Scenario D. Moderate Strategy Strong Culture

The Organizational Context

This scenario describes the situation in a struggling business unit within a larger thriving organization. The parent organization has a strong and dominant culture. The business unit was created 20 years ago with an innovative cross-disciplinary focus intended to serve as an incubator for new policy ideas and serious research. The initial business strategy was well formulated around a vision of the founding manager. The unit's focus on policy and research has been aligned with a particular national culture and national-focused business environment.

The Business Challenge

The founding manager had a strong vision but lacked the skills to turn the vision into a practical strategy. The unit was initially successful in establishing a community and network across the campus but neglected the core business strategy of the organization in setting its business goals. The management did not effectively support the strategies of new staff within the unit. As a result, many of those individuals failed to succeed within the larger organization. There were high levels of turnover, with temporary staff becoming the dominant influence in the network. Over time some less than effective hiring decisions were made, which further weakened the business goals of the unit and put the unit at risk of surviving within the larger organization. The parent organization valued the original business goals and could see how they aligned with changes to the external business environments. It was in the parent organization's interests to strengthen the unit and ensure its success. The parent organization introduced a new manager from within the organization's network – a manager with stature in both the profession and the local community. This new manager had the support of the parent institution and was knowledgeable in leveraging the culture and strategy to stabilize the unit. The unit culture was rebuilt around internal collaboration and cross-support, where it was clear to individuals what they needed to do to succeed. It was clear that the age composition of the unit needed to reflect the increasingly younger population of the parent organization – so crucial new staff were hired, mentored, and coached by the new manager. As each new staff succeeded, their success was promoted and celebrated. The traditional individual competition was not rewarded. Instead, culture became a tool that ensured success.

The Result

The culture is now strong, and the unit has stabilized. The journey has taken more than a decade, though, and now the lead manager is retiring back to his original department. While a new manager was hired from within the ranks of the current team, it is not yet clear whether this individual will have the reputation and individual management style to continue to expand the unit culture. The unit's success within the organization is assured for another ten years – but the definition of success primarily is focused on the success of key individuals. Whether the unit will continue to expand its "business base" with the outside business community is yet to be seen

Scenario E. Moderate Strategy Moderate Culture

The Organizational Context

This organization is in a mature phase of development – in term of the nature of the its work and the its life within the larger organization. The unit's work is crucial to the success of the organization, but it is not considered a core capability – leaders see the value of the unit's work but do not have an understanding of it. Strategy always comes from above. At the unit level, strategy takes the form of activity planning and short term deliverables. In essence, there is little strategic thinking at the unit level. Unit level strategies are effective where subgroup managers or individuals are effective at managing unit or top-level management. Strategic support often comes through political and social network connections that are outside of the standard chain of command. The unit's work is dependent upon innovation and managing risk – but innovation breakthroughs come only after significant investments and exploration. There is a time element to the unit's work that is out of alignment with the expectations and operations of the larger organization. The unit's cultural composition is drawn from a single country, and its gender composition is primarily male. Its age composition is mature to nearing retirement. In some ways, the unit is at risk of declining unless younger staff are brought in to continue the work – particularly given the long timelines involved in developing new products. Leadership at the top changes on a fairly regular basis – the goal is to ensure that there is a steady rotation of knowledge across the whole organization – this often means that there are frequent changes in leadership at the unit level. Managers, though, are career employees – they may be reassigned to other units or promoted, but they do not tend to leave the organization. Managers of units such as the one represented in the scenario must translate and broker demands from top-level leaders to research managers. This means unit managers must have not only competencies in the unit's business but also strong communication competencies and strong personnel management skills. Unfortunately, managers are not chosen for these competencies but more often for their political connections and networks. They are often removed from their positions when these connections are lacking. As a result, individuals in the unit must reserve about 30% of their time and attention to reading and adapting to management requirements. This means increased stress and tension at all levels. It tends to promote a competitive rather than a collaborative management philosophy. The culture begins to degrade as a result and has an impact on strategy. Open communications with other researchers are essential to building a knowledge base for innovation.

The Business Challenge

The new unit manager is appointed who comes from a robust command and control background. He immediately cuts off all travel for the unit and strains the network relationships that are so critical to the knowledge flows required for innovation. With the decreased knowledge base, the quality of the unit's work begins to suffer. The unit manager's lack of knowledge of the work became clear to the top leadership. Additionally, as critical researchers request transfers to other more high profile research units within the larger organization, it is clear that the unit's capabilities are declining. Some individuals maintain their networks by leveraging annual events and through peer review activities. However, what was once an influential culture becomes a more typical culture for the organization. What was once seen as a strong business strategy also declines to moderate.

The Result

The organization realizes the misalignment of the manager to the unit's work and mission and reassigns the manager. A new manager is assigned, who immediately introduces a more inclusive culture grounded on recognition and rewards that have value to the individuals. Gradually, the old culture is rebuilt and a new research breakthrough results. The strategy is redefined, and confidence in the unit's capabilities are strengthened. New and younger researchers are now attracted to the unit, and there is sufficient overlap in the transition to allow them to acclimate to existing work and to introduce their new ideas. Gender composition remains a challenge, but with the younger workforce, there is an opportunity for future growth. The experienced researchers are comfortable retiring, assured that the strategy would continue to be supported. They remain part of the external network

Scenario F. Moderate Strategy Weak Culture

The Organizational Context

This scenario describes a business unit that has reached a mid-life cycle phase. We cannot say it has achieved maturity because the core focus of the unit has not yet stabilized or coalesce to a point where the organization recognizes its value and function. It is at a point where the strategy needs to be updated and reinforced. The work of the previous manager – who consolidated several units and created a new vision – is a good starting point for a new strategy. The unit that was previously a high profile unit perhaps more for its culture and the willingness of its staff to work with and support other units. It had a true service and support culture across the organization and was often engaged in those services. In the past, the unit's work was pivotal in designing the new internal document management system and the emerging intranet and web architectures. Previously the unit was managed by a charismatic leader who had an extensive social network throughout the organization and developed a unit culture that was inclusive and learning focused.

The Business Challenge

With the retirement of the previous manager, the division manager decides to break up the unit and to assign some previous subgroups to other units. This means that the unit has shrunk in size as a result of the redefinition. The new manager has strong ties to data and selected business units – but does not have a broad background in all kinds of content. The new manager does not have architecture experience or training, so the core competency of the previous unit must be supported by the staff who remain assigned to the unit. The new manager is promoted to this new position based on work done in installing and consolidating a new financial management system. This project is seen as a significant success initially, but as time passes and the organization realizes how consolidation was achieved – the short cuts and poor decisions are exposed. As a result of these evolving discoveries, the stature of the unit leader declines and the unit as well. Subnetworks strengthen as a result of weakening the unit – and individuals with particular competencies are drawn in as support to projects in other units and departments. In particular, opportunities open for individuals to build their network across the organization. In the decline of the unit's stature, motivated individuals strengthen their positions across the organization. While some individuals build new networks, other individuals fall back on social cultures and networks – and strengthen their ties to well-placed individuals throughout the organization. Individuals who have neither specialized competencies nor strong network ties are at higher risk as the organization moves towards downsizing staff and reducing the financial burdens of staff salaries. There is disruption at the division level, and the unit manages to weather three changes in division management in under a year. Two of the changes were interim assignments, and one was the result of dismissal due to security breaches of financial systems. Before dismissal, the third CIO recruited a new unit manager from outside the organization. This individual was aligned with his management control philosophy. The philosophy was one of firm control and direction – a culture very different from the previous division or unit manager. This culture was shaken when the division manager was dismissed for poor control over financial system security. The new unit manager had a strong law enforcement philosophy and heritage – which was not only at odds with the unit culture but also with the organization culture as a whole.

The Result

Over time, the unit's disintegration and fragmentation grow despite an increased budget, an increase in staffing, in physical space allocations, and titles and promotions. The new unit manager was unable to build a cohesive culture. When the unit manager received a vote of no confidence, the previous unit manager is reinstated as an interim. However, the internal relationships are shaken, and critical staff leave the unit leaving it further vulnerable to reduced support capacity. Within two years, the business strategy of the unit collapses. Its culture collapsed with the introduction of the new unit manager. There is little left to build upon, and eventually, the unit's staff are absorbed into other units or leave the organization entirely. The function disappears from the organization's landscape.

Scenario G. Weak Strategy Strong Culture

The Organizational Context

Strategy: This organizational unit is one of the oldest areas of practice in the organization. The organization is close to two centuries old with a single focus and concentration over its entire history. It is considered to be the premier institution to work for in the profession. This organizational unit has two business goals – (1) to establish policies that support collaboration and exchange among other institutions in the profession at the national, state and local level; and (2) to create production records for unique resources to make those records available to information brokers and redistributors. The work of this unit is intended to support all markets and is generally regarded as the highest quality. As a result, there are strong strategies that have grown up around both the establishment of policies and procedures. These strategies are so strong that they have been tightly integrated into the culture of the unit. The work itself has become a tradition within the organization. While this supports quality, it creates a management philosophy that can be resistant to change. Culturally, managers and staff are proud to work for this unit, and there are strong personal and professional networks established within the unit and from the unit external to other institutions. The culture is risk-averse, deeply tied to the profession, and heavily class and credential-based. This means that opinions are typically only expressed by senior members of the community. New members of the network need to prove their worth over the years before they have a voice. The stature of the organization has shielded it from cultural shifts and market pressures. Traditionally, there has been a gender composition conundrum. The majority of the workforce has been female, while the leader selected has always been male and from outside the profession. This has created a discrepancy in assumptions and beliefs between leaders and workers. Additionally, the leader has been a figurehead rather than a true manager.

The Business Challenge

Because the culture has been resistant to new and younger voices, the organization is not prepared to compete in the new information and knowledge economy. Any new focus or areas of practice must be additive rather than expansions or extensions of current activities. The culture has been focused heavily on print products, preservation, and conversation of historical print products. The culture required to support strategies for dynamic and mutable information and knowledge products. As a result, the organization has ceded this new business area to the commercial market. As a result, the focus has shifted away from this institution. Traditionally, the top leadership of the organization has been drawn from the literary and academic worlds. This type of leadership aligned well with the traditional print, preservation, and conservation focus of the organization. As the organization has visibly lost stature and relevance in a changing world, though, it was clear that both a strategic and a cultural change were needed. However, given the well-entrenched culture and strategies, making this shift presented significant challenges. A new leader was brought in from within the profession but from a service and public-facing aspect of the profession. This choice was well-received internally by the staff who saw one of their own being elevated to the highest position. At the same time, though, it signaled a shift in focus from backroom operations and "safe choices" of static products to active engagement around information and an opportunity to refocus on a broader spectrum of products. Additionally, the new leader was now the traditional end-of-career appointment but a mid-career professional. This meant the new leader was still active in the profession with an active network from which to draw. This network and the enthusiasm around this new leader made it easier for her to bring in younger talent more in tune with the new information environment. The professional recognition, though, also made retirements and realignments easier to accept and accomplish.

The Result

This transition is in progress and will take many years to accomplish. In this case, the challenge the new leader faces is reinventing the business strategy and strengthening the staff commitment to that strategy. The strength of the traditional culture must be carefully managed, in any case. Any resistance to the cultural front will sink any new business strategy. In effect, the culture needs to be calibrated to support the new strategy each step of the way. Moreover, the calibration needs to happen at the business unit level to ensure it is sustainable and stable. The new leader was a good choice because she has sufficient career years left to see the transition through to a good result. By bringing in younger advocates – and providing more gender diversity – she also has the opportunity to build a good succession plan. This may pre-empt any future 'outside the profession' choices for new leadership.

Scenario H. Weak Strategy Moderate Culture

The Organizational Context

This scenario comes from a 250-year-old institution with strong traditions and well-established competencies. Competencies are acquired from selected academic institutions, and field experience is critical. Competencies also tend to favor a particular social and economic background since negotiations are generally between individuals drawn from social and economic classes of power. Language experience is critical – as is cultural knowledge of the organization is deeply embedded in the language of diplomacy and the language of the country and region. The craft can only be learned on the job and in the field, so it takes years to become proficient in the practice. Proficiency is also dependent on having good mentors and coaches, so networks become critical aspects of one's professional development. The strategy may shift on a routine basis as leadership changes, but these shifts have not represented core or fundamental changes like the work or the practice. There has never been a shift so dramatic as to bring into question the work of the organization. The organization's culture is deeply grounded in values and behaviors of respect, patience, listening, understanding, accommodation, and solid communication competencies. Many of these competencies are inherent to the nature and personality of the individual. Conversely, some personality types are not well suited to the practice. Forceful behaviors or agendas that are supportive of a specific industry or entity other than the nation are discouraged. Traditions are well established within and across the organization. Culture is built and reinforced over the career life of staff – as they are rotated from post to post and increase their levels of knowledge and responsibilities. The culture is shifting – a decade ago, it was a culture where young professionals did not raise a voice until they had ten years of experience. Today, though, young professionals are increasingly given opportunities to explore new networking and diplomatic methods leveraging social media, artificial intelligence, and digital learning environments. Traditionally, leaders of the organization have been symbolic and supportive. Recently, though, leaders have engaged directly in diplomatic work – setting an example for other managers throughout the organization to follow. This has a substantial impact on middle managers and mid-career professionals in particular to more actively engage in diplomatic outreach and efforts.

The Business Challenge

This scenario describes the events of a specific business unit in the larger organization. The unit was dedicated to maintaining diplomatic ties with a specific region and country. With the most recent change, the strategy has shifted from a focus on all countries and a corps of competencies across the organization and the world to a single country focus The single country focus requires a particular skill set in negotiating through challenges and impediments because the country of focus has a poor history of honoring business contracts. This makes it challenging for diplomatic staff to set the stage or establish a dialog for negotiations to proceed. A single-focus strategy aligned with the regional culture and a single industry – oil and gas. An executive brought in from industry that introduces a private-sector resource investment strategy that is not well aligned with or integrated into the historical business of diplomacy and representing the nation's broader interests. It has been the case that the primary focus os the relationship has been broad-based – spanning from academic and research collaboration to building business infrastructures to selected joint military engagements. The business challenge arose when a new leader of the organization was brought in with a single business goal of opening oil and gas resource markets to selected companies. The new leader was a former corporate manager from one of these companies. While the new leader had some knowledge of business negotiations and establishing legal rights and contracts, the individual had no experience with other areas of collaboration and exchange. The combination of well-entrenched and well-established strategies and cultures at first attempts to accommodate the new priorities but then begins to push back. When the new leader meets with resistance from the unit, he removes key diplomatic personnel and replaces them with political appointments. Initially, these are at the support level. When the leader comes under increasing pressure to remove top-level individuals and fails, he is removed from his position. For the second time in the organization's history, an individual from the military services is brought in to accomplish the business goal.

The Result

Having experienced an earlier military regime at the top management level, the organization's career professionals begin a concerted effort to push back and expose the internal activities of the organization. While the culture had recovered from the previous military management, it was still in the process of growth and rejuvenation. A select set of individuals put career shift strategies in place and take up the challenge of exposing the ethical and legal violations they have been asked to support. The remaining career professionals form invisible and hidden strategies to survive the new leadership. The business strategy of the top leadership does not move forward, generating more considerable animosity between leadership and staff. The strategy should be the first focus on reconstruction, leveraging the culture to achieve the preferred results. Management needs to rethink their internal strategy as well as its external business strategy. While the adopted strategy may be perceived as strong in a private sector business context, it is a weak strategy in the diplomatic environment

Scenario I. Weak Strategy Weak Culture

The Organizational Context

In terms of strategy, this scenario describes an organizational unit whose work has been contracted out to a services support vendor. This means a double layer management structure and a two-faceted business strategy. One strategy is that of the parent or contracting organization. The second strategy is that of the contractor organization. The contracting organization originally defined the contract to develop a new system to support the management of retirement investments for a particular economic sector. As a result, the business unit's strategy was primarily focused on a technical solution. The contracting organization hired a project manager with strong technical skills. However, the project manager also had a particular management philosophy and control approach that was strongly influenced by the engineering culture. As a result, every solution to every problem was technical and rigidly engineered. Because of the nature of the parent organization's business – retirement investment management – the dominant strategy was that of low risk. Business goal was on the low risk management of pension funds and careful tracking of investments and growth. This would have been a straight forward business strategy and philosophy in a non-contact environment. However, the two-tiered contract environment exacerbated existing project team tensions. In any contracting environment, there there are two levels of management and two strategies at play - the strategy of the parent organization and the strategy of the contracting organization. The business goals of these two organizations are not always aligned. It is the role of the onsite business manager for the contractor to ensure that there is a seamless integration of the organization's business strategy and the contracting organization's strategy. There is little room for individual strategies or business goals in this environment – the contract is a service contract, which means that professional and business goals of individuals are often set aside or achieved indirectly. It takes a particular set of people skills and competencies to manage strategies well in this context. The differentiated strategy was further undermined by the culture of the contract project team. The project team manager adopted a robust command and control – follow the directions of the manager was the preferred behavior. Survival was dependent upon understanding the manager's idea of a solution and being able to make that happen. The culture of the parent organization was not able to filter through as the contract manager monitored and guarded communications carefully – there was no outlet for staff working on the contract. This management philosophy had an impact on strategy because it meant that contract staff was not in a position to act as conduits for good ideas and suggestions from stakeholders or clients – all these ideas had to be channeled to the manager who then filtered them for their technical value.

The Business Challenge

Salaries of contract managers are often below those of permanent managers, and as a result, contracting organizations often select managers who do not have strengths in all areas. In this case, the contractor saw the main challenge as improving the support systems and therefore focused on technical competencies in a manager. What was needed, though, was a better balance of people and technical skills. The support staff was highly qualified but young and eager to learn. Learning opportunities were constrained to learning what the manager needed them to learn. The manager was not a good mentor or coach but was instead accustomed to a formal academic instructor role – which did not fit well in a work environment. Medical issues among the staff – stress-related

– eventually forced the contract management to reassign the manager to another project.

The Result

In this scenario, the contracting organization failed to take action either in the form of coaching the manager or in reassuring the staff. The manager gave the contracting officer an ultimatum to replace staff or accept her resignation – they reassigned her to another project – and gave the staff additional support. The interim manager was brought in who reviewed the strategy and expanded it to include factors beyond its original strict technical systems focus. This expansion of strategy provided greater breathing space for the degraded culture to begin to rebuild. The intervention came too late, though, and the damage to the contractor's reputation was notable. The manager did not work well with the new project team and was encouraged to leave the contracting company. Eventually, the individual established a consulting business and returned to the academic sector to continue teaching.

BALANCING STRATEGY AND CULTURE AT THE UNIT AND TEAM LEVEL

What have we learned from scenarios at the business unit and team level? We note the importance of team composition in achieving balance. Whether strategy or culture is dominant appears to depend more on the cultural factors influencing the team – and the level of support between the team and the leader. Stability of the unit – its life cycle stage and prominence in the organization - also plays a critical role. The alignment of management cultures between top and unit leadership appears to be a key element – where there is a discrepancy, and the discrepancy is managed to by the unit manager, the unit culture will survive. Where the top management culture is at odds with the unit culture, the unit culture will prevail. The exception here is when the unit level management leaves, retires, or is removed. Management culture philosophies vary with regional differences as well as national differences some regional variations may be stronger than national variations. It is also clear that we need to understand better how culture and strategy affect the relationships of business unit managers and organization level managers –

where these relationships are well managed – generally by the unit manager – there is a better chance of alignment.

At this level, alignment does not necessarily mean total agreement or synchronization – unit cultures and strategies must be allowed some level of latitude in defining their cultures and in interpreting strategy if they are to succeed. We also note that rigid alignment – controlled or forced alignment – are not true alignments – any alignment you strive to achieve should be negotiated and managed. If there are on-going management and adaptation of these alignments across levels, the chances of sustainable success are more significant for the organization as a whole. Another observation is the importance of having variation in the key factors to ensure different views and gaps – the importance of designing intentional variations into your organizational cultures. Those organizations that have realized the importance of balanced teams – whether they be work teams or management teams and networks – rather than entirely similar teams – may have a better chance of sustaining and surviving in the knowledge economy. These organizations have designed adaptability and flexibility into their staffing strategies. This is different from merely aiming for "diversity" in a team – because what appears to be an apparent diversity may mask similar management philosophies and business goals. Organizations that aim for the coherence of thinking but diversity in appearance will not be as successful in this new economy as those who aim for diversity in thought and approach regardless of appearance. What does this mean for unit leaders? What does this mean for staff in business units?

CONCLUSION

After reading this chapter, you should be able to:

- Explain why we care about aligning unit and team level strategies and cultures
- Adapt the framework to the unit and team levels
- Apply the framework to the unit and team levels
- Document the unit and team level cultures and strategies
- Identify the gaps and pain points across the organization

ADDITIONAL READING

Ang, S., & Inkpen, A. C. (2008). Cultural intelligence and offshore outsourcing success: A framework of firm-level intercultural capability. *Decision Sciences*, *39*(3), 337–358. doi:10.1111/j.1540-5915.2008.00195.x

Ang, S., & Van Dyne, L. (2015). *Handbook of cultural intelligence: Theory, measurement, and applications*. Routledge. doi:10.4324/9781315703855

Ang, S., Van Dyne, L., & Koh, C. (2006). Personality correlates of the four-factor model of cultural intelligence. *Group & Organization Management*, *31*(1), 100–123. doi:10.1177/1059601105275267

Ang, S., Van Dyne, L., Koh, C., Ng, K. Y., Templer, K. J., Tay, C., & Chandrasekar, N. A. (2007). Cultural intelligence: Its measurement and effects on cultural judgment and decision making, cultural adaptation and task performance. *Management and Organization Review*, *3*(3), 335–371. doi:10.1111/j.1740-8784.2007.00082.x

Apud, S., Lenartowicz, T., & Johnson, J. P. (2003). Intercultural competence: what do practitioners really know? *Proceedings, Academy of International Business South-East Region Conference*.

Bellot, J. (2011). Defining and assessing organizational culture. *Nursing Forum*, *46*(1), 29–37. doi:10.1111/j.1744-6198.2010.00207.x PMID:21306393

Betancourt, J. R., Green, A. R., Carrillo, J. E., & Owusu Ananeh-Firempong, I. I. (2016). Defining cultural competence: A practical framework for addressing racial/ethnic disparities in health and health care. *Public Health Reports*. PMID:12815076

Bhui, K., Warfa, N., Edonya, P., McKenzie, K., & Bhugra, D. (2007). Cultural competence in mental health care: A review of model evaluations. *BMC Health Services Research*, *7*(1), 15. doi:10.1186/1472-6963-7-15 PMID:17266765

Brislin, R., Worthley, R., & Macnab, B. (2006). Cultural intelligence: Understanding behaviors that serve people's goals. *Group & Organization Management*, *31*(1), 40–55. doi:10.1177/1059601105275262

Brouthers, K. D., & Brouthers, L. E. (2001). Explaining the national cultural distance paradox. *Journal of International Business Studies*, *32*(1), 177–189. doi:10.1057/palgrave.jibs.8490944

Bu-Qammaz, A., Dikmen, I., & Birgonul, M. T. (2006). Cultural risk assessment in construction projects. *CCIM2006 Sustainable Development through Culture and Innovation.*

Campinha-Bacote, J. (2002). The process of cultural competence in the delivery of healthcare services: A model of care. *Journal of Transcultural Nursing*, *13*(3), 181–184. doi:10.1177/10459602013003003 PMID:12113146

Cooke, R. A., & Szumal, J. L. (2000). Using the Organizational Culture Inventory to understand the operating cultures of organizations. Handbook of organizational culture and climate, 4, 1032-1045.

Crandall, S. J., George, G., Marion, G. S., & Davis, S. (2003). Applying theory to the design of cultural competency training for medical students: A case study. *Academic Medicine*, *78*(6), 588–594. doi:10.1097/00001888-200306000-00007 PMID:12805037

de la Garza Carranza, M. T., & Egri, C. P. (2010). Managerial cultural intelligence and small business in Canada. *Management Revue*, 353-371.

Earley, P. C., & Mosakowski, E. (2002). Linking culture and behavior in organizations: Suggestions for theory development and research methodology. In *The many faces of multi-level issues* (pp. 297–319). Emerald Group Publishing Limited. doi:10.1016/S1475-9144(02)01038-X

Earley, P. C., Murnieks, C., & Mosakowski, E. (2007). Cultural intelligence and the global mindset. In *The global mindset* (pp. 75–103). Emerald Group Publishing Limited. doi:10.1016/S1571-5027(07)19004-5

Elenkov, D. S., & Manev, I. M. (2005). Social Culture Intelligence, Top-Level Leadership And Innovation Influence: An International Study. In Academy of Management Proceedings (Vol. 2005, No. 1, pp. F1-F6). Briarcliff Manor, NY: Academy of Management.

Elenkov, D. S., & Manev, I. M. (2009). Senior expatriate leadership's effects on innovation and the role of cultural intelligence. *Journal of World Business*, *44*(4), 357–369. doi:10.1016/j.jwb.2008.11.001

Emirbayer, M., & Goodwin, J. (1994). Network analysis, culture, and the problem of agency. *American Journal of Sociology*, *99*(6), 1411–1454. doi:10.1086/230450

Fowler, S. M., & Mumford, M. G. (1999). *Intercultural Sourcebook: Cross-Cultural Training Methods* (Vol. 2). Yarmouth, ME: Intercultural Press, Inc.

Gallego-Toledo, J. M. (2015). Cultural profiling and a Chinese experience. *Journal of Chinese Human Resource Management*, *6*(2), 120–132. doi:10.1108/JCHRM-09-2015-0014

Gelfand, M. J., Imai, L., and Fehr, R. (2008). Thinking intelligently about cultural intelligence. *Handbook on cultural intelligence: Theory, measurement and applications*, 375-388.

Glenn, S. S. (1988). Contingencies and metacontingencies: Toward a synthesis of behavior analysis and cultural materialism. *The Behavior Analyst*, *11*(2), 161–179. doi:10.1007/BF03392470 PMID:22478011

Glisson, C. (2007). Assessing and changing organizational culture and climate for effective services. *Research on Social Work Practice*, *17*(6), 736–747. doi:10.1177/1049731507301659

Groves, K. S., & Feyerherm, A. E. (2011). Leader cultural intelligence in context: Testing the moderating effects of team cultural diversity on leader and team performance. *Group & Organization Management*, *36*(5), 535–566. doi:10.1177/1059601111415664

Hofstede, G. (1980). Culture and organizations. *International Studies of Management & Organization*, *10*(4), 15–41. doi:10.1080/00208825.1980.11656300

Hofstede, G. (1984). *Culture's consequences: International differences in work-related values*. Beverly Hills, CA: Sage.

Hofstede, G. (2001). *Culture's consequences: Comparing values, behaviors, institutions and organizations across nations*. Thousand Oaks, CA: Sage.

Hofstede, G., Hofstede, G. J., & Minkov, M. (2010). *Cultures and organizations: Software of the mind (revised and expanded)*. New York, NY: McGraw-Hill.

Imai, L., & Gelfand, M. J. (2010). The culturally intelligent negotiator: The impact of cultural intelligence (CQ) on negotiation sequences and outcomes. *Organizational Behavior and Human Decision Processes*, *112*(2), 83–98. doi:10.1016/j.obhdp.2010.02.001

Jang, H. Y., & Barnett, G. A. (1994). Cultural differences in organizational communication: A semantic network analysis 1. *Bulletin of Sociological Methodology. Bulletin de Methodologie Sociologique*, *44*(1), 31–59. doi:10.1177/075910639404400104

Janssens, M., & Brett, J. M. (2006). Cultural intelligence in global teams: A fusion model of collaboration. *Group & Organization Management, 31*(1), 124–153. doi:10.1177/1059601105275268

Johnson, J. P., Lenartowicz, T., & Apud, S. (2006). Cross-cultural competence in international business: Toward a definition and a model. *Journal of International Business Studies, 37*(4), 525–543. doi:10.1057/palgrave.jibs.8400205

Kendra, K., & Taplin, L. J. (2004). Project success: A cultural framework. *Project Management Journal, 35*(1), 30–45. doi:10.1177/875697280403500104

King, T., & Byers, J. F. (2007). A review of organizational culture instruments for nurse executives. *JONA: The Journal of Nursing Administration, 37*(1), 21–31. doi:10.1097/00005110-200701000-00005 PMID:17172969

Kirmayer, L. J. (2012). Rethinking cultural competence. *Transcultural Psychiatry, 49*(2), 149–164. doi:10.1177/1363461512444673 PMID:22508634

Koh, C., Joseph, D., & Ang, S. (2009, February). Cultural intelligence and collaborative work: intercultural competencies in global technology work teams. In *Proceedings of the 2009 international workshop on Intercultural collaboration* (pp. 261-264). ACM. 10.1145/1499224.1499271

Koutroumanis, D. A., & Alexakis, G. (2009). Organizational Culture In The Restaurant Industry: Implications For Change. *Journal of Organizational Culture, Communications and Conflict, 13*(2).

Kumas-Tan, Z., Beagan, B., Loppie, C., MacLeod, A., & Frank, B. (2007). Measures of cultural competence: Examining hidden assumptions. *Academic Medicine, 82*(6), 548–557. doi:10.1097/ACM.0b013e3180555a2d PMID:17525538

Lamal, P. A. (Ed.). (1997). *Cultural contingencies: Behavior analytic perspectives on cultural practices*. Greenwood Publishing Group.

Lie, D. A., Lee-Rey, E., Gomez, A., Bereknyei, S., & Braddock, C. H. III. (2011). Does cultural competency training of health professionals improve patient outcomes? A systematic review and proposed algorithm for future research. *Journal of General Internal Medicine, 26*(3), 317–325. doi:10.100711606-010-1529-0 PMID:20953728

Livermore, D., & Soon, A. N. G. (2015). *Leading with cultural intelligence: The real secret to success*. Amacom.

Livermore, D., Van Dyne, L., & Ang, S. (2012). Cultural intelligence: Why every leader needs it. *Intercultural Management Quarterly*, *13*(2), 18–21.

MacNab, B., Brislin, R., & Worthley, R. (2012). Experiential cultural intelligence development: Context and individual attributes. *International Journal of Human Resource Management*, *23*(7), 1320–1341. doi:10.1080/09585192.2011.581636

MacNab, B., Brislin, R., Worthley, R., Galperin, B. L., Jenner, S., Lituchy, T. R., ... Bess, D. (2007). Culture and ethics management: Whistle-blowing and internal reporting within a NAFTA country context. *International Journal of Cross Cultural Management*, *7*(1), 5–28. doi:10.1177/1470595807075167

Mannion, R., Konteh, F. H., & Davies, H. T. O. (2009). Assessing organisational culture for quality and safety improvement: A national survey of tools and tool use. *BMJ Quality & Safety*, *18*(2), 153–156. doi:10.1136/qshc.2007.024075 PMID:19342532

Maznevski, M. (2008). Cultural intelligence: Domain and assessment. *International Journal of Cross Cultural Management*, *8*(2), 123–143. doi:10.1177/1470595808091787

Morosini, P., Shane, S., & Singh, H. (1998). National cultural distance and cross-border acquisition performance. *Journal of International Business Studies*, *29*(1), 137–158. doi:10.1057/palgrave.jibs.8490029

Mosakowski, E., Calic, G., & Earley, P. C. (2013). Cultures as learning laboratories: What makes some more effective than others? *Academy of Management Learning & Education*, *12*(3), 512–526. doi:10.5465/amle.2013.0149

Mtolo, S. G. (2017). *The Influence of Cultural Intelligence on the relationship between Social Capital and Entrepreneurial Performance: A study of foreign traders in Johannesburg's informal economy* (Doctoral dissertation).

Mueller, S. T., Sieck, W. R., & Veinott, E. (2007). *Cultural metrics: A finite mixture models approach* (Technical Report DAAD19-01-2-0009). Fairborn, OH: Klein Associates Division of ARA.

Mueller, S. T., & Veinott, E. S. (2008). Cultural mixture modeling: Identifying cultural consensus (and disagreement) using finite mixture modeling. *Proceedings of the Cognitive Science Society*.

Ng, K. Y., Van Dyne, L., & Ang, S. (2009). From experience to experiential learning: Cultural intelligence as a learning capability for global leader development. *Academy of Management Learning & Education*, *8*(4), 511–526. doi:10.5465/amle.8.4.zqr511

Ng, R. (2013). Cultural intelligence. *The encyclopedia of cross-cultural psychology*, 310-313.

Norton, W. (1995). Behavior Analysis and the Cultural Geographic Study of Place. *Journal of Cultural Geography*, *15*(2), 1–15. doi:10.1080/08873639509478351

O'Reilly, C. A. III, Caldwell, D. F., Chatman, J. A., & Doerr, B. (2014). The promise and problems of organizational culture: CEO personality, culture, and firm performance. *Group & Organization Management*, *39*(6), 595–625. doi:10.1177/1059601114550713

Oolders, T., Chernyshenko, O. S., & Stark, S. (2008). Cultural intelligence as a mediator of relationships between openness to experience and adaptive performance. Handbook of cultural intelligence: Theory, measurement, and applications, 145-158.

Pavlidis, G., Koutsoudis, A., Arnaoutoglou, F., Tsioukas, V., & Chamzas, C. (2007). Methods for 3D digitization of cultural heritage. *Journal of Cultural Heritage*, *8*(1), 93–98. doi:10.1016/j.culher.2006.10.007

Peterson, B. (2011). *Cultural intelligence: A guide to working with people from other cultures*. Nicholas Brealey.

Pieraccini, M., Guidi, G., & Atzeni, C. (2001). 3D digitizing of cultural heritage. *Journal of Cultural Heritage*, *2*(1), 63–70. doi:10.1016/S1296-2074(01)01108-6

Purnell, L. (2002). The Purnell model for cultural competence. *Journal of Transcultural Nursing*, *13*(3), 193–196. doi:10.1177/10459602013003006 PMID:12113149

Rasmussen, L. J., Sieck, W. R., & Osland, J. (2010). *Using cultural models of decision making to develop and assess cultural sensemaking competence. Advances in Cross-Cultural Decision Making*. Boca Raton, FL: CRC Press, Taylor and Francis Group.

Rockstuhl, T., Dulebohn, J. H., Ang, S., & Shore, L. M. (2012). Leader–member exchange (LMX) and culture: A meta-analysis of correlates of LMX across 23 countries. *The Journal of Applied Psychology*, *97*(6), 1097–1130. doi:10.1037/a0029978 PMID:22985117

Rockstuhl, T., Seiler, S., Ang, S., Van Dyne, L., & Annen, H. (2011). Beyond general intelligence (IQ) and emotional intelligence (EQ): The role of cultural intelligence (CQ) on cross-border leadership effectiveness in a globalized world. *The Journal of Social Issues*, *67*(4), 825–840. doi:10.1111/j.1540-4560.2011.01730.x

Seufert, S. (2002). Cultural perspectives. In *Handbook on information technologies for education and training* (pp. 411–421). Berlin: Springer. doi:10.1007/978-3-662-07682-8_26

Shenkar, O. (2001). Cultural distance revisited: Towards a more rigorous conceptualization and measurement of cultural differences. *Journal of International Business Studies*, *32*(3), 519–535. doi:10.1057/palgrave.jibs.8490982

Sieck, W. R., Rasmussen, L. J., & Smart, P. (2010). Cultural network analysis: A cognitive approach to cultural modeling. In *Network science for military coalition operations: Information exchange and interaction* (pp. 237–255). IGI Global. doi:10.4018/978-1-61520-855-5.ch011

Sousa, C. M., & Bradley, F. (2006). Cultural distance and psychic distance: Two peas in a pod? *Journal of International Marketing*, *14*(1), 49–70. doi:10.1509/jimk.14.1.49

Stanco, F., Battiato, S., & Gallo, G. (Eds.). (2011). *Digital imaging for cultural heritage preservation: Analysis, restoration, and reconstruction of ancient artworks*. CRC Press.

Sue, D. W. (2001). Multidimensional facets of cultural competence. *The Counseling Psychologist*, *29*(6), 790–821. doi:10.1177/0011000001296002

Sue, D. W., & Torino, G. C. (2005). Racial-cultural competence: Awareness, knowledge, and skills. Handbook of racial-cultural psychology and counseling: Training and practice, 2, 3-18.

Tarique, I., & Takeuchi, R. (2008). Developing cultural intelligence: The roles of international nonwork experiences. Handbook of cultural intelligence: Theory, measurement, and applications, 56-70.

Thom, D. H., Tirado, M. D., Woon, T. L., & McBride, M. R. (2006). Development and evaluation of a cultural competency training curriculum. *BMC Medical Education*, *6*(1), 38. doi:10.1186/1472-6920-6-38 PMID:16872504

Thomas, D. C. (2006). Domain and development of cultural intelligence: The importance of mindfulness. *Group & Organization Management*, *31*(1), 78–99. doi:10.1177/1059601105275266

Thomas, D. C. (2015). Cultural intelligence. Wiley Encyclopedia of Management, 1-3.

Thomas, D. C., Elron, E., Stahl, G., Ekelund, B. Z., Ravlin, E. C., Cerdin, J. L., ... Brislin, R. (2012). Development of the cultural intelligence assessment. In *Advances in global leadership* (pp. 155–178). Emerald Group Publishing Limited. doi:10.1108/S1535-1203(2012)0000007011

Triandis, H. C. (2006). Cultural intelligence in organizations. *Group & Organization Management*, *31*(1), 20–26. doi:10.1177/1059601105275253

Triandis, H. C. (2008). Cultural intelligence. Handbook of cultural intelligence.

Van Dyne, L., Ang, S., & Koh, C. (2015). Development and validation of the CQS: The cultural intelligence scale. In *Handbook of cultural intelligence* (pp. 34–56). Routledge.

Van Dyne, L., Ang, S., Ng, K. Y., Rockstuhl, T., Tan, M. L., & Koh, C. (2012). Sub-dimensions of the four factor model of cultural intelligence: Expanding the conceptualization and measurement of cultural intelligence. *Social and Personality Psychology Compass*, *6*(4), 295–313. doi:10.1111/j.1751-9004.2012.00429.x

Wagner, W., & Yamori, K. (1999). Can culture be a variable? Dispositional explanation and cultural metrics. *Progress in Asian social psychology, 2.*

Chapter 9
Balancing Individual Strategies and Cultures

ABSTRACT

Strategies may be formulated and published by senior leaders; they may be supported by line managers and by teams. The success of a strategy comes down to the actions of individuals. In particular, the authors are interested in managing those risks result from an individual's day-to-day behaviors and actions. What changes at this level? Two things change. First, who conducts the assessment changes? The individual must take responsibility for knowing the organization's strategies, becoming aware of their personal strategies, and their own cultures. The individual must drive this process. Second, the individual must have a clear understanding of which individuals are responsible for which strategies.

WHY DO WE CARE ALIGNING AT THIS LEVEL?

Strategies may be formulated and published by senior leaders; they may be supported by line managers and by teams. Ultimately, though, the success of a strategy comes down to the actions of individuals. Individuals must be invested in a strategy; it must align with their individual beliefs, assumptions, and values. Moreover, it must be reflected in their actions and behaviors. When these do not align, we have a risk. Small risks accumulate and add up to unrealized or contradicted strategies. These risks are different for every individual in every unit. The risks we encounter at these levels when strategies

DOI: 10.4018/978-1-7998-4315-3.ch009

and cultures are not aligned may have higher business costs because this is the level at which work happens. We will not repeat those arguments and justifications in this chapter, but we do remind the reader that they apply to these levels as well.

There are two dimensions to risk at this level. First, an individual may not buy into the organization's strategies. Their actions may not impede those strategies, but they may not support them. This is a clear example of how culture might undermine strategy. Second, an individual may have their business strategies, and these may run counter to the organization's, or they may support the organization's but only in a way that benefits that individual. When these do not align, we have a risk. Small risks accumulate and add up to unrealized or contradicted strategies. These risks are different for every individual in every unit. In contrast, as individuals engage and become invested in the organization's strategies and adopt its cultures, the organization's behavior begins to change. Our goal as business and information managers is to find a fit that grows our information and business cultures and supports our business and information strategies.

The goal is to identify ways to reduce the risk of strategic failures at the person or individual level. In particular, we are interested in managing those risks result from an individual's day to day behaviors and actions. It is at this level that we face the most significant risks. All of the arguments and justifications we laid out in Chapters 7 and 8 are valid at this level. The framework we introduced in Chapters 7 and 8 holds at this level, with a few changes.

What changes at this level? Two things change. First, who conducts the assessment changes. The individual must take responsibility for knowing the organization's strategies, becoming aware of their personal strategies, and their own cultures. The individual must drive this process. Second, the individual must have a clear understanding of which individuals are responsible for which strategies. This means the organization must be clear about responsibility and accountability for strategies and must communicate this clearly to individuals. This means that ultimately there must be a strong management model supporting each strategy. Armed with this information, and when provided with self-assessment tools and incentives, it is up to the unit, the team, and the local manager to shape all of those individual assessments into something that supports the immediate strategy and culture. Perhaps the best way to accomplish this is to build it into the periodic performance appraisal process. This is not, though, a one-time effort. Shaping and adapting is a continuous effort, requiring continuous support from the organization – because it is part of the way we work. Norms and behaviors are not mandated and achieved in a single day. Instead, they are adapted and adjusted incrementally.

The framework and methodology we follow to identify misalignments, to develop target lists of strategies at risk are the same at these lower levels. What is different is the breadth and depth of business strategies we have to work with, the nature of the impact of lacking or sub-optimized information strategies at the operational level, and the cultural factors we need to see and shape.

What is different is who is responsible and accountable for applying the framework, and for shaping culture to support strategy. Ideally, we establish a general methodology around the framework at the organization level and promote that methodology throughout the organization. We apply the framework and shape the culture only at strategic points in the organization. Furthermore, we put the process in the hands of those who are responsible for achieving the strategic goals and objectives. Managers who are responsible for developing strategies should now be responsible for integrating cultural analysis into the strategy development and management process. Then each leader, each division, each unit – designs a fit to support the current business need. Over time this approach gradually creates a new business methodology. It shifts the nature of strategic planning always to include culture shaping. Shaping our culture becomes part of the way we work.

ADAPTING THE FRAMEWORK TO INDIVIDUAL LEVELS

How do we adapt the framework? Of the seven steps, which steps change, and which remain the same? For those that change, what changes?

Table 1. Adapting the Seven-Step Methodology

Step 1. Assess the Current Risks (Pain Points) in our Business Strategies
• *Individual take responsibility for their self-assessments of their support for the local business strategy, for the local information strategy, for exposing and adapting their strategies and behaviors, and for growing their self-awareness of their cultures;*
Step 2. Assess the Current Risks (Pain Points) in our Information Strategies
• *Individuals begin with self-assessments – possibly with structured questionnaires focused on business and information strategies;*
Step 3. Identify Common Risks (Pain Points) in Business and Information Strategies
• *Ideally, individuals initiate the discovery of risks or misalignments because they need to engage around these areas and propose ways to achieve a better fit;*
Step 4. Assess the Current State of Business Cultures (Leverage Points)
• *Individuals should have the opportunity to share their assumptions and beliefs about the business and the information strategies;*
Step 5. Assess the Current State of Information Cultures (Leverage Points)
• *This is a critical step in the alignment process because information strategies are rarely implemented at this individual level – it is most often the case that individual information cultures take precedence;* • *In order to assess individual information strategies and cultures, the organization must develop a clear statement of what these are – and these statements must be actionable and practical;* • *Abstract policy statements must be translated into actual assessment methods and models that individuals can use for guidance;* • *Allowing individuals to describe their inherent information cultures creates an opportunity for the organization – it provides a foundation for understanding what needs to be adapted and shaped to support the business strategy.*
Step 6. Identify Common Cultural Leverage Points for Strategies at Risk
• *Individuals should identify cultural aspects they can leverage to support the unit;* • *There should be an open discussion of these points of leverage across the unit;* • *Ultimately, the individuals in the unit should reach a consensus on these points of leverage and how to adapt them – the consensus should be the point that maximizes the advantage and minimizes risks to individuals*
Step 7. Align The Cultural Points of Leverage With Strategic Risks and Pain Points
• *Unit managers and staff integrate cultural analysis into strategic planning processes and adopt it as a standard business process*

STEP 1: ASSESS THE CURRENT RISKS (PAIN POINTS) IN OUR BUSINESS STRATEGIES

The objective of this step is comparable to that at the organization and the unit level. An additional challenge is that we expect there will be more strategies at this level, and we will need to have a reliable and representative list of what exists. The challenge here, though, is that every individual in the unit has their individual and potentially invisible strategies.

There is no point in having individual self-assess if there is no process in place for units to support and leverage these assessments. Units must support individuals in their self-assessments, and commit to developing a cohesive business and information strategy and culture at the unit level. It is the organization's responsibility to clarify individuals' roles in any strategy, and to identify supporting roles where they are missing;

The unit and individuals need to determine what norms and behaviors are supportive and which impede strategy at this level.

STEP 2: ASSESS THE CURRENT RISKS (PAIN POINTS) IN OUR INFORMATION STRATEGIES

This will be challenging at the individual level if there is no practical or applicable translation of information policies. Structured questionnaires may be useful in helping individuals to understand what strategies exist, what form they take, and how they can best support them The point of this step is to help individuals "see" their assumptions, beliefs, and values and to compare them with the expectations of their units. Individuals are dependent upon the unit and the organization for making explicit any relevant business strategies so they can use this information in their self-assessments. Part of this step may also be engaging an institutional expert on cultures – to advise and guide individuals in their self-assessments and to act as a coach in interpreting the results.

STEP 3. IDENTIFY COMMON RISKS (PAIN POINTS) IN BUSINESS AND INFORMATION STRATEGIES

This step also follows the framework and methodology established at the organization level, but its success is entirely dependent on a close working relationship among unit-level business managers, staff, and information professionals. Ideally, individuals initiate the discovery of risks or misalignments because they need to engage in these areas and propose ways to achieve a better fit. Individuals should also have the opportunity to define the level of risk – because they are best positioned to understand – at a work level – what the consequences might be.

STEP 4: ASSESS THE CURRENT STATE OF BUSINESS CULTURES (LEVERAGE POINTS)

This step is more challenging at this level than it is at the organization level. It is challenging for two reasons. The first reason is that we have a different set of cultural factors to consider (Table 2). The second reason is that while there are many cultural assessment tools available, they tell us little about how an individual's business culture aligns with that of the unit or the organization. This is a step the unit members must design and conduct internally.

Table 2. Individual culture factors of interest

• What is the individual's gender, and how does it align with the unit?
• What is the individual's national culture? How does it fit with the unit?
• What is the age, and how does it fit with the unit?
• What are the individual's roles and status in the unit?
• What relationships and networks do individuals hold? What value do they have for the unit?
• What is an individual's language, and how does it align with the unit?

Individuals should have the opportunity to share their assumptions and beliefs about business and information strategies. Individuals should have the opportunity to explain whether their values are aligned with those of the unit and organization, and if not, why not. This source of information can help us to understand some crucial aspects of the unit and organization cultures – are those values, assumptions, and beliefs espoused or actual? We can take as input the individual cultural profiles, but it is only through comparison to espoused and actual cultures that we learn whether we have gaps and risks. To accomplish this step, we must have a strong toolkit of culture assessment tools available across the organization.

STEP 5. ASSESSING IDENTIFY COMMON CULTURAL LEVERAGE POINTS FOR STRATEGIES AT RISK

The factors for assessing the information culture of the unit or team are consistent with those of the organization. This is a critical step in the alignment process because information strategies are rarely implemented at this individual level – it is most often the case that individual information cultures take precedence. In order to assess individual information strategies and cultures, the organization must develop a clear statement of what these are – and these statements must be actionable and practical. Abstract policy statements must be translated to actual assessment methods and models that individuals can use for guidance. Allowing individuals to describe their inherent information cultures creates an opportunity for the organization – it provides a foundation for understanding what needs to be adapted and shaped to support the business strategy.

STEP 6. IDENTIFY COMMON CULTURAL LEVERAGE POINTS FOR STRATEGIES AT RISK

Just as at the organization level, this is a joint effort at the unit level. Individuals should identify cultural aspects they can leverage to support the unit. There should be an open discussion of these points of leverage across the unit. Ultimately, the individuals in the unit should reach a consensus on these points of leverage and how to adapt them – the consensus should be the point that maximizes the advantage and minimizes risks to individuals.

STEP 7. ALIGN THE CULTURAL POINTS OF LEVERAGE WITH STRATEGIC RISKS AND PAIN POINTS

At this point, the task is to determine how to best integrate individual strategies and cultures into the business and information strategy development and management process. What kind of business risk do individual strategies present? What is the business value of that risk? How much of that risk is the organization willing to accept? What is the direct cost of building cultural analysis into the early stages of strategy development? What are the indirect costs – what incentives are necessary to encourage individuals to contribute and adapt?

The challenge here is far greater than what we described at the organization or the unit level because of the sheer scale of this effort. Consider that this process will play out for every individual across the organization. At the organization level, there is an added challenge of ensuring that all of these new processes and 'fits' also connect to the organization level.

SCENARIOS DRAWN FROM REAL WORLD EXPERIENCES

While there is much in the text to which a reader might relate, the authors thought it might be useful to provide some scenarios drawn from their real-world experiences. The intent is to illustrate the challenges we have faced when strategies and cultures have different strengths. Each experience is represented as a scenario in which the strategy or the culture is at a different level of strength. In a concise narrative, we consider the effect on the business environment of a realignment and balancing of culture and strategy. While the scenarios are grounded in the authors' real experiences, no single scenario is an accurate representation of any event, any organization, unit, or individual. Each scenario has been edited and changed to illustrate the point. We present nine scenarios – ranging from scenarios with well-aligned and balanced cultures and strategies to scenarios with disconnected weak cultures and weak strategies. These scenarios are all focused on the individual level.

Figure 1. Matrix of scenarios at the individual level

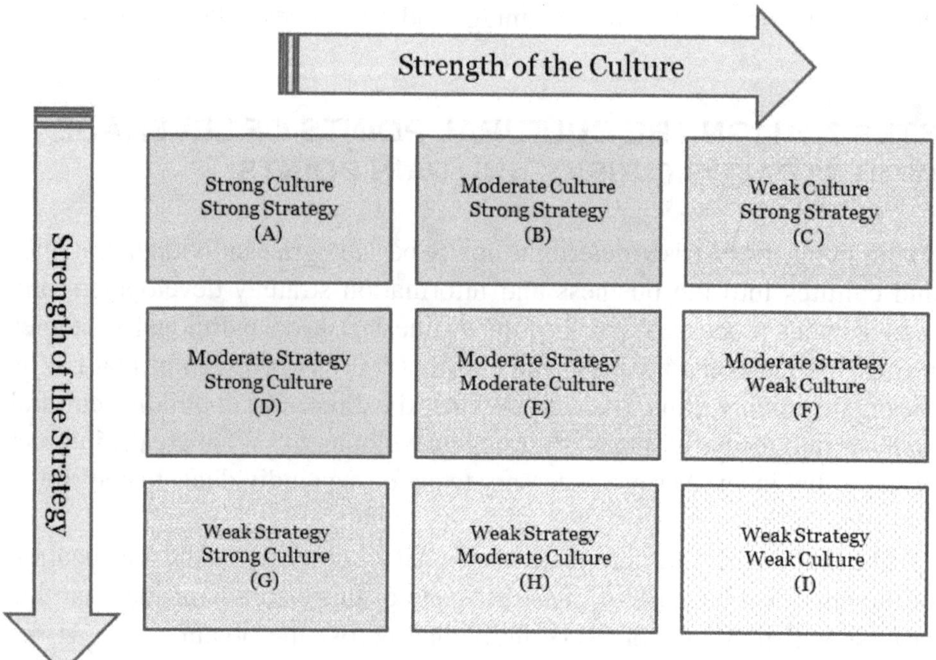

Scenario A. Strong Strategy Strong Culture

The Organizational Context

This scenario represents a political organization. The individual profiled is the primary leader or candidate of the political organization. The individual stature, level of expertise, and roll are essential to understand the degree of influence that the individual has in the organization. In this case, the individual would be considered a leader though there is not a strict organizational structure to the organization. There is not a top-level a mid-level and a lower level where everyone is required to report up, and everyone's livelihood depends upon how they behave within the organization. What is notable is that the success of the organization is dependent here on the personality and the strategies of the individual because, in this case, they determine the agenda for the organization. In other words, they define the business goals and the business strategy for the organization. Ideally, there is a larger organization supporting this individual. Furthermore, that larger organization would be responsible for taking the vision of the individual and translating it into a strategy that is then operationalized by a larger group of individuals. So, in this case, the personal strategy of the individual we are profiling is a robust economic agenda. The individual believes there is a dominant strategy that will help to achieve the vision for a large number of individuals. The culture of the organization is open and participative. There is extensive communication and social engagement across all roles, levels, and locations. The challenge is that the culture is ultimately defined around the candidate. If there is a change in who is in the lead role, the culture is likely to break down. In other words, if something were to happen to the candidate, it is not clear that another individual could step into that role and continue to advance the business goals. While there may be a clear strategy, that strategy is so tightly integrated with culture, and the culture is so dependent upon the individual, but it is not clear that either the strategy or the culture could survive without the individual.

The Business Challenge

The business challenge here is how do we stabilize this organization to ensure that there is continuity in an additional succession planning almost for this lead individual and how do we do that in a way that does not look like the individual is being supplanted. The best approach to achieving this aspect of the strategy would be to have the candidate himself or herself identify the Heir Apparent and the person or persons who would best be positioned to carry out the vision and to continue to and nourish the culture. The challenge is that the individual in question may believe that they are the only person who can achieve the business vision. There may not be a level of trust in other individuals to identify successors. If this case, it is unlikely that the strategy will be wholly achieved or that the culture will be cohesive in the end because this is not how organizations will work in the knowledge economy. In this case, what would appear to be an open and Democratic organization, an open and fair process among the staff, is an intense following around the individual.

The Result

If this individual does not identify successors or heirs to carry out the business vision, the culture will not survive. It will be intense for a short period of time. Ultimately the organization will not achieve its goals in the longer term. The knowledge economy requires that organizations have opportunities for stakeholders, partners, and even competitors to engage in the business activity, whatever that business activity may be, whether it is politics, private sector marketing, or education. The command and control structures of industrial organizations are not conducive to the creation and open flow of knowledge. Ultimately, this organization will collapse under its unfulfilled expectations.

Scenario B. Strong Strategy Moderate Culture

The Organizational Context

This scenario describes an individual who has a powerful sense of business strategy. Moreover, that business strategy is aligned with and supportive of the organization's business strategy. This individual is in a support services business unit. He is not in a line management position. He is the manager of a small unit, however. He has no permanent staff reporting to him, but he has many staff on detail reporting to him. In this case, it is essential to have a strong sense of the organization's business strategy as well as the business strategies of all the units. The reason this strong understanding is essential is that individuals need to feel that their temporary assignments to this unit have value to their originating unit. They will go back to that unit, and when they return, they need to be able to demonstrate what their work produced value for that original business unit. The success of the profiled individual is due to his ability to not insert himself into either the culture or the strategy but to be a catalyst and an enabler for others. Everyone who works with this individual sees value and benefit because they are supported, and they can develop under this person's leadership. The culture of the support services unit is open, communicative, and learning. This unit must assume a moderate-risk strategy as the organization is for safety and risk aversion conscious. So this individual is good at exposing what he does not know. This individual is explaining what it is he wants to and needs to learn. This individual is good at admitting his mistakes and learning from his mistakes. This personal culture and this personal learning strategy set the tone for the business strategy and the culture of the whole unit.

The Business Challenge

For five years, this individual has had a very supportive direct line manager. Recently though, that manager has retired. Rather than a sign the whole unit to the new director - retaining the line reporting structure - your organization decided to reassign this unit to report to the head of the project management office. This is a significant shift in the reporting structure for this individual and the unit. The business challenge here is that the project management office is not open to experimentation, learning, and any degree of risk-taking. Instead, the project management office has strict procedures and guidelines for project oversight, reporting, and structures. The management philosophy of the project management office is more command and control for the simple reason that most of the staff in that office are former military personnel. Their official training and their network are tightly connected to military communities. Luckily the individual we are profiling in this scenario is adaptable and flexible and does not put his strategies and cultures before those of units. As a result, this individual is going to develop strong relationships with the new manager of the project management office, to adapt his style in the unit's culture to ensure that the new manager continues to support the work of the unit. We know that this individual will create a low-risk environment for the project management office personnel, well still supporting some degree of experimentation and learning within the support services unit.

The Result

Because of this individual's personal qualities and characteristics, the support services unit continues to thrive within the organization. It continues to provide critical Support Services related to Knowledge Management within the organization. Over time, this individual can unobtrusively coach and mentor the manager of the project management office in the basic tenets of Knowledge Management. In the end, the manager of the project management office becomes an advocate for the work of the unit. Because the project management office has been able to achieve a broad infiltration to all areas of the organization, Vishnu and strong alignment open new doors for the support services unit. In the end, the connections the individual has been able to leverage in the project management office extends the reach of his unit.

Scenario C. Strong Strategy Weak Culture

The Organizational Context

The individual profiled in this scenario has a long history of promoting others and positioning himself as a catalyst and mentor. He is in peak career – having already held several pivotal positions within the organization. He is widely respected and admired throughout the organization. He has a strong network within and outside the organization. This individual is good at formulating a business vision and turning it into a strategy. His personal goals do not enter the picture for this individual – he is firmly committed to the organization and, over the years, has been a driving force for innovation. He works best when there are supportive leaders in the picture, which allows him to focus on those who work for and report to him. If the broader culture is conducive, he will build an influential unit culture. He will also cultivate individuals who have strong potential. He also has a strong sense of ethics and values and will step in to support those who have been treated poorly. As a result, strong loyalties are surrounding this individual. The business strategy he is responsible for is an important one for the larger organization. To move this strategy forward, the individual splits his time between advancing the business agenda and building a robust divisional structure. He redesigns the environment to reinforce the new innovative culture, defines new job classifications, and promotes individuals within the division. This allows individuals to advance their own career goals while contributing to the business goals of the division. There is strong support for the business agenda, and the division achieves its goals.

The Business Challenge

This is an unusual business challenge. The success of the division is noteworthy due to the strong alignment of the division's strategy and culture. The division is held up to other divisions as a model to emulate. Unfortunately, the other units are not capable of moving in the same direction because their strategies and cultures are not as well balanced. Additionally, the critical support services needed to complete the division's business agenda are lacking in the technology division. As a result, the division has to build its internal technical team and infrastructure. This presents a conflict and contention with the larger organization. The other units begin to push back against this division. In the end, the internal politics put the top leaders of this division at risk. A weak corporate management structure and a weak organizational culture create pressures that are so great that the top manager is fired, and the individual profiled is reassigned to a client-focused role. The culture that grew around the division sustains, but the business strategy is redefined. The internal technical team and infrastructure are absorbed into the larger organizational structure and are lost in the existing culture and strategy.

The Result

Different individuals come to different conclusions and learn different lessons from this experience. Some individuals learn that it is not wise to be exploratory, innovative, or experimental. This is the lesson learned by mid-career professionals in the division. Those who were more aligned with the business strategy learn that it is safer to align themselves with individuals who are in the network of the corporate leadership. Perhaps the most significant impact, though, is the impact on the reputation of the larger organization. Corporate management failed to understand the extended networks of the two top managers of the division. They failed to see what impact – strategically and culturally – their actions would have on existing clients, stakeholders, and partners. This impact on the organization's reputation was significant.

Scenario D. Moderate Strategy Strong Culture

The Organizational Context

This individual is charged to lead a cross-agency team to develop a new job series that will better position each agency to weather the changes coming in the knowledge economy. Each agency has its own unique business goals and strategies, and its own cultures. There is an underlying goal of service, but this is interpreted in different ways by different agencies. This is not the first time this effort has been attempted. Two previous efforts have failed. The two earlier failures were due in part to the individuals tasked to lead them. In both cases, those individuals saw the success of the project as a career milestone and career promotion opportunity for themselves. This individual is in the late stages of their career and sees this as an essential business goal for the larger organization. She sees her role as that of catalyst and facilitator rather than "leader." As a result, she assembles a large panel of experts and ensures that none of these experts will use the assignment to advance their own goals. The previous events that shape the group's strategy are focused on learning events to ensure that the expert team level sets their background and expectations. In the process, a collaborative and supportive culture is created which bridges existing cultures.

The Business Challenge

Because of the two earlier failures, it is essential that the expert panel adopt a new and different approach. Because the leader has established a learning agenda for the experts, they have the space to rethink and refine their goals. This is an essential strategy because the agency they need to lobby to adopt their proposed new classification is under new leadership and is resistant to any further growth of the organization, or any new job series. This presents a significant challenge before the panel begins its work. The leader's flexibility in allowing the panel to explore new strategies highlights a possible new path – rather than hit the end goal head-on and push for a full new classification – the panel decides to address a core element of all job series – competencies. It is much less intrusive and threatening to lobby to add new competencies to all classes.

The Result

This is a winning strategy arrived at because the new leader created a panel culture that allowed this ground-breaking idea to emerge. By establishing these competencies, the panel will achieve its long term goal in a much more extensive way than by having established a dedicated, and thus more isolated, job series. By supporting an open and learning culture among experts – this individual created a winning strategy. Every expert on the panel can take this strategy back to their agency and lobby successfully for its adoption. This was a low-key effort that had significant, long term impacts.

Scenario E. Moderate Strategy Moderate Culture

The Organizational Context

The individual is an excellent catalyst and facilitator. She leads a unit that provides services to a large and historically well established public service agency. Her busy strategy – and challenge – is to bring the services strategy into the digital environment. The work of the unit is fragmented and represents nine different areas of practice, each firmly entrenched in their professions. The individual's facilitation competencies are essential to building bridges across these different communities. The individual has wisely devoted attention to strengthening the unit culture in hopes of creating an environment in which a common strategy will emerge. The culture did grow over five years, but the strategy has not grown internally at the same pace.

The Business Challenge

The challenge is that this individual does not have a firm grounding in any of these areas of practice. There is a heavy reliance on external experts as coaches and mentors. The individual has a strong social network within the agency, but this network does not extend beyond the headquarters location. To advance the strategy, this individual has reached out to respected experts and consultants in the field. This provides the strategic support needed, but it comes at a high cost. It is only available when the individual has a significant budget to leverage. In increasingly constrained economic times, the strategy stalls. This presents both challenges and opportunities. If the individual had a stronger grounding in the profession, they would be better positioned to advance the strategy and operationalize it. The challenge is comes from the outside. There is little ownership or uptake of the strategy among internal teams. Fortunately, the personal qualities of this individual incentivize her to pick up the challenge directly and advance the strategy. She adopts a focused personal learning strategy and increases her knowledge base in those areas that are the most pivotal for the strategy. Then she reaches out to those individuals who have the most influence in those communities to develop business strategies. In other words, she shifts her focus from continuing to advance the culture to bringing the strategy at least to the same level of the culture. Once these are balanced, she can move them forward.

The Result

For some time, this individual may be less visible on the national stage, or even on the state level stage. Instead, time and effort are devoted to deeper dives into strategy development and adoption across the agency. This means more visibility among those communities that "own" the fundamental strategies. And, more direct engagement with these communities. Given this individual's personality and professional goals, the expected result is the cultivation and promotion of a few key individuals who can form a critical support team for this individual when she returns to advance both the strategy and culture. The dedicated and focused support team will be critical to ensuring sustainability and

Scenario F. Moderate Strategy Weak Culture

The Organizational Context

This scenario describes a mid-tier academic institution striving to remake its image and reposition itself as a digital learning environment. New initiatives around special projects to raise the profile of the university. Private school so donated funds and resources and private interests will be dominant. The business strategy of the larger institution is good though it does not address the fundamental learning, teaching, and research capabilities of the institution. The strategy focuses on building the profile around high profile researchers, topics, or spaces. One of the new initiatives is around a 21st-century digital learning space – new concepts around access to resources, ways of engaging with students, and ways of learning – the redefinition of these underlying assumptions is of interest to younger professionals and younger generation students. The business strategy of the unit is defined by this individual and in collaboration with the organization's top leadership and selected new staff hired to support the initiative. Staff who are aligned with this individual's thinking are promoted to new leadership roles. In other words, this individual uses his personality and personal networks to build a new staffing support structure around the new facility. This effort to redefine the staff is also intended to shift the very traditional and conservative culture of the unit. The shift is effective for a year, and progress towards a new set of beliefs, values, and behaviors is evident. The transition to this new culture, though, is not yet fully adopted across the whole faculty and staff of the unit. There are traditional protections in place to ensure the security of existing faculty. The only way to change these positions and move out those who are not adopting the new culture and strategy appears to be to eliminate their base. The effort to consolidate what was a very distributed unit begins.

The Business Challenge

These are underway, and fears and concerns have begun to build particularly in the more senior faculty, when the unit leader – the individual who leads this effort over the past five years, receives an offer for a top leadership position at another top tier institution. This is a huge career advancement for the individual, and there is only one logical choice. The challenge is that the individual has devoted all his time to strategy and to cultivating a new staff to support the strategy. He has just begun to reorient and balance the culture when he leaves. There is no apparent successor to continue to move the culture development forward. The business strategy is completed, and a new leader takes ownership of that strategy. This individual is also charismatic, but is new to the institution and is still regarded with suspicion by the senior faculty. Also, the second-tier managers represent the cultures of their business areas – and reveal a culture that is much more fragmented than the institutional management previously understood. The interim appointment of a new leader is not effective, so the parent organization recruits a new leader from outside. During the recruitment process, a charismatic individual is recruited, who few realize is highly political. The new individual has ambitions beyond the current institution and has personal business goals and strategies that are not focused on completing the cultural realignment. Instead, the new leader builds internal coalitions at a level above his position and uses that leverage to eliminate any internal competition simply. The new leader and former heir apparent leader are dismissed under a cloud, several senior managers are encouraged to leave, and the tenured status of senior faculty is threatened. Most senior faculty take early retirement or accept lower-level positions.

The Result

The institution achieves just the opposite result as initially intended. Rather than promote the institution as a 21st-century innovative culture and strategy, all of the internal struggles and scandals are exposed to the outside world. The new leader recruited from the outside continues to consolidate his power within the organization and creates a new corporate-level role for himself. This allows him to step out of the unit daily and to create a new structure of technology-focused colleagues across the organization. He builds a new network. The new leader leverages the network to make a jump to a top administrative position in another organization, leaving the business unit to continue to decline and the reputation of the organization in shambles. His charismatic personality diverts attention to himself and allows others to believe the unit failures are attributable to the unit's culture.

Scenario G. Weak Strategy Strong Culture

The Organizational Context

This scenario presents a profile of an individual who is a member of a small internal-client focused unit within a larger organization. The organization has many internal stakeholders. The primary service these clients need is technical support for operations, e.g., workflow and process management. The organization has detailed requirements for project management and complicated guidelines for managing projects. Each project is designed to support a unique external environment, and it is essential to track the different players as well as the data and information generated by the project. The organization also has rigorous internal reporting requirements. The unit tasked to develop the solution is the unit to which this individual has been assigned. There is a clear business strategy laid out by the clients, and the organization supports this strategy. Delivering on the strategy, though, is not trivial because it requires collecting and synthesizing requirements from many different stakeholders. The manager of the business unit is a very mild-mannered mid-career man. The manager represents a different national culture and management control philosophy than this individual. The other members of the teamwork well with the manager but are not as dominant personalities as this individual. The individual represents a culture where men are dominant, and particularly men from a particular economic and social class. There is a cultural clash within the unit, created by this one individual. He continually challenges the manager internally and has begun to challenge him in other settings. The top-level manager has tried to coach and mentor him, but because he is from a lower social and economic class in the same culture, he does not challenge or reprimand the individual. The individual learns that adopting aggressive behavior within the division gains exposure. Cycle by cycle, he improves his standing until he pushes the manager out of the unit. In effect, he has reshaped the unit culture to support his personal business goals. He has created a culture of personality within his unit. Outside of the division, he has built a strong social and personal network with key clients and strengthened his profile. In this scenario, the organization has a clear and intentional business strategy. The individual also has a clear and intentional business strategy. He manages to align these two in the eyes of the client. Moreover, the culture has been redefined to support the strategy. So, it would appear that we have achieved a balance. Where is the challenge?

The Business Challenge

The challenge has existed over the years but has been hidden from all but a few individuals. Client expectations have been created for a fully functional internal work process support application that would also produce required reports automatically, and track progress against goals. The business challenge is that the individual who has maneuvered himself into a position of authority and responsibility has no technical background and does not work well with or communicate well with others. To the extent that he can "talk about" what he will deliver rather than to "do design" or "engineer a solution," he succeeds. The challenge becomes apparent when developers begin to voice concerns about the specifications they have been given to work with. The challenge grows when a development and migration environment is created, and no contingency or fall back options are defined before migration. No full testing regime is put in place to ensure the applications will work as promised. To ensure deadlines are met, the migration of data from existing sources to the new application is launched – with no backup. A major component fails, and ten years of historical data are accidentally lost with no backup. The mistake is hidden from clients. Only after roll-out do clients discover they are unable to access some of their historical information. When asked about the challenge, the division continues to hide the problem and the cause.

The Result

Every organization has formal and informal cultures. In this case, the formal culture is not one that will call out and punish an individual for making a mistake. When a significant challenge arises, the individual responsible is reassigned to another project or unit, offered early retirement, or simply moved to another division in the organization. In other words, they become invisible. Because of the individual's stature, he was simply reassigned to a new role where he could lead an existing function that was working well. This was not the end of the story, though, as the animosity that he had created through his 'strong-arm' tactics encouraged those involved in the migration to share details about what happened through their informal networks. Ultimately, the informal culture exposed the cause and effect. The division relied on a small group of individuals to come in and remedy the problems created during migration. In the end, the reputation of the division suffered significantly. The message communicated to the internal client base was that relying on the division carried risks

Scenario H. Weak Strategy Moderate Culture

The Organizational Context

In this scenario, we describe the impact of an individual whose personal goals are to secure an administrative position to achieve financial security. The individual has no specific business strategy other than to take advantage of conflict and disruption in the environment to advance. The individual targets a position as Director of Information Technology but has no background in either information or technology. Initially, the individual is in a mid-level position, which she achieved through political and social connections. To achieve a culturally supportive position, the individual has hired people who are dependent upon her for their positions – not top-level individuals in the field, but they are politically and socially supportive. The individual does not attempt to build a knowledge base from which to operate but instead attempts to promote herself as an expert in the community – she secures keynote roles and teaching positions – but does not deliver on those roles. She takes advantage of internal chaos and conflict to mask these insecurities and continue to rely on the existing social and political network she has created.

The Business Challenge

The individual is moved into the director position on an interim basis, but the lack of a business strategy and the exclusive culture result in new recruitment. An individual from another area of the organization is chosen for the position, and this individual leaves the institution. She remains in the area, though, and retains a role in the political and social network. Being the only professional in the new organization, she is more successful and has a better opportunity to learn in a less public way.

The Result

The new director redefines the information technology strategy, but much of the work and foundation that was put in place in previous years has eroded and is now outdated. Given the internal chaos and conflict, there are few resources available to rebuilt or redefine a new strategy. The strategy must be strengthened, but the only option is to adopt and replace it with an existing strategy from the larger organization. In the end, the function stabilizes but does not advance. The unit fails to achieve the original business vision. The unit culture is continued by a few professionals who remain in place, but the culture and strategy are not aligned. The strategy reflects external cultures, and the internal culture is more aligned with the historical strategy

Scenario I. Weak Strategy Weak Culture

The Organizational Context

The individual profiled in this scenario has an uneven career path over the past thirty years. Initially coming from a mathematical sciences background, the individual moved into a data analytics position for a significant scientific agency. While the individual had strong professional and academic competencies, management, and people skills were lacking. These were not essential in the positions she held early in her career. As she attempted to advance, though, along a management path, the lack of competencies presented a challenge. A strong family and social grounding in the law enforcement community was a personal culture that was in conflict with the unit and organizational culture. While the individual had never been in the military, family, and community structure tended to favor strict command and control.

Additionally, the most highly valued aspect of the new unit culture was that of loyalty to those in positions of power. As the individual advanced through management positions, staff were favored and promoted for their loyalties. At a critical point in her career, she was recruited for a significant management position in a high profile organization. Her recruitment was in large part due to her strong law enforcement management philosophy. This approach served her well for the first six months of her tenure at the new organization. While her culture was in contrast to the culture of the organization, it aligned with the culture of the CIO. Any conflicts that arose were smoothed over by the CIO. The business challenge arose when the CIO was dismissed for a significant error in judgment. After that, the support network for this individual was no longer in place.

The Business Challenge

The business challenge existed both within and outside the business unit. The individual had identified individuals who were pliable and likely to be loyal to her – and dependent upon her for career advancement. The previous manager, while demoted, was retained within the unit. This individual was dependent upon the new manager for continued residency in the country. New individuals were added to the unit, who owed their position to the new manager. There were two individuals in the unit, though, who were not reliant on the new manager, and they were targeted for removal early in her tenure. The internal cultural challenges were exposed when it became clear that the new manager did not have a practical strategy to advance. Instead, the practical strategy came from one of the individuals the manager had targeted for removal. There was a temporary reduction in hostilities so the manager could adopt and claim the new strategy. The challenge came when it was clear that she did not have the competencies to gain adoption of the strategy. This responsibility was given to the individual she had targeted for removal. When it became clear that the manager was unlikely to succeed, she shifted the strategy and brought in a commercial company to define and advance an industry strategy. This approach was supported.

The Result

Unfortunately, it also became clear that there was a behind the scenes negotiation to over-compensate the company for their efforts and a strategic alliance between the manager and the company to train and position the manager as a future corporate executive. This constituted a breach of ethics and was the final straw for the organization. The manager was notified that her probationary period would not be approved and that her contract would be terminated. The individual reached outside of the organization to a political contact from the law enforcement and military community to put pressure on the organization to reassign her to a different area of the organization. It took another two years before the individual was terminated. The impact on the unit was dissolution and destruction. The unit was eliminated, and individual staff were reassigned to different teams. Two critical individuals left before the termination struggles began. The function has never been reconstituted. In this scenario, we see how the personal strategies and cultures of an individual can have a significant, negative impact on a business unit and an organization as a whole. This should be but is not an uncommon scenario.

BALANCING INDIVIDUAL LEVEL CULTURES AND STRATEGIES

The view from this perspective is different from that of the unit or the organization level because it is the individual characteristics and propensities that dominate here. It is also different from the unit level, though individuals can have a significant effect on the strategy and culture of the unit and team. What does balancing mean at this level? Balancing could mean learning how to leverage the qualities of a dominant individual, learning how to strengthen the qualities of an individual, knowing when those qualities are simply not suitable, and providing advice and guidance to the individual on tempering, growing, or leveraging their qualities. Balancing also means understanding the role that the individual plays in the unit and the organization – and how to assess the impact – positive or negative – resulting from changes you might make. What have we learned from these scenarios? We can see how an individual with strong personal business goals and a strong ability to build a culture around themselves and their agenda can affect the unit and the organization. What happens if the individual is removed? Or if they are transferred? What happens if the individual is promoted? What happens if the individual is absent from the scene for some time? Removing or transferring such an individual can have a significant impact on the unit and the organization. In the industrial economy, removing a "damaged" or "malfunctioning" component or resource will improve the result. This is not always the case when the component is the knowledge capital of an individual. Before any actions are taken – positive or negative – the unit and the organization should consider the potential impacts. How dependent is the unit or organization on this individual? If a founder, what will happen when they leave or retire? If an innovator, what happens if they are shifted to management? These are all new questions we need to consider when we focus on balancing culture and strategy at the individual level.

CONCLUSION

After reading this chapter, you should be able to:

- Explain why we care about aligning strategies and cultures at the individual level
- Adapt the framework to the unit and team levels
- Apply the framework to unit and teams in your organization
- Document the assessment for units and teams
- Identify gaps and pain points across the organization

ADDITIONAL READING

Ang, S., & Inkpen, A. C. (2008). Cultural intelligence and offshore outsourcing success: A framework of firm-level intercultural capability. *Decision Sciences*, *39*(3), 337–358. doi:10.1111/j.1540-5915.2008.00195.x

Ang, S., & Van Dyne, L. (2015). *Handbook of cultural intelligence: Theory, measurement, and applications*. Routledge. doi:10.4324/9781315703855

Ang, S., Van Dyne, L., & Koh, C. (2006). Personality correlates of the four-factor model of cultural intelligence. *Group & Organization Management*, *31*(1), 100–123. doi:10.1177/1059601105275267

Ang, S., Van Dyne, L., Koh, C., Ng, K. Y., Templer, K. J., Tay, C., & Chandrasekar, N. A. (2007). Cultural intelligence: Its measurement and effects on cultural judgment and decision making, cultural adaptation and task performance. *Management and Organization Review*, *3*(3), 335–371. doi:10.1111/j.1740-8784.2007.00082.x

Apud, S., Lenartowicz, T., & Johnson, J. P. (2003). Intercultural competence: what do practitioners really know? *Proceedings, Academy of International Business South-East Region Conference.*

Bellot, J. (2011). Defining and assessing organizational culture. *Nursing Forum*, *46*(1), 29–37. doi:10.1111/j.1744-6198.2010.00207.x PMID:21306393

Betancourt, J. R., Green, A. R., Carrillo, J. E., & Owusu Ananeh-Firempong, I. I. (2016). Defining cultural competence: A practical framework for addressing racial/ethnic disparities in health and health care. *Public Health Reports.* PMID:12815076

Bhui, K., Warfa, N., Edonya, P., McKenzie, K., & Bhugra, D. (2007). Cultural competence in mental health care: A review of model evaluations. *BMC Health Services Research*, *7*(1), 15. doi:10.1186/1472-6963-7-15 PMID:17266765

Brislin, R., Worthley, R., & Macnab, B. (2006). Cultural intelligence: Understanding behaviors that serve people's goals. *Group & Organization Management*, *31*(1), 40–55. doi:10.1177/1059601105275262

Brouthers, K. D., & Brouthers, L. E. (2001). Explaining the national cultural distance paradox. *Journal of International Business Studies*, *32*(1), 177–189. doi:10.1057/palgrave.jibs.8490944

Bu-Qammaz, A., Dikmen, I., & Birgonul, M. T. (2006). Cultural risk assessment in construction projects. *CCIM2006 Sustainable Development through Culture and Innovation.*

Campinha-Bacote, J. (2002). The process of cultural competence in the delivery of healthcare services: A model of care. *Journal of Transcultural Nursing*, *13*(3), 181–184. doi:10.1177/10459602013003003 PMID:12113146

Cooke, R. A., & Szumal, J. L. (2000). Using the Organizational Culture Inventory to understand the operating cultures of organizations. Handbook of organizational culture and climate, 4, 1032-1045.

Crandall, S. J., George, G., Marion, G. S., & Davis, S. (2003). Applying theory to the design of cultural competency training for medical students: A case study. *Academic Medicine*, *78*(6), 588–594. doi:10.1097/00001888-200306000-00007 PMID:12805037

de la Garza Carranza, M. T., & Egri, C. P. (2010). Managerial cultural intelligence and small business in Canada. *Management Revue*, 353-371.

Earley, P. C., & Mosakowski, E. (2002). Linking culture and behavior in organizations: Suggestions for theory development and research methodology. In *The many faces of multi-level issues* (pp. 297–319). Emerald Group Publishing Limited. doi:10.1016/S1475-9144(02)01038-X

Earley, P. C., Murnieks, C., & Mosakowski, E. (2007). Cultural intelligence and the global mindset. In *The global mindset* (pp. 75–103). Emerald Group Publishing Limited. doi:10.1016/S1571-5027(07)19004-5

Elenkov, D. S., & Manev, I. M. (2005). Social Culture Intelligence, Top-Level Leadership And Innovation Influence: An International Study. In Academy of Management Proceedings (Vol. 2005, No. 1, pp. F1-F6). Briarcliff Manor, NY: Academy of Management.

Elenkov, D. S., & Manev, I. M. (2009). Senior expatriate leadership's effects on innovation and the role of cultural intelligence. *Journal of World Business*, *44*(4), 357–369. doi:10.1016/j.jwb.2008.11.001

Emirbayer, M., & Goodwin, J. (1994). Network analysis, culture, and the problem of agency. *American Journal of Sociology*, *99*(6), 1411–1454. doi:10.1086/230450

Fowler, S. M., & Mumford, M. G. (1999). *Intercultural Sourcebook: Cross-Cultural Training Methods* (Vol. 2). Yarmouth, ME: Intercultural Press, Inc.

Gallego-Toledo, J. M. (2015). Cultural profiling and a Chinese experience. *Journal of Chinese Human Resource Management*, *6*(2), 120–132. doi:10.1108/JCHRM-09-2015-0014

Gelfand, M. J., Imai, L., & Fehr, R. (2008). Thinking intelligently about cultural intelligence. *Handbook on cultural intelligence: Theory, measurement and applications*, 375-388.

Glenn, S. S. (1988). Contingencies and metacontingencies: Toward a synthesis of behavior analysis and cultural materialism. *The Behavior Analyst*, *11*(2), 161–179. doi:10.1007/BF03392470 PMID:22478011

Glisson, C. (2007). Assessing and changing organizational culture and climate for effective services. *Research on Social Work Practice*, *17*(6), 736–747. doi:10.1177/1049731507301659

Groves, K. S., & Feyerherm, A. E. (2011). Leader cultural intelligence in context: Testing the moderating effects of team cultural diversity on leader and team performance. *Group & Organization Management*, *36*(5), 535–566. doi:10.1177/1059601111415664

Hofstede, G. (1980). Culture and organizations. *International Studies of Management & Organization*, *10*(4), 15–41. doi:10.1080/00208825.1980.11656300

Hofstede, G. (1984). *Culture's consequences: International differences in work-related values*. Beverly Hills, CA: Sage.

Hofstede, G. (2001). *Culture's consequences: Comparing values, behaviors, institutions and organizations across nations*. Thousand Oaks, CA: Sage.

Hofstede, G., Hofstede, G. J., & Minkov, M. (2010). *Cultures and organizations: Software of the mind (revised and expanded)*. New York, NY: McGraw-Hill.

Imai, L., & Gelfand, M. J. (2010). The culturally intelligent negotiator: The impact of cultural intelligence (CQ) on negotiation sequences and outcomes. *Organizational Behavior and Human Decision Processes*, *112*(2), 83–98. doi:10.1016/j.obhdp.2010.02.001

Jang, H. Y., & Barnett, G. A. (1994). Cultural differences in organizational communication: A semantic network analysis 1. *Bulletin of Sociological Methodology. Bulletin de Methodologie Sociologique*, *44*(1), 31–59. doi:10.1177/075910639404400104

Janssens, M., & Brett, J. M. (2006). Cultural intelligence in global teams: A fusion model of collaboration. *Group & Organization Management*, *31*(1), 124–153. doi:10.1177/1059601105275268

Johnson, J. P., Lenartowicz, T., & Apud, S. (2006). Cross-cultural competence in international business: Toward a definition and a model. *Journal of International Business Studies*, *37*(4), 525–543. doi:10.1057/palgrave.jibs.8400205

Kendra, K., & Taplin, L. J. (2004). Project success: A cultural framework. *Project Management Journal*, *35*(1), 30–45. doi:10.1177/875697280403500104

King, T., & Byers, J. F. (2007). A review of organizational culture instruments for nurse executives. *JONA: The Journal of Nursing Administration, 37*(1), 21–31. doi:10.1097/00005110-200701000-00005 PMID:17172969

Kirmayer, L. J. (2012). Rethinking cultural competence. *Transcultural Psychiatry, 49*(2), 149–164. doi:10.1177/1363461512444673 PMID:22508634

Koh, C., Joseph, D., & Ang, S. (2009, February). Cultural intelligence and collaborative work: intercultural competencies in global technology work teams. In *Proceedings of the 2009 international workshop on Intercultural collaboration* (pp. 261-264). ACM. 10.1145/1499224.1499271

Koutroumanis, D. A., & Alexakis, G. (2009). Organizational Culture In The Restaurant Industry: Implications For Change. *Journal of Organizational Culture, Communications and Conflict, 13*(2).

Kumas-Tan, Z., Beagan, B., Loppie, C., MacLeod, A., & Frank, B. (2007). Measures of cultural competence: Examining hidden assumptions. *Academic Medicine, 82*(6), 548–557. doi:10.1097/ACM.0b013e3180555a2d PMID:17525538

Lamal, P. A. (Ed.). (1997). *Cultural contingencies: Behavior analytic perspectives on cultural practices*. Greenwood Publishing Group.

Lie, D. A., Lee-Rey, E., Gomez, A., Bereknyei, S., & Braddock, C. H. III. (2011). Does cultural competency training of health professionals improve patient outcomes? A systematic review and proposed algorithm for future research. *Journal of General Internal Medicine, 26*(3), 317–325. doi:10.100711606-010-1529-0 PMID:20953728

Livermore, D., & Soon, A. N. G. (2015). *Leading with cultural intelligence: The real secret to success*. Amacom.

Livermore, D., Van Dyne, L., & Ang, S. (2012). Cultural intelligence: Why every leader needs it. *Intercultural Management Quarterly, 13*(2), 18–21.

MacNab, B., Brislin, R., & Worthley, R. (2012). Experiential cultural intelligence development: Context and individual attributes. *International Journal of Human Resource Management, 23*(7), 1320–1341. doi:10.1080/09585192.2011.581636

MacNab, B., Brislin, R., Worthley, R., Galperin, B. L., Jenner, S., Lituchy, T. R., ... Bess, D. (2007). Culture and ethics management: Whistle-blowing and internal reporting within a NAFTA country context. *International Journal of Cross Cultural Management*, *7*(1), 5–28. doi:10.1177/1470595807075167

Mannion, R., Konteh, F. H., & Davies, H. T. O. (2009). Assessing organisational culture for quality and safety improvement: A national survey of tools and tool use. *BMJ Quality & Safety*, *18*(2), 153–156. doi:10.1136/qshc.2007.024075 PMID:19342532

Maznevski, M. (2008). Cultural intelligence: Domain and assessment. *International Journal of Cross Cultural Management*, *8*(2), 123–143. doi:10.1177/1470595808091787

Morosini, P., Shane, S., & Singh, H. (1998). National cultural distance and cross-border acquisition performance. *Journal of International Business Studies*, *29*(1), 137–158. doi:10.1057/palgrave.jibs.8490029

Mosakowski, E., Calic, G., & Earley, P. C. (2013). Cultures as learning laboratories: What makes some more effective than others? *Academy of Management Learning & Education*, *12*(3), 512–526. doi:10.5465/amle.2013.0149

Mtolo, S. G. (2017). *The Influence of Cultural Intelligence on the relationship between Social Capital and Entrepreneurial Performance: A study of foreign traders in Johannesburg's informal economy* (Doctoral dissertation).

Mueller, S. T., Sieck, W. R., & Veinott, E. (2007). *Cultural metrics: A finite mixture models approach* (Technical Report DAAD19-01-2-0009). Fairborn, OH: Klein Associates Division of ARA.

Mueller, S. T., & Veinott, E. S. (2008). Cultural mixture modeling: Identifying cultural consensus (and disagreement) using finite mixture modeling. *Proceedings of the Cognitive Science Society*.

Ng, K. Y., Van Dyne, L., & Ang, S. (2009). From experience to experiential learning: Cultural intelligence as a learning capability for global leader development. *Academy of Management Learning & Education*, *8*(4), 511–526. doi:10.5465/amle.8.4.zqr511

Ng, R. (2013). Cultural intelligence. *The encyclopedia of cross-cultural psychology*, 310-313.

Norton, W. (1995). Behavior Analysis and the Cultural Geographic Study of Place. *Journal of Cultural Geography, 15*(2), 1–15. doi:10.1080/08873639509478351

O'Reilly, C. A. III, Caldwell, D. F., Chatman, J. A., & Doerr, B. (2014). The promise and problems of organizational culture: CEO personality, culture, and firm performance. *Group & Organization Management, 39*(6), 595–625. doi:10.1177/1059601114550713

Oolders, T., Chernyshenko, O. S., & Stark, S. (2008). Cultural intelligence as a mediator of relationships between openness to experience and adaptive performance. Handbook of cultural intelligence: Theory, measurement, and applications, 145-158.

Pavlidis, G., Koutsoudis, A., Arnaoutoglou, F., Tsioukas, V., & Chamzas, C. (2007). Methods for 3D digitization of cultural heritage. *Journal of Cultural Heritage, 8*(1), 93–98. doi:10.1016/j.culher.2006.10.007

Peterson, B. (2011). *Cultural intelligence: A guide to working with people from other cultures*. Nicholas Brealey.

Pieraccini, M., Guidi, G., & Atzeni, C. (2001). 3D digitizing of cultural heritage. *Journal of Cultural Heritage, 2*(1), 63–70. doi:10.1016/S1296-2074(01)01108-6

Purnell, L. (2002). The Purnell model for cultural competence. *Journal of Transcultural Nursing, 13*(3), 193–196. doi:10.1177/10459602013003006 PMID:12113149

Rasmussen, L. J., Sieck, W. R., & Osland, J. (2010). *Using cultural models of decision making to develop and assess cultural sensemaking competence. In Advances in Cross-Cultural Decision Making*. Boca Raton, FL: CRC Press, Taylor and Francis Group.

Rockstuhl, T., Dulebohn, J. H., Ang, S., & Shore, L. M. (2012). Leader–member exchange (LMX) and culture: A meta-analysis of correlates of LMX across 23 countries. *The Journal of Applied Psychology, 97*(6), 1097–1130. doi:10.1037/a0029978 PMID:22985117

Rockstuhl, T., Seiler, S., Ang, S., Van Dyne, L., & Annen, H. (2011). Beyond general intelligence (IQ) and emotional intelligence (EQ): The role of cultural intelligence (CQ) on cross-border leadership effectiveness in a globalized world. *The Journal of Social Issues, 67*(4), 825–840. doi:10.1111/j.1540-4560.2011.01730.x

Seufert, S. (2002). Cultural perspectives. In *Handbook on information technologies for education and training* (pp. 411–421). Berlin: Springer. doi:10.1007/978-3-662-07682-8_26

Shenkar, O. (2001). Cultural distance revisited: Towards a more rigorous conceptualization and measurement of cultural differences. *Journal of International Business Studies, 32*(3), 519–535. doi:10.1057/palgrave.jibs.8490982

Sieck, W. R., Rasmussen, L. J., & Smart, P. (2010). Cultural network analysis: A cognitive approach to cultural modeling. In *Network science for military coalition operations: Information exchange and interaction* (pp. 237–255). IGI Global. doi:10.4018/978-1-61520-855-5.ch011

Sousa, C. M., & Bradley, F. (2006). Cultural distance and psychic distance: Two peas in a pod? *Journal of International Marketing, 14*(1), 49–70. doi:10.1509/jimk.14.1.49

Stanco, F., Battiato, S., & Gallo, G. (Eds.). (2011). *Digital imaging for cultural heritage preservation: Analysis, restoration, and reconstruction of ancient artworks*. CRC Press.

Sue, D. W. (2001). Multidimensional facets of cultural competence. *The Counseling Psychologist, 29*(6), 790–821. doi:10.1177/0011000001296002

Sue, D. W., & Torino, G. C. (2005). Racial-cultural competence: Awareness, knowledge, and skills. Handbook of racial-cultural psychology and counseling: Training and practice, 2, 3-18.

Tarique, I., & Takeuchi, R. (2008). Developing cultural intelligence: The roles of international nonwork experiences. Handbook of cultural intelligence: Theory, measurement, and applications, 56-70.

Thom, D. H., Tirado, M. D., Woon, T. L., & McBride, M. R. (2006). Development and evaluation of a cultural competency training curriculum. *BMC Medical Education, 6*(1), 38. doi:10.1186/1472-6920-6-38 PMID:16872504

Thomas, D. C. (2006). Domain and development of cultural intelligence: The importance of mindfulness. *Group & Organization Management, 31*(1), 78–99. doi:10.1177/1059601105275266

Thomas, D. C. (2015). Cultural intelligence. Wiley Encyclopedia of Management, 1-3.

Thomas, D. C., Elron, E., Stahl, G., Ekelund, B. Z., Ravlin, E. C., Cerdin, J. L., ... Brislin, R. (2012). Development of the cultural intelligence assessment. In *Advances in global leadership* (pp. 155–178). Emerald Group Publishing Limited. doi:10.1108/S1535-1203(2012)0000007011

Triandis, H. C. (2006). Cultural intelligence in organizations. *Group & Organization Management*, *31*(1), 20–26. doi:10.1177/1059601105275253

Triandis, H. C. (2008). Cultural intelligence. Handbook of cultural intelligence.

Van Dyne, L., Ang, S., & Koh, C. (2015). Development and validation of the CQS: The cultural intelligence scale. In *Handbook of cultural intelligence* (pp. 34–56). Routledge.

Van Dyne, L., Ang, S., Ng, K. Y., Rockstuhl, T., Tan, M. L., & Koh, C. (2012). Sub-dimensions of the four factor model of cultural intelligence: Expanding the conceptualization and measurement of cultural intelligence. *Social and Personality Psychology Compass*, *6*(4), 295–313. doi:10.1111/j.1751-9004.2012.00429.x

Wagner, W., & Yamori, K. (1999). Can culture be a variable? Dispositional explanation and cultural metrics. *Progress in Asian social psychology, 2.*

Section 5

Managing Strategic and Cultural Risks

Chapter 10
Strategic and Cultural Risk

ABSTRACT

This chapter explores the concepts of harm and risk and translates them to the strategy and culture context. The peer-reviewed and gray literature speak to generic hazards and threats whose consequences might be amplified by cultural and information behaviors and actions. This chapter takes the discussion of hazards and risks one step further by speaking to specific hazards and threats related to organizations' business and information cultures and information strategies. The business literature tells us that the rate of strategic failure is somewhere between 60% and 90%. The authors describe several common risk factors that can be addressed by redefining the strategic planning process. The ISO 31000/31010 risk management process is adapted to account for these factors.

HARM AND RISK – DEFINITION AND CHARACTERIZATION

What do we mean by harm? What do we mean by risk? Both of these concepts are context and time-specific. The peer-reviewed and gray literature speak to generic hazards and threats whose consequences might be amplified by cultural and information behaviors and actions. This text takes the discussion of hazards one step further by speaking to specific hazards and threats that are germane to an organization's business and information cultures, and its information strategies. This presents a challenge for the authors – we must translate those generic definitions and discussions of hazards and threats to a cultural and information context. This is the starting point for this chapter.

DOI: 10.4018/978-1-7998-4315-3.ch010

Harm is defined as the negative impacts that might result in the organization, the unit or team, or the individual if our business or information strategies fail. What kinds of harm can a strategy-culture failure produce? If culture undermines the organization's strategy, it can affect any functions that are strategy-dependent or strategy-drive. This means all functions. Because strategies speak to an organization's fundamental business success and performance, any kind of failure or suboptimal realization of a strategy will impact the organization's health or well-being. We want to minimize risk, and particularly those forms of risk that may be attributed to the use or misuse of information to the organization. What are the most common reasons business strategies fail? What are the most common reasons information strategies fail?

Risk is measured by degrees of harm. We can never eliminate risk, but we can identify the levels of harm that are likely to occur and the degree of harm we can and cannot tolerate. How do business managers think of risk?

Business managers and accountants look at risk from a practical perspective, in a specific context, and at a specific point in time. Business and financial managers look at risk as a threat of liability, loss, or another occurrence that is caused by internal or external vulnerabilities. Most commonly, business managers and accountants focus on financial risk or risks associated with investments and return on the investment. Managers gauge whether a risk is worth taking based on the expected value – of both a positive and a negative result. Business managers assess and analyze risks and make investment decisions based on their knowledge of the possible outcomes, the probability that each of those outcomes will occur, and the value of each outcome. For physical and financial capital investments and risks, we have built-in standard controls and remedies. We can buy insurance, or we have a depreciation model that allows us to manage risks over time.

Economists tend to look at risk on a more macro level than do business managers and accountants. Economists tend to look at risk at a sector or an industry level, or based on the behavior of a particular economic factor. Economists factor in uncertainty (e.g., lack of information or varying qualities of information) and culture as ancillary or side effects of risk. These are essential considerations, but they look at knowledge indirectly – not as a commodity or capital but as an input to a business decision. They offer some guidance, but they are not direct translations or solutions to the challenges we raise in this text.

The goal of effective risk management is to understand and manage uncertainty effectively. Executives have to be the integrators of the different risk positions of the organization and its internal and external environments. Cultural and information risk models and methods need to be designed for integration into the organization's overall risk portfolio.

MANAGING STRATEGIC RISK

Strategic risks occur for many reasons (Borek Parlikad and Woodall, 2011; Borek, Woodall and Parlikad, 2011; Borek et al., 2011; Clark, 2013; Hardy and Williams, 2010; Jarvelainen, 2012; Khidzir, Arshad and Mohamed, 2010; Lemieux, 2004; Mitchell, 2009). At this stage in the process, we want to identify the reasons and design a remedy that will reduce the risk to a level we can tolerate. The business literature tells us that the rate of strategic failure is somewhere between 60% and 90%. These levels of failure are neither acceptable nor sustainable in the knowledge economy. It is critical to business success that we identify and reduce the most common risk factors. The authors highlight the most common risk factors referenced in the literature. These risk factors will be very familiar to the reader at this point.

Risk Factor 1. Strategies are Defined Prematurely

Resources are not available, information is not thoroughly identified or leveraged, and culture is not aligned with the business. Ideas, dreams, and visions are essential starting points, but they must be translated into goals and objectives and then be supported with a strategy. There is a period of learning and positioning that must precede the development of a strategy. Business strategies must be grounded in reliable information, and strong information strategies must support them. For a practical example, we refer the reader to Chapter 9 Scenario E.

Risk Factor 2. The Wrong People are Involved in Developing or Implementing the Strategy

Strategic plans are too often defined by a few senior managers and published for others to carry out. Those tasked to operationalize the strategy have little input. The strategy will be interpreted and translated at the unit or the team level, or it will be ignored at these levels. It is not that senior managers are the wrong people but that there might have been significant gaps in information when the strategy was formulated. Senior management may have knowledge gaps when it comes to the detail required to build the strategy for units and teams. Without including functional level managers, important questions might not be asked. Strategies should always be grounded on input from those who have front line and firsthand knowledge. The people who execute the strategy have first-hand knowledge and generally the best understanding of how to achieve the objectives in their area. For a practical example, we refer the reader to Chapter 7 Scenario D, and Chapter 8 Scenario A.

Risk Factor 3. Right People are not Involved in Developing or Implementing the Strategy

When the right people are not included in strategy creation, it can be detrimental to the success of the strategy. When the strategic planning circle is too small, and managers from different levels in the organization are not included in the formulation, critical pieces of knowledge and ideas are forgone. A small strategic planning circle also hinders buy-in from the rest of the organization. If employees are not allowed to be involved in the creation stage, it is going to be a lot harder to gain their buy-in, in the implementation stage. Opening up the strategic planning phase and extending the conversation to the rest of the organization will not only give you great suggestions and feedback but once the strategy is released, the buy-in will be easier to achieve. For a practical example, we refer the reader to Chapter 9 Scenario F.

Risk Factor 4. The Strategy is Too Abstract or General

Strategies fail when they lack focus and detail. Abstract strategies that fail to nail down any concrete actions, goals, or projects. Strategies should be specific, measurable, achievable, realistic, and timely. For a practical example, we refer the reader to Chapter 7 Scenario F.

Risk Factor 5. The Strategy is Not Honest

Strategies should be realistic and practical. They should clearly define limitations. Make sure there is a real consensus among those who will be tasked with realizing it. While strategic objectives may stretch the organization, they still must be realistic. Make sure that those impacted by it are committed to it. This speaks to culture – and the alignment of cultures – of units and individuals. It is essential that individuals not feel marginalized when it comes to supporting the strategy. Units and individuals must feel empowered and engaged. For a practical example, we refer the reader to Chapter 9 Scenario G.

Risk Factor 6. The Strategy Does Not Align With Core Business Competencies

The misalignment between a new strategy and the core competencies of a company is a primary cause of failure. This speaks to the alignment of organization and unit level strategies. Organizational strategies should build upon and leverage unit level strategies. For a practical example, we refer the reader to Chapter 7 Scenario C, Chapter 8 Scenarios D and F.

Risk Factor 7. Organization's Culture is Resistant to Change

The best strategies will fail unless they have a supportive culture. By definition, strategies are about change. Moreover, people are not always anxious to change. Some people will always be more comfortable with what is familiar. This is an opportunity to review the culture and why people across the organization are resistant to change. For a practical example, we refer the reader to Chapter 8 Scenario G.

Risk Factor 8. The Strategy Does Not Have Rigorous Management or Operations Plan

Creating a strategy is the first step in a longer process. Translating your strategy to a plan and tactics requires buy-in and support. It means assigning roles and responsibilities for realizing the strategy, and for gaining buy-in across the organization. For a practical example, we refer the reader to Chapter 7 Scenario G.

Risk Factor 9. The Strategy Sets Unrealistic Goals and Cannot Be Achieved

Unrealistic goals are a big problem in many strategies. When your goals are unrealistic, they will seem un-achievable and end up demoralizing your people. While your unrealistic goals may look good on paper, they can be quite challenging for those who are charged to execute them. If goals seem unattainable, employees will lose enthusiasm and may turn toward resentment instead. Realistic strategies are based on a good understanding of past performance, current resources, and organizational information. For a practical example, we refer the reader to Chapter 8 Scenario E.

Risk Factor 10. The strategy Has no Accountability – No One is Responsible for its Success or Failure

Alignment of strategies across all three levels and the assignment of responsibilities for strategies are critical success factors. When it is not clear who owns the different parts of the strategy, it is easy for goals and objectives to slip through the cracks and miss their deadlines. Accountability is not about having someone to blame but ensuring there is someone who owns and takes the lead on realizing the goals. Periodic meetings, reports, and course corrections are essential. Ensure that every goal, objective, and project has at least one owner. Ensure that each manager at each level is clear about the accountabilities and authorities they have for strategy implementation; it is about all managers understanding their role as a people manager. If people are not clear of their role and their accountabilities for strategy delivery or are not held accountable for their work, it will be business as usual for all but a few frustrated individuals. Clear accountability helps drive change. For a practical example, we refer the reader to Chapter 8 Scenario B.

Risk Factor 11. Lack of Communication

Communication helps with organizational alignment. If a plan does not get communicated to employees, they will not understand their role or how they contribute to achieving the organization's strategy. For a practical example, we refer the reader to Chapter 8 Scenario I.

Risk Factor 12. Failure to Align Values and Behaviors with Strategy

Managers are often consumed by daily operational problems and lose sight of long-term goals. Unless there is an organizational focus on strategy implementation, managers will focus on their day-to-day work. Poor strategic implementation hinders the ability of a formal strategy to affect what the company does in practice. Too often day to day activities and behaviors are only somewhat aligned with the organization's strategy. In many cases, day to day activities are unaligned. Lack of alignment may be an indication of what Mintzberg refers to as an emergent strategy. For a practical example, we refer the reader to Chapter 8 Scenario H.

MANAGING BUSINESS AND INFORMATION CULTURE RISKS

Culture risk is created when there is a misalignment between an organization's values and leader actions, employee behaviors, or organizational systems. Cultural risk is recognized as a significant management factor in the ISO 3100/31010 standard (de Oliveria et al., 2017; Gierdrum and Peter, 2011; IEC, 2008; International Standards Organization, 2009; Alina, 2012; Ansaldi et al., 2012; Luko, 2014; Popov, Lyon and Hollcroft, 2016; Valis and Koucky, 2009). Specifically, this standard advises organizations to align cultural risk considerations with their overall risk profile and strategy. Risks introduced by business and information cultures are among the most impactful but the least recognized. Information culture risks can be as damaging as business culture risks. Information culture risks are less visible and less well known than business culture risks, but their consequences can be significant in a knowledge economy. Consider the implications of the examples offered below. These are all common information behaviors developed in the industrial economy. If not controlled or managed, their impacts in a knowledge economy can have costly and lasting impacts for an organization.

In these situations, the business cannot function at optimal capacity. On the other hand, a unit or team leader can create a productive and inclusive work culture that incentivizes all team members to adjust their behaviors.

The business adage – culture eats strategy for breakfast every day – speaks directly to this risk. Culture – whether formal or informal – can override strategy and behaviors. Cultures that are anti-knowledge, that reward secrecy and hiding rather than sharing and use can introduce significant business risk. They can create an environment where all of the risks described above may flourish. A cultural risk can be:

- A trigger for new hazards;
- An amplifying factor for general consequences of a threat/hazard;
- A diminishing factor for general consequences of a threat/hazard

Leaders who purposefully align values, beliefs, and actions with macro-level activity and messaging within their organization tend to be more effective in executing business strategies. It starts by identifying desired cultural attributes. Then they are institutionalized through purpose-built mechanisms that encourage expected behaviors and discourage actions that produce suboptimal outcomes. Moreover, leaders who are also monitoring and measure reputation risk and culture can use those indicators as guideposts for ongoing improvements.

Example 1. Macro Business Issues

Macro business culture risks include cost and regulatory pressures, digital disruption, cyber threats, talent shortages, and others—have clear cultural implications.

Example 2. High Employee Turnover

Employees are the primary source of information and knowledge about our organizations, their business processes, products, and outcomes. When organizations experience high rates of staff turnover, this means we have significant information losses and leakages. This can have a direct and indirect effect on the organization. Direct effects take the form of loss of productive capacity, possible loss of production level knowledge, and product quality. Indirect costs take the form of the additional time and effort the organization must expend to rebuild this information and knowledge capacity.

Example 3. Corrosive Cultures

Corrosive cultures can prevent individuals from working together, from learning continuously together, from transferring and sharing information and knowledge, improving processes, or generally trusting others.

Example 4. Risk Preference or Aversion Behaviors

Attitudes and behaviors can introduce significant positive and negative risks. Where individuals are willing to experiment and take reasonable risks, new business value may result. Where individuals are unwilling to share their knowledge or use the knowledge created by others, they can create impediments for the business. Every organization has individuals whose individual behaviors create tension or discord within a team or unit.

Example 5. Intentional Use of Suboptimal Business Information

Individuals and organizations can create procedural knowledge risks. An individual can fail to use vetted organizational knowledge when it is available and accessible – only because it does not represent "their working knowledge." Individuals can create procedural knowledge risks by failing to note errors, faults, or discrepancies where they occur for fear of being held accountable for those conditions. The business can create procedural knowledge risks by continuing to use or promote process knowledge that is simply wrong or inaccurate – which contains mistakes, errors, gaps. The business may fail to manage the risks associated with core knowledge and business capabilities or fail to safeguard the knowledge of innovations. A significant risk can result where the business fails to acquire and absorb new knowledge, which would allow it to remain competitive in the industry.

Example 6. Misuse of Sensitive Information

Sensitive information may take the form of a business-critical process or product information. It might take the form of national security or market intelligence information. It might also have personally sensitive value or may harm an individual if revealed. These types of risks may be created by accident, deliberately or without malice. Regardless of intent or cause, though, their effects can be significant.

Example 7. Information Theft

Information theft may occur in any situation. Perhaps the most noteworthy is the theft of subject matter expertise or advanced knowledge. Subject matter and experts offer insights into why they are sometimes reluctant to share their tacit knowledge. They are concerned that if it is exposed, it might be misrepresented, misused, or misunderstood. They worry that tacit knowledge can be stolen or appropriated by another source – that it will not be adequately attributed to its source. Where tacit knowledge is not traceable, this is a significant risk. The impact of these concerns is that individuals may be unwilling to share their knowledge.

Example 8. Failure to Share Knowledge and Information

An organization or a business process may be at risk because some are working with incomplete understanding. Some individuals concerned about how they will be treated or rewarded for their work may hold it close to retain power and leverage. The business can make decisions or take actions that result in unintentional or unrecognized tacit knowledge loss. These might include creating an environment that encourages individuals to leave and take their tacit knowledge to another business. Simple internal promotions or job reassignments can result in a loss of access to tacit knowledge – individuals have to "file that knowledge away Tacit knowledge risks can also result from positive actions. Less intentional risks can occur when individuals access and use tacit knowledge with an incomplete understating. Alternatively, where tacit knowledge is known but insufficient well understood to realize its full relevance. Perhaps the simplest form of tacit knowledge risk is that individuals are simply unaware of what they know and fail to share it as a result.

Example 9. Deliberate Loss of Business Information

Perhaps the most classic business activity that generates business risk, though, is the outsourcing or offshoring of business processes. This could result in a complete loss of access to process knowledge and supporting tacit knowledge, skills, and competencies. Offshoring or outsourcing for cost efficiency can have high direct and indirect costs. Risks to core operations can result if an organization cannot leverage, mobilize, or exploit the knowledge it already possesses. What level of risk results when process knowledge is not coordinated across functions or where errors occur and are not reported to other units? How much may productive capacity be wasted where procedural knowledge must be reinvented or duplicated? What is the risk to decision-makers where the full process knowledge is not shared with decision-makers, and suboptimal decisions are made?

Example 10. Information Hoarding or Hiding

Consider the impact where an individual maintains personal copies of all documents and publications. This takes time away from projects and processes; it can confuse if the versions are out of date, or even introduce legal challenges where the individual does not have a right to use the document. If these are single-source copies, it means others cannot access them. Consider the instance where the organization uses network drives to maintain its business documentation. However, the drive is not indexed by the enterprise search engine. There is no protocol for naming or maintaining folders, or for adding or deleting documents and publications. There is the appearance of management, but in fact, all the information on the drive is at risk. Consider the consequences of an infrastructure failure if individual network drives are not mirrored or backed up.

Example 11. Poorly Designed Information Infrastructure

The most common form of risk, though, is where repositories or organizational solutions are poorly designed – where information is hard to find, where information is lost in an organizational migration, where documents are retained without review, where outdated or invalidated information is retained and is discoverable. Consider the risk of discoverable documents and reports that contain uncertain, erroneous, or merely faulty knowledge.

DESIGNING CULTURAL ASSESSMENT INTO STRATEGIC PLANNING PROCESSES

There is no silver bullet solution to these challenges. Each organization must begin the process of exposing its strategies, improving strategy formulation, aligning business and information strategies, and ensuring that every strategy has a supportive business and information culture. Success is only guaranteed if the organization incorporates cultural analysis and alignment into every one of its strategy development and implementation processes. What does this look like? Moreover, how can you design this in a way that allows you to track and measure your progress? Let us begin by reviewing the strategic planning process and determine what needs to be adapted to incorporate cultural analysis and alignment.

Figure 1. Traditional strategic planning process

Step 1. Identify Your Strategic Position
Step 2. Gather People and Information
Step 3. Perform a SWOT Analysis
Step 4. Formulate a Strategic Plan
Step 5. Execute Your Strategic Plan
Step 6. Constantly Monitor Performance

Figure 2. Modified and adapted strategic planning process

Step 1. Identify Your Strategic Goals and Objectives
Step 2. Identify Relevant Information Strategies and Strategic Information Assets
Step 3. Identify Strengths, Weaknesses, Opportunities, and Threats
Step 4. Formulate a Strategy
Step 5. Develop an Implementation Plan
Step 6. Identify Relevant Units and Individuals
Step 7. Identify Relevant Cultures
Step 8. Assign Responsibilities and Accountabilities
Step 9. Launch the Strategic Plan
Step 10. Constantly Monitor Performance

The strategic planning process is essentially a list of six steps that managers should follow to complete and implement a strategy within a company. The most common process includes six high-level steps (Figure 1). How should we redefine this process to account for information strategies for business and information cultures?

As we noted earlier in the chapter, several common risk factors can be addressed by redefining the strategic planning process. For example, the process might be redefined to include ten steps (Figure 2).

The modified and adapted strategic planning process makes room for and accommodates our cultural and information risk management and mitigation concerns. Each of the ten steps is described below.

Step 1. Identify Your Strategic Position

The first stage prepares you for the rest of the strategic planning process. To achieve your goals, you must first have a clear vision. Start by defining both your short-term and long-term objectives. In short, what do you hope to achieve? Next, determine what steps you will take to accomplish these objectives. When identifying your strategic position, remember that your goals should be realistic and measurable. For help with this step, look back to your mission statement, corporate values, and work culture.

Step 2. Identify Relevant Information Strategic and Strategic Information Assets

You will also want to bring in as much up-to-date information to the table as possible. Ensure that any data you use is accurate so that you make informed decisions backed up by facts.

Step 3. Perform a SWOT Analysis

SWOT, which is an acronym for strengths, weaknesses, opportunities, and threats, acts as a powerful tool during the strategic planning process. A SWOT analysis is often performed to help identify the strengths and weaknesses of a business, as well as identify any opportunities and threats that could arise. Once the team has identified all strengths, weaknesses, opportunities, and threats, you can work together to develop new goals that will help your business face these possibilities more positively. A SWOT analysis can also lead you in the right direction and towards your goals. Once you have people and information to draw from, examine any internal or external issues that could affect your objectives.

Step 4. Formulate a Strategic Plan

Once you have successfully identified your strategic position and have a set of goals that align with your company's mission, you can begin working on your strategic plan. When developing your plan, consider which initiatives will have the most significant impact on your business and which will help improve your position the most. Also, consider which initiatives are most urgent and put these at the front of the line. To ensure that your strategic plan is working, you will need to determine the best way to measure your progress. With measurable goals you can visibly see improvements as they happen.

Step 5. Implementation Plan

Develop a plan to communicate about implementation and evaluation. No matter how basic or complex, a communication plan is useful in organizing activities related to reporting about your progress and process to the community. Your communication plan should allow for two-way communication so that as you share information, there is also an opportunity for stakeholder input and engagement.

Step 6. Identify Relevant Units and Individuals

It is critical to ask other people in areas and functions relevant to the strategy for their input. This includes employees, customers, or partners. Once you have established your strategic position, you will want to bring in the people who will be involved in the planning process. Additionally, your strategic planning process will not be effective unless everyone is doing their part. This requires you to monitor and manage performance continually and tweak any components that are not leading to satisfactory results. It is also essential to hold those involved in the strategic planning process accountable for their assigned tasks. Know that it may be necessary to repeat the strategic management process if any corrective actions you take are not successful. Continue to collect new and relevant data to help with any future strategic planning that may occur.

Step 7. Assess Relevant Cultures

This is a critical new step. It is at this point that you call into action all of those structural and dynamic factors we identified in Chapters 3 through 9, and put operationalized them. This means building institutional capacity for cultural assessment, analysis, and modeling. It means defining and developing those capabilities that can provide cultural assessment and coaching services across the organization. It also means understanding the nature of cultural intelligence and competencies needed to support these capabilities over time.

Step 8. Assign Responsibilities and Accountabilities

Determine who is accountable. This is how you are going to get to where you want to go. The strategies, action plans, and budgets are all steps in the process that effectively communicates how you will allocate time, human capital, and money to address the priority issues and achieve the defined objectives.

Step 9. Execute Your Strategic Plan

Once you have your strategic plan in place, you are ready to implement it. This step is the action phase of the strategic planning process. Start by making everyone involved in the plan aware of your strategy. Ideally, you want to distribute tasks among different individuals or departments to prevent one person or group of people from becoming overwhelmed. Also, take the time to check back with these individuals or groups to ensure that you are staying on track. If you find that you are not meeting your objectives, make any necessary changes.

Step 10. Constantly Monitor Performance

All aspects of the plan, and the identified tasks and timelines, should be monitored for progress, and adjustments should be made when indicated to ensure that the plan remains relevant. Changes should be developed in collaboration with partners and stakeholders involved in the planning process. As mentioned previously, evaluation results can be used not only to monitor your progress but also to improve and revise action plans as progress is made, and changes occur. Be prepared to learn and adapt as you move forward. Be prepared to make mid-course corrections based on evaluation results. Effective, implemented plans are dynamic. The plan may need revision based on a completed objective, a newly identified priority, a change in responsibilities, or a change in resources and assets. To ensure the plan performs as designed, you must hold regularly scheduled formal reviews of the process and refine it as necessary. We suggest at least once a quarter.

CONCLUSION

After reading this chapter, you should be able to:

- Define harm and risk
- Describe examples of business culture and information culture risks
- Explain why it is essential to manage strategic risk
- Describe the ten-step methodology for integrating culture into strategic planning

REFERENCES

Alina, S. (2012). Risk management: An integrated approach to risk management and assessment. *Annals of the University of Oradea, Economic Science Series Annals of the University of Oradea Economic Science Series*, *21*(2), 776–781.

Ansaldi, S., Monti, M., Agnello, P., & Giannini, F. (2012). An ontology for the identification of the most appropriate risk management methodology. In *OTM Confederated International Conferences "On the Move to Meaningful Internet Systems"* (pp. 444-453). Springer. 10.1007/978-3-642-33618-8_60

Borek, A., Parlikad, A. K., & Woodall, P. (2011). Towards a process for total information risk management. ICIQ.

Borek, A., Woodall, P., Gosden, M., & Parlikad, A. K. (2011). *Managing information risks in asset management experiences from an in-depth case study in the utility industry*. Academic Press.

Borek, A., Woodall, P., & Parlikad, A. K. (2011). A risk management approach to improving information quality for operational and strategic management. *Proceedings of the 18th EUROMA conference: exploring interfaces.*

Hardy, C. A., & Williams, S. P. (2010). Managing Information Risks and Protecting Information Assets in a Web 2.0 Era. In Bled eConference (p. 25). Academic Press.

IEC. (2008). *ISO 31010—Risk Management—Risk Assessment Techniques.* Geneva: International Electrotechnical Commission.

International Standards Organization. (2009). 31010: Risk management—Risk assessment techniques. Event (London). Geneva, 552.

Khidzir, N. Z., Arshad, N. H. H., & Mohamed, A. (2010). Information security risk management: An empirical study on the importance and practices in ICT outsourcing. In *2010 International Symposium on Information Technology* (Vol. 3, pp. 1610-1615). IEEE. 10.1109/ITSIM.2010.5561646

Lemieux, V. L. (2004). Two approaches to managing information risks. *Information & Management, 38*(5), 56.

Luko, S. N. (2014). Risk assessment techniques. *Quality Engineering, 26*(3), 379–382. doi:10.1080/08982112.2014.875769

Lyon, B. K., & Popov, G. (2016). The art of assessing risk. *Professional Safety, 61*(03), 40–51.

Mitchell, S. (2009). *Managing information risk: a director's guide.* IT Governance Ltd.

Popov, G., Lyon, B. K., & Hollcroft, B. (2016). *Risk assessment: A practical guide to assessing operational risks.* John Wiley & Sons.

Valis, D., & Koucky, M. (2009). Selected overview of risk assessment techniques. *Problemy eksploatacji*, 19-32.

ADDITIONAL READING

Clarke, R. (2013). Data risks in the cloud. *Journal of Theoretical and Applied Electronic Commerce Research, 8*(3), 59–73. doi:10.4067/S0718-18762013000300005 de Oliveira, U. R., Marins, F. A. S., Rocha, H. M., & Salomon, V. A. P. (2017). The ISO 31000 standard in supply chain risk management. *Journal of Cleaner Production*, *151*, 616–633. doi:10.1016/j.jclepro.2017.03.054

Gjerdrum, D., & Peter, M. (2011). The new international standard on the practice of risk management–A comparison of ISO 31000: 2009 and the COSO ERM framework. *Risk Management*, *31*(21), 8–12.

Järveläinen, J. (2012). Information security and business continuity management in interorganizational IT relationships. *Information Management & Computer Security*, *20*(5), 332–349. doi:10.1108/09685221211286511

Wright, T. (2015). *10 Reasons why 70% of Strategies Fail*. Access online on July 20, 2018 at https://www.executestrategy.net/blog/7-top-reasons-why-strategic-plans-fail

Chapter 11
Managing Cultural Risks

ABSTRACT

Risk assessment is a process that allows us to understand risks, define risk criteria, assess the probability and the consequences of that risk occurring, define a level of risk we can tolerate and afford, and define a cost-effective and efficient mitigation treatment. The authors provide a risk assessment and analysis method that the reader can use to (1) build cultural risk into your organizational risk management profile and (2) adapt the organization's risk management profile to include cultural risks. The method builds upon but extends the ISO 31000/31010 risk management methodology to determine the level of cultural risk your organization is carrying. The authors walk through and translate each of the seven steps to account for cultural risks.

RISK ASSESSMENT – DEFINITION AND CHARACTERIZATION

Risk is inherent in everything that we do. Risk management helps us make better decisions in specific contexts. Risk management helps us to manage our organizations in real-world situations. Strategies are often formulated for ideal situations or the best of all possible worlds. This means that in formulating strategies, organizations fail to consider the everyday risks involved in conducting the organization's business. Risk assessment is a process that allows us to understand risks, define risk criteria, assess the probability and the consequences of that risk occurring, define a level of risk we can tolerate and afford, and define a cost-effective and efficient

DOI: 10.4018/978-1-7998-4315-3.ch011

mitigation treatment. Chapter 10 provided a high-level description of the types of risks an organization might encounter – risks generated by suboptimal formulation and management of strategy, and risks generated by ignoring or failing to recognize the influence of culture. In this chapter, we describe how to translate those generic hazards and risks into actual risk calculations. The authors recommended aligning your strategic and cultural risks with the organization's risk management profile.

In this chapter, the authors provide a risk assessment and analysis method which the reader can use to (1) build cultural risk into your organizational risk management profile, and (2) adapt the organization's risk management profile to include cultural risks. This methodology is consistent with the treatment of cultural risk management highlighted in ISO 31000 Risk Management and ISO 31010 – Risk Assessment Techniques ((IEC, 2008; International Standards Organization, 2009). The methodology explains how to integrate specific cultural behaviors into an overall risk assessment methodology, and how to define and model tangible and intangible aspects of cultural behavior (i.e., loss of reputation, risk perception, awareness as mitigation, and so on). These translations and interpretations are specific and unique to an organization and a point in time. The authors can provide general guidance, but it is up to the reader to design a solution that suits the context.

The authors translate the ISO 31000/31010 risk management methodology into a seven-step methodology; you can follow to determine the level of cultural risk your organization is carrying. This methodology presumes that you will follow the authors' guidance and integrate cultural analysis and risk management into your strategic planning process. It also presumes that you will elevate the role of information strategies and integrate those strategies into the organization's strategic planning process.

The translation assumes that culture and information are essential risks and targets them as part of the organization's core risks. While ISO recognizes the importance and harm that can result from cultural risks, they are considered only as a potential factor that may trigger or amplify another risk. The authors presume that the full risk assessment methodology will be applied to cultural and information risks.

Figure 1. Translation of ISO 31000/31010 risk assessment methods

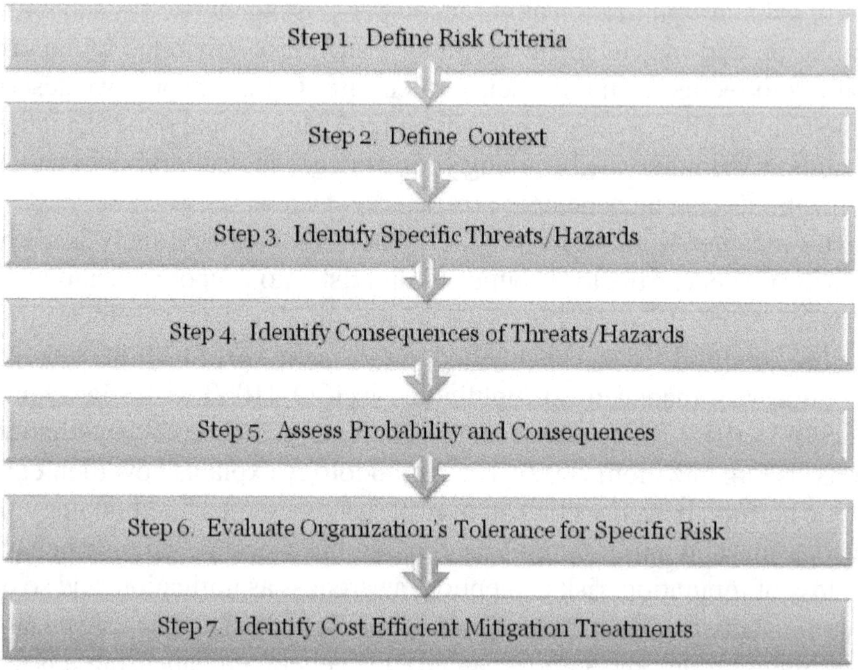

Starting from those vantage points, the authors' interpretation of the ISO 31000/31010 methodology includes the following seven steps. Each step is discussed in detail below.

Step 1. Define Risk Criteria
Step 2. Define the Strategic Context
Step 3. Identify Specific Threats/Hazards
Step 4. Identify Consequences of Threats/Hazards
Step 5. Assess Probability and Consequences
Step 6. Evaluate Organization's Tolerance for Specific Risk
Step 7. Identify Cost-Efficient Mitigation Treatments

STEP 1. RISK CRITERIA

Risk criteria define the frame of reference used to evaluate the significance or importance of an organization's risks. The risk criteria help to determine whether an evaluated level of risk is acceptable or tolerable. Risk criteria should reflect the industry, the organization's values, policies, and objectives should consider the views of all the stakeholders, and should be derived from standards, laws, policies, and other requirements. The criteria will encompass the organization/industry operation and type of risks.

We use risk criteria need to determine thresholds of predicted or projected risks. This means that business and information managers need to have a good understanding of (1) general principles of risk control, (2) risk envelopes; (3) average or peak/extreme risks; (4) risk measures; and (5) risk limits and values. The place to begin is by understanding how your organization understands and each of these criteria. Who in your organization has the answers to these questions?

- How does your organization think about and approach Risk Control?
- What is your organization's Risk Envelope?
- How do you determine Average or Peak/Extreme Risks?
- What Risk Measures does your organization currently use?
- How does your organization define Risk Limits and Values?

This will vary with each organization. Organizations should ensure that any new initiative or change initiative is aligned with the existing culture. This most critical step then is to gain the support of whoever handles and manages risk at your organization. These individuals are most likely in financial, legal and regulatory, corporate insurance, or reputation management.

The result of Step 1 is an identification of risk managers throughout the organization and answers to the five key questions. Once we have this level of understanding, we have a foundation for managing and mitigating cultural risks.

STEP 2. DEFINE THE RISK CONTEXT

Chapters 5, 6, 7, 8, and 9 were designed to help us to understand the context in which these risks might occur. In those chapters, the authors suggested that you think in terms of structural factors (e.g., levels of the organization) and dynamic factors (e.g., relevant factors at each level). The authors also suggested that culture is elusive and challenging to manage – trying to manage culture outside of a specific business context can be a high-risk venture in itself – because it is unlikely to succeed and very likely to have high direct and indirect costs. Furthermore, they suggested that the most effective context for managing cultural risk is to design it to suit each business context – to support each actual and practical business strategy. We assume that the reader will take every precaution to ensure the strategy is in good shape and has every chance of success. The context, therefore, will always be – what is the nature of the culture we need to support the business strategy? This is a question only an individual manager or team can ask and answer in a specific situation at a given point in time

STEP 3. THREATS AND HAZARDS IDENTIFICATION

Hazard identification means establishing what could go wrong with the strategy. Therefore, there is a need to identify all the ways in which these risks may occur. You want to ensure that all the vulnerabilities have been correctly identified and prioritized.

STEP 4. IDENTIFY EFFECTS OF THE HAZARD

The consequences of a risk occurring depend on the situation and the context. The effects of a cultural risk can be estimated using the scale presented in Table 1. Every organization must define the effects based on their knowledge of the context and the factors involved.

This step involves modeling the nature of the risk and determining its effects. In the work of risk management, this translates to risk models and risk analytics. Remember that at this point, we are focused on the risk itself, rather than the remedy. When considering cultural and information risks, it is essential to consider both qualitative and quantitative modeling methods. If you followed the author's guidance in Chapters 7, 8, and 9, you have reasonably proper documentation of the nature of your risks and the factors that create those risks. You can leverage this documentation to create your risk models. In constructing a cultural risk model or an information risk model, you are interested in understanding the impact that culture and information risks (as independent variables or factors) have on your business strategies (as a dependent variable). Your task is to take what you have learned in Chapters 3 through 6 and model – either qualitatively or quantitatively – those factors that will affect strategy and the effect they might have. Over time your risk model should evolve based on what you learn and the remedies or controls you put in place.

Table 1. Effects of the risk and nature of the harm

Effect of the Risk	Description of the Harm	The object of the Harm
Irreparable Harm	· May result in a costly loss of significant tangible assets or resources. · May significantly violate, harm, or impede mission, reputation, or business interest. · May create significant legal or regulatory liabilities. · May result in serious physical harm or injury.	May impact the organization generally, specific business units or teams, individuals within the organization. May impact organization stakeholders, including partners, stewards, clients, or customers.
Significant Harm	· May result in a costly loss of tangible assets or resources. · May violate, harm, or impede mission, reputation, or business interest. · May create significant legal or regulatory liabilities. · May result in severe and tangible injury.	Harm may occur to selected aspects of the organization's operations, internal or external stakeholders. The impact is likely to be significant but more targeted in its effect.
Moderate Harm	· May result in loss of some tangible assets and resources. · May noticeably affect an organization's mission, reputation, or business interest. · May create noticeable legal and regulatory liabilities.	The harm may result to any of the stakeholders, or particular aspects of the organization's business.
Little Harm	· Unlikely to cause any harm to the organization, its functions or individuals, or external stakeholders.	

These models of risks and their consequences are the basis for risk analytics and evaluation. Risk models help us to determine the total effect we might incur from a specific risk. Risk models can be qualitative, quantitative, or hybrid. Qualitative risk models are based on subjective and simulated identification of threats and consequences, and human or machine-assisted categorization of the degree of harm. Initially, you will likely need to rely on qualitative or hybrid methods when considering risks resulting from cultural or information misalignments. We say initially because, over time, as you learn how to translate what you learn from using qualitative methods into quantitative patterns. You should strive for quantitative models and methods in the following situations:

- when there are concerns that qualitative approaches may overlook significant hazards;
- where there may be uncertainties over the likelihood or consequence (or both) in a context and where quantifying these may reduce uncertainty;

- where qualitative assessments indicate a significant number of risks in a given context, and there is a need to prioritize risk reduction or mitigation using more robust techniques (i.e., where high dollar investments are involved)

There is a rich set of well established quantitative models related to risk analysis, including market risks, value at risk, historical simulation, or extreme value theory to analyze the consequences of harm to a financial portfolio. Any context where you can translate the risk consequences or effects into quantitative measures or dollar values, you are well-positioned to use quantitative models and methods. It is also highly likely that the risk models and analytical methods your organization relies on will be quantitative.

STEP 5. RISK PROBABILITY AND LIKELIHOOD ASSESSMENT

It is necessary to estimate the risk for each hazard identified. In this step, you will identify and select the scales for the likelihood that the risk will occur and the consequence if that risk does occur. The likelihood of a hazard identified occurring is a function of the probability of the resulting consequences materializing. It is also a function of the subject being exposed at a given location and time. ISO 31000/31010 suggests four levels of likelihood (Table 2).

Table 2. ISO 31000/31010 Risk Likelihood Scale

Likelihood	Scale	Likelihood of Occurrence
Highly Probably/Likely	10	1 per day – Very likely risk
Medium/Possible	5	1 per week – Possible risk
Low/Remote	2	1 per month – Remote risk
Negligible/Unlikely.	1	1 per year or less – Unlikely Risk

These levels are (1) Highly Probably/Likely; (2) Medium/Possible; (3) Low/Remote; and (4) Negligible/Unlikely. Risks that are highly probable or likely to occur might create hazards at the rate of one per day. Those risks that have a medium/possible occurrence might occur weekly. Risks that might only occur monthly are rated as low/remote. Finally, risks that have a negligible rate of occurrence might present annually or less. Because of the nature of cultural and information risks, and the way they present – in everyday actions and decisions - you should not be surprised if your probability and likelihood assessment finds many risks at the Highly Probable/Likely level. This may be alarming, so it is essential to be clear and honest about the

STEP 6. RISK EVALUATION AND TOLERANCE

Risk evaluation and analysis is determined by the consequences of the effect of the risk (Table 1) and the probability of that risk occurring (Table 2). These are not trivial tasks, but once you have established the effect and the probability, you can evaluate the level of risk using a risk matrix (Table 3).

Table 3. Consequences of risks

Likelihood	Scale	Description of the Harm
Highly Probably/Likely	10	· May result in a highly costly loss of significant tangible assets or resources. · May significantly violate, harm, or impede mission, reputation, or business interest. · May create significant legal or regulatory liabilities. · May result in serious physical harm or injury.
Medium/Possible	5	· May result in a costly loss of tangible assets or resources. · May violate, harm, or impede mission, reputation, or business interest. · May create significant legal or regulatory liabilities. · May result in severe and tangible injury.
Low/Remote	2	· May result in loss of some tangible assets and resources. · May noticeably affect an organization's mission, reputation, or business interest. · May create noticeable legal and regulatory liabilities.
Negligible/Unlikely.	1	· Unlikely to cause any harm to the organization, its functions or individuals, or external stakeholders.

Just as it is essential to anchor risk criteria, characteristics, effects, and probabilities in a given context, it is also essential to define the degree of tolerance for those risks. The organization, the unit, or the individual must decide whether the cost of the risk is tolerable or affordable. If it is not affordable, then a cost-efficient and cost-effective risk control or risk remedy must be defined. In order to make that determination, you need to know the nature of the risk control or remedy and its costs.

At this point, you have accumulated a rich set of risk-related insights. What should you do with those insights? Once you have completed Steps 1 through 6, you are ready to perform risk analysis. Risk analysis pulls all of these factors together to help you determine where your most significant culture and information risks exist, what the aggregate impact of those risks might be, and where you can most effectively propose and apply controls and remedies.

STEP 7. RISK CONTROLS AND REMEDIES

In Chapter 1, we established the fact that trying to change an organization's whole culture is neither an affordable nor practical remedy for cultural risks. Every cultural risk remedy will be evaluated in the context of its business and information value and its cost to implement. Anywhere risk levels and consequences exceed what the organization can tolerate, risk control or remedy needs to be proposed. When assessing the risk, each aspect of risk must be evaluated separately because each risk might require a different metric and a different analytical model.

We agree that risk is the product of likelihood and consequence. To reduce risks, you have two essential choices: you can reduce the likelihood of a risk occurring, or you can change the context to reduce the impact of the risk. For each context and each risk, you should identify risk controls and remedies that are consistent with your organization's risk management approach. Risk controls and remedies translate to the following options:

- elimination of the risk or substitution of a remedy for the full risk;
- risk is controlled or managed to a tolerable level;
- risk cannot be eliminated or controlled, but measures are defined to recover from a potential occurrence;
- the risk is identified and transferred to another party or entity, e.g., an insurance policy or company

These remedies should allow you to reduce the risks to an acceptable level. Do not assume that you will be able to eliminate the risk, but rather aim for a level that is affordable and tolerable in your context. Remember that as you reduce risks and address aspects of the culture, the culture and the business will change. What is tolerable today may not be tolerable six months from now.

You should expect that over time, as you learn from your controls and remedies, the risk models and analytics will become part of your organization's risk management approach. Reporting on cultural and information risks should be a part of your management communications. These models and methods should become institutional tools that can be used in any situation that has strategic value and cultural or information risks. Also, keep in mind that these models and analytical methods may be the most effective tools you have for influencing and shaping your organization's culture.

CONCLUSION

After reading this chapter, you should be able to:

- define risk assessment
- describe the ISO 31000/31010 risk assessment methodology
- describe the expanded cultural risk assessment methodology
- Apply the expanded cultural risk assessment methodology to your organization
- Describe common risk controls and remedies

REFERENCES

IEC. (2008). *ISO 31010—Risk Management—Risk Assessment Techniques.* Geneva: International Electrotechnical Commission.

International Standards Organization. (2009). 31010: Risk management—Risk assessment techniques. Event (London). Geneva, 552.

Chapter 12
Building and Managing Cultural Capacity

ABSTRACT

Cultural risks can be managed to create value, or they can be ignored to create liabilities. To manage cultural risks, organizations must have a cultural capacity from which to draw. Building cultural capacity is a three-pronged effort. It means building capacity at a strategic level, at an individual level, and collectively. Cultural capacity is achieved through strategic, collective, and individual actions. This chapter considers how organizations can build cultural capacity strategically, collectively, and individually.

CULTURAL CAPACITY – DEFINITIONS AND CHARACTERIZATION

Cultural capacity is an emerging concept. Cultural capacity is defined as the ability of an organization to manage and leverage its whole culture to support its goals and objectives. Cultural capacity means:

- Understanding culture at all levels
- Ensuring all information and business cultures support the organization's business and information strategies;
- There is an alignment of strategies and cultures at all levels of the organization;

DOI: 10.4018/978-1-7998-4315-3.ch012

- That managers and staff know what culture is and the role it plays in supporting or impeding strategies;
- Every individual across the organization engages in and supports cultural assessment and growth.

Building cultural capacity is a three-pronged effort. It means building capacity at a strategic level, at an individual level, and collectively. What does this look like on a practical level? Cultural capacity building means that organizations should have a strong foundation of cultural capital and cultural capabilities. This means going beyond a simple one-time cultural assessment project or initiative to ensuring that culture is an essential element of the strategic, core, and enabling capabilities. It also means that cultural competencies are built into the organization's roles and responsibilities for leaders, for line managers, internal staff, and external stakeholders.

Cultures are dynamic – they vary with the business environment, the business goals of the organization, the organization's leadership, and all those other facts we reviewed in Chapter 5. Cultures play a critical role in supporting or impeding business strategies. Cultural risks can be managed to create value, or they can be ignored to create liabilities. To manage cultural risks, organizations must have a cultural capacity from which to draw. Cultural capacity is comprised of institutional support. Cultural capacity is achieved through strategic, collective, and individual actions. How do we build cultural capacity strategically? How do we build it collectively? And Individually?

Figure 1. Cultural capacity building

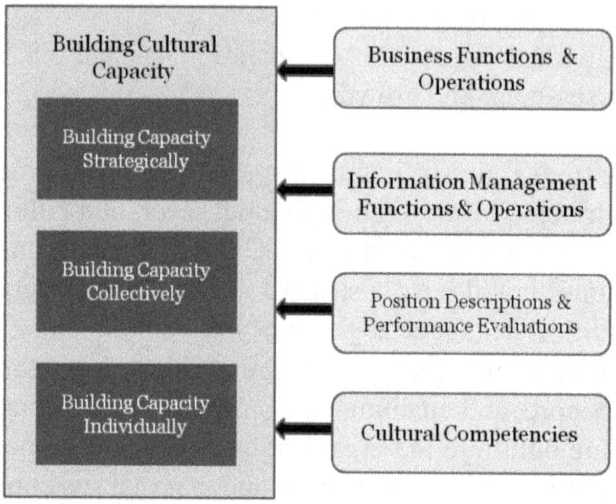

BUILDING CULTURAL CAPACITY STRATEGICALLY

Organizational leaders – whether defined as leaders by their title or role or simply respected as a leader for their actions – play a critical role in establishing a robust and sustainable business and information culture. An essential first step in building cultural capacity is to identify these leaders and ensure that they understand their role and their responsibilities for building cultural capacity. Moreover, leaders must take on the role of capable champions who contribute to cultural capacity through their ability to attract, retain, and empower leaders (Huy 2003; Kantor 1983).

How do leaders build culture strategically? They build an organization's cultural capacity by consciously taking every opportunity to increase their awareness of their assumptions, beliefs, values, and behaviors, to develop their cultural competencies, and to influence the attitudes and behaviors of others through example. It means instilling respect for and secure custodianship of information. It means actively contributing to procedural knowledge – to questioning how and why we do things, admitting mistakes, and learning from their mistakes. It means sharing their networks and continuing to build relationships. There are some classic constructive examples of strategic culture capacity building in the popular press. We would refer the reader to the cultural leadership of James D. Wolfensohn, President of the World Bank from 1995-2005, and his work to create the 'knowledge bank.' We would refer the reader to the strategic leadership at organizations like Google, where both business and information culture capacities are strategic advantages.

Organizations need to learn how to leverage and build the cultural capacity of their internal workforce and their external stakeholders. Simply put – learning how to build cultural capacity is a critical new business capability. Organizations need to grow, invest in, manage, and leverage their business and information cultures. Its collective cultures define an organization's cultural capacity.

Trustworthy leadership is key to building cultural capacity. Senior executives can earn the trust of the organization and lead the organization by practical and honest example, and through periods of tumultuous change. This means that an organization's leaders need to not only talk a good game about leveraging knowledge, but they need to demonstrate their knowledge capital attributes every day. This factor aligns with organization culture because it speaks to how leaders can create fundamental beliefs and assumptions about the value of knowledge to the business, how those beliefs can be turned into practical behaviors and closely held values, and how the environment reflects those beliefs. Knowledge capacity is built through practice. Capacity will not grow where trust does not exist (Bass 1990; Kotter 1996).

BUILDING ORGANIZATIONAL CAPACITY COLLECTIVELY

The most significant way cultural capacity grows is through the active and collective engagement of individuals in shaping and adapting the culture. Idiosyncratic and individual behaviors no longer define the culture – instead, cultures emerge around units, teams, and communities. Cultural capacity becomes an essential aspect of organizational citizenship. These collective values and behaviors become norms and find their way into recognized roles and responsibilities. As these roles and responsibilities are normalized, they reinforce and further shape the culture. Norms are an expression of the organization's values and establish what sort of behaviors agents can expect from one another (Hatch & Cunliffe, 2006). When they interact, exchange knowledge, and experience new rewards and recognitions, an individual's understanding of what the organization values will change. Individuals at all levels will modify their understanding of what the organization values to reinforce the culture. Modified roles and changing norms are reciprocally reinforcing. When this happens, the organization's cultural capacity increases.

Middle managers, in particular, have a significant role to play in increasing the collective cultural capacity of the organization. Consider their ability to network effectively across levels of the organization to establish and reinforce cultural attitudes, beliefs, values, and behaviors. Middle and front line behaviors have the most significant contact with front line staff and stakeholders. They are well-positioned to reinforce or correct cultural norms and behaviors. It is also these middle managers who can reinforce or impede cultures through their everyday decision making (Floyd and Wooldridge 1996; Oshry 1996).

Trusting followers is another critical aspect of building cultural capacity. It speaks to the ability of the organization to collectively and constructively dissent from or follow a new path advocated by leaders. This factor is critical to building cultural capacity in particular. Culture is grounded in assumptions, beliefs, and values – if the organization does not recognize and respect the assumptions, beliefs, and values of the internal workforce, there will be little trust. Trusting followers must feel safe to agree, disagree, rethink, and expose mistakes constructively, to learn, unlearn, and relearn (Bass 1990; Kelley 1992).

Innovative cultures are essential to the 21st-century knowledge economy. They are not the purview of a few 'high performing' individuals. Instead, they are the norm for the full workforce. They are also not limited to 'technical competencies' – innovation means learning how to grow and evolve all forms of knowledge capital (Kotter and Heskett 1992; Hamel 2000).

BUILDING CULTURAL CAPACITY THROUGH INDIVIDUAL ACTIONS

An individual's culture is implicit and inherent to who they are. It is embedded in the person; it is an essential attribute of that person. A person's culture may be shared with others, but it cannot – by definition – be separated from the person. When we talk about an individual's contribution to cultural capacity, we are talking about the cultural attributes they bring to the organization. An individual's culture is influenced by the business and information cultures of their working environments. Individuals make decisions to adapt, grow, or expand these inherent cultural attributes. Growing cultural capacity individually means taking primary responsibility for investing, leveraging, and assessing our cultures. The individual is the primary actor. The organization is the secondary or supporting actor, but not the primary actor. While leaders may set an example through their behavior, it is the individual actions of the full workforce that creates the full cultural capacity of an organization. Individuals who take responsibility for growing their knowledge capital will, by definition, contribute to the organization's overall capacity.

The leadership qualities of the traditional industrial economy – reserved for a few high performers – are now common attitudes and behaviors, skills, and competencies required of everyone. An environment where anyone can have a new idea, where anyone can see a way to improve 'the way we work' – is an environment of knowledge leaders and idea generators (Huy, 2003; Kantor, 1983).

Accountable cultures are equally important. Accountable culture is the ability of the organization to hold responsible for each individual for knowledge capital. This means that individuals must take responsibility for acknowledging, growing, and investing in their knowledge capital. It means that everyone plays a role in building the organization's knowledge capital and has some responsibilities for ensuring that capital is safeguarded – just as they would any other type of capital investment (Pfeiffer and Sutton, 2000; Ulrich et al. 1999).

BUSINESS AND INFORMATION CULTURAL CAPABILITIES

Throughout the text, the authors have highlighted the importance of learning to see business and information cultures. Learning to see these cultures is not a onetime effort. It is a continuous capability. Business and information cultures are dynamic and require continuous monitoring, management, and analysis. Every organization needs to have some form of sustainable cultural capability. What is a capability? Moreover, what is cultural capability?

Cultural capability is an emerging concept. It is not yet treated as an organizational capability. Instead, it is a separate and fragmented area of research – mainly in the organizational culture domain. Looking across the organizational culture domain, the authors suggest cultural capabilities might include:

- Development and communication of the organizations core cultural assumptions, beliefs, norms, and values – espoused and actual
- Cultural analysis as a core capability in all business functions
- Cultural risk modeling
- Cultural risk assessment methods

- Cultural profile development
- Cultural competence training and coaching
- Individual cultural performance methods
- Cultural metrics for individuals, units and teams, and at the organization level
- Development and monitoring of rewards and recognitions for supportive cultural behaviors
- Routine cultural health reporting and communication

In smaller organizations, these capabilities might be integrated into an important role. In larger organizations, these capabilities might be introduced as new functions. If an organization cannot afford to add these capabilities as routine functions, they should identify external sources and services that can be called upon to support capacity building.

Cultural capabilities include the ability to coach and support individuals in developing their cultural competence. This means having access to cultural trainers to having internal cultural coaches and mentors. It also means building rewards and incentives into existing performance assessment methods.

BUSINESS AND INFORMATION CULTURE ROLES AND RESPONSIBILITIES

One way to reinforce this is to establish an organization-wide expectation for cultural capacity building responsibilities and to assign some form of these to every individual. In this way, knowledge capacity building becomes part of the assessment culture. It ensures that every individual has a clear understanding of their knowledge capital expectations, that every individual has the opportunity to develop it, and is committed to contributing to the knowledge capital of colleagues. We refer to responsibilities generally for the simple reason that organization vary in how they define competencies and how they hold individuals accountable. The critical point is to ensure that these responsibilities are assigned equitably and fairly across the organization.

In some cases, cultural capacity building may require the development of specialized roles and responsibilities. These roles are strategic in the sense that they are leverage points for enabling knowledge capital growth throughout the organization. A more extensive discussion of these roles is presented in Chapter 5.

CULTURAL COMPETENCE

The traditional definition of cultural competence pertains to the conventional definition of cultures as national and social cultures, and the variations in assumptions, beliefs, values, and behaviors these cultures might introduce. Traditionally, cultural competence was defined as the ability to understand, communicate with, and effectively interact with people across cultures. Cultural competence encompasses being aware of one's world view. And, it means developing positive attitudes towards cultural differences. This traditional definition is essential to building an organization's cultural capacity, but it is only one small part of that whole culture. In the context of a 21st-century knowledge economy and a knowledge organization, cultural competence also includes being aware of the value and liabilities culture can pose to business and information strategies. It also includes an individual's ability to adapt and shape one's cultural norms and behaviors to support the organization.

CONCLUSION

After reading this chapter, you should be able to:

- Define cultural capacity
- Explain how to build cultural capacity strategically
- Explain how to build cultural capacity collectively
- Explain how to build cultural capacity individually
- Describe emerging information culture capabilities
- Describe emerging information culture competencies

REFERENCES

Bass, B. (1990). *Bass and Stogdill's handbook of leadership* (3rd ed.). New York: Free Press.

Floyd, S. W., & Wooldridge, B. (1996). *The strategic middle manager: How to create and sustain competitive advantage*. Jossey-Bass Publishers.

Hamel, G. (2000). *Leading the revolution*. Boston: Harvard Business School Press.

Huy, Q. N. (2001). In praise of middle managers. *Harvard Business Review*, *79*(8), 72–79. PMID:11550632

Kantor, R. M. (1983). *The change masters*. New York: Touchstone.

Kelley, R. (1992). *The power of followership*. New York: Currency Doubleday.

Kilmann, R. H., & Kilmann, I. (1989). *Managing beyond the quick fix: A completely integrated program for creating and maintaining organizational success*. Jossey-Bass.

Kotter, J. P. (1996). *Leading change*. Boston, MA: Harvard Business School Press.

Kotter, J. P. (2008). *Corporate culture and performance*. Simon and Schuster.

Oshry, B. (1996). *Seeing systems*. San Francisco: Berrett-Koehler.

Ulrich, D., Zenger, J., & Smallwood, N. (1999). *Results-based leadership*. Harvard Business Press.

ADDITIONAL READING

Cunningham, C. E., Woodward, C. A., Shannon, H. S., MacIntosh, J., Lendrum, B., Rosenbloom, D., & Brown, J. (2002). Readiness for organizational change: A longitudinal study of workplace, psychological and behavioural correlates. *Journal of Occupational and Organizational Psychology*, *75*(4), 377–392. doi:10.1348/096317902321119637

Elenkov, D. S., Judge, W., & Wright, P. (2005). Strategic leadership and executive innovation influence: An international multi-cluster comparative study. *Strategic Management Journal*, *26*(7), 665–682. doi:10.1002mj.469

Grant, R. M. (1995). *Contemporary strategy analysis*. Oxford: Blackwell.

Kouzes, J. M., & Posner, B. Z. (2002). *The leadership challenge*. San Francisco, CA.

Oxtoby, B., McGuiness, T., & Morgan, R. (2002). Developing organisational change capability. *European Management Journal*, *20*(3), 310–320. doi:10.1016/S0263-2373(02)00047-6

Pfeffer, J., & Sutton, R. I. (2000). *The knowing-doing gap: How smart companies turn knowledge into action*. Harvard Business Press.

Senge, P. (1990). The leader's new work: Building learning organizations. *Sloan Management Review*, *32*(1), 7–23.

Appendix:
Sample Project Plan for Balancing Cultural Risks

This appendix contains a template for a project plan to guide an organization through the process of thinking about, designing, and developing an approach that brings cultural risk in line with strategies. The appendix explains how the plan is organized. Suggestions for how to use the project plan are also provided.

EXPLAINING THE PROJECT PLAN

What is a project plan? A project plan is a simple aid for managing a complex set of tasks. Project plans are intended to help the reader plan and track progress toward establishing a holistic sustainable remedy for strategy and culture misalignments. Following the project plan can help you identify stakeholders, raise awareness of key topics, communicate the importance of business and information strategies, business and information cultures, and risks created by misalignments. The project plan can help you define the actions that are essential to developing and sustaining a balanced solution.

The project plan presented in this appendix (Table A1) is a synopsis of the issues and topics that have been discussed throughout the book. An organization might begin its journey by using the project plan as a roadmap. Each task in the project plan refers back to an individual chapter – as a reference for further study and consideration. The project plan is designed to be used over time and as needed to ensure an organization continues to move its approach forward and to ensure it continues to be relevant to and supportive of business goals. The project plan is designed to be adapted to your organization and to be adapted to include what you learn as you move forward.

The project plan is ordered logically into 12 tasks. Each task is broken down into subtasks or steps which align with the topics discussed in the individual chapters.

- Tasks 1 and 2 are intended to help you decide how you want to design your audits and to decide what you want to audit. These tasks focus on raising awareness of what an audit is, how to prepare for, conduct, and report on the results of an audit. These tasks will ensure that you consider – and decide – which of the three kinds of knowledge audits are most important to your organization.
- Tasks 3 and 4 focus on
- Tasks 5 and 6 focus on Tasks 5, 6 and 7 focus on three important building blocks that should be in place before you consider an audit. Task 5 guides you through determining the knowledge assets you have. Task 6 helps to increase awareness of the source and ownership of these assets. Task 7 determines the useful business life of these assets in your context.
- Tasks 7, 8 and 9 focus on a step by step methodology for focus on the how you manage your knowledge assets. Task 8 raises your awareness of how assets are used in your business processes. Task 9 helps you to discover how you currently manage those assets. Task 10 focuses on exposing any risks associated with your knowledge assets. Finally, Task 11 will guide you through the development of an investment and growth strategy for your knowledge assets.
- Tasks 10, 11 and 12 will help you examine how you currently account for your knowledge assets. Task 12 includes steps that will expose how you currently value your knowledge assets. Task 13 will help you to define and track knowledge asset costs. Finally, Task 14 will be important to organizations who need to track and account for the revenue and profit potential of their knowledge assets.

HOW TO USE THE PROJECT PLAN

Chapter by chapter, the book has walked the reader through the key issues and activities. The authors realize that the book will be used by organizations that are at different stages of preparing for and conducting strategic and cultural risks. For this reason, the reader may want to consider using the project plan to assess where you stand. The project plan is a blank form which can be expanded to suit your business needs. The project plan is a reminder that your strategy, your culture and your risk thresholds are unique to your organization. Your solutions must be your own and they must align with and be relevant to your business environment. Organizations can use the project plan to do the following:

- Assess and assign responsibility for determining the current state of the organization in identifying and managing strategy and culture alignment risks.
- Identify and involve all stakeholders, both current and future, in the practicalities of planning and accomplishing your goals and solutions.
- Define the actions and activities that need to be completed in order to support your remedies. The topics covered in the individual chapters should provide practical guidance on what you need to know in order to develop remedies that suit your business goals.
- Align each task in the project plan with the concepts discussed presented in the corresponding chapter.
- Finally, formulate a strategy and culture risk management solution for the near and the long term.

Table 1.

Task 1. Develop an understanding of the relationship of culture and strategy	Start	Finish	Predecessor	Assigned To	% Complete	Status	Comments
Raise the organization's understanding of the role of information in new economy							
Raise awareness of the relationship of business and information cultures and strategies							
Select an alignment approach that works for your organization							
Develop an understanding of what you need to know to align culture and strategy							
Raise awareness of what is involved in integrating cultural analysis and strategy development							
Task 2. Raise awareness of the basic elements of culture							
Develop a high level narrative explanation of why Culture Matters to your Organization							
Prepare easily understood definitions and examples of culture relevant to your organization							
Develop a concise introduction to the Elements of Culture for business managers							
Review and adapt Culture Models and Typologies to your organization							
Task 3. Identify the Organization's Business Strategies							

continued on following page

Appendix

Table 1. Continued

Identify and engage the key stakeholders of business strategies							
Develop a concise but comprehensive overview of Business Strategies							
Develop easy to use self-learning materials to raise awareness of the forms strategies can take							
Raise awareness and build a dialog around how the organization formulates and leverages strategies							
Task 4. Identify the Organization's Information Strategies							
Identify and engage the key stakeholders of information strategies							
Develop a concise but comprehensive overview of information strategies							
Develop easy to use self-learning materials to raise awareness of the forms information strategies can take							
Raise awareness and build a dialog around how the organization formulates and leverages information strategies							
Task 5. Identify the Organization's Business Cultures							
Expand and engage your community of stakeholders to include human resource experts, ethics and learning experts							
Develop a concise by comprehensive overview of business cultures							
Develop easy to use self-learning materials to raise awareness of the elements of business culture							
Engage business managers and key stakeholders in a discussion around the business cultural factors at play at the organization level							
Engage business managers and key stakeholders in a discussion around the business cultural factors at play at the unit, team and group level							
Engage business managers and key stakeholders in a discussion around the business cultural factors at play at the individual level							
Task 6. Identify the Organization's Information Cultures							
Expand and engage yoru community of stakeholders to include information professionals and practitioners from across the organization							
Develop a concise but comprehensive overview of information cultures							
Develop easy to use self-learning materials to raise awareness of the elements of information cultures							
Engage business managers and key stakeholders in a discussion around the information cultural factors at the organization level							
Engage business managers and key stakeholders in a discussion around the information cultural factors at the unit, team and group level							

continued on following page

Table 1. Continued

Engage business managers and key stakeholders in a discussion around the information cultural factors at the individual level							
Task 7. Balance the Organization Strategies and Cultures							
Adapt the step by step methodology for balancing cultures and strategies at the organization level							
Identify business managers at the organization level with significant imbalances and past challenges							
Develop a project to test and adapt the methodology							
Review the project results and update the methodology							
Communicate the results to other stakeholders at the organization level							
Task 8. Balance the Unit and Team Strategies and Cultures							
Adapt the step by step methodology for balancing cultures and strategies at the unit, group and team level							
Identify managers of business units with significant imbalances and past challenges							
Develop a project to test and adapt the methodology							
Review the project results and update the methodology							
Communicate the results to other stakeholders at the unit level							
Task 9. Balance Individual Strategies and Cultures							
Adapt the step by step methodology for balancing cultures and strategies at the individual level							
Identify key individuals who represent strong alignments of culture and strategy to use as good practice test cases							
Develop a project to test and adapt the methodology							
Review the project results and update the methodology							
Engage the individuals to develop a strategy for sharing the results with human resource, ethics, learning experts and with business unit managers							
Task 10. Identify the Organization's Strategic and Cultural Risks							
Raise awareness of the ISO 31010 Risk Management Methodology							
Adapt the organization's strategy development process to include cultural analysis							
Identify the organization's cultural risk thresholds							
Integrate the cultural risk management methodology into the organization's risk management models							

continued on following page

Table 1. Continued

Develop a methodology for integrating risk assessment strategies across all three levels of the organization								
Task 11. Managing the Organization's Cultural Risks								
Adapt strategic planning metrics and reports to include expanded coverage of all forms and types of strategies								
Adapt strategic planning metrics and reports to include coverage of key cultural factors at all three levels								
Develop a publishing and communication approach for new metrics and reports								
Build a management level dialog around the new and expanded metrics and reports								
Task 12. Build and Manage the Organization's Cultural Capacity								
Identify areas of institutional capacity that need to be strengthened to support the new risk management methodology								
Identify learning and training gaps required to support new capabilities								
Identify adjustments to individual investment and performance processes								

About the Authors

Denise A. D. Bedford is currently an Adjunct Professor, Georgetown University's Communication Culture and Technology program; Visiting Scholar at the University of Coventry, and a Distinguished Practitioner/Virtual Fellow with the U.S. Department of State. In 2010, Dr. Bedford retired from the World Bank where she had been Senior Information Officer for 15 years. In this capacity she was responsible for information and business architecture, search architecture, enterprise taxonomies and core metadata. In 2015, she retired from her role as Goodyear Professor of Knowledge Management, Kent State University where she developed and directed a master's level curriculum in knowledge management. Dr. Bedford has also worked for Intel Corporation, NASA, University of California Systemwide Administration, and Stanford University. She currently serves as an Associate Editor of the Journal of Knowledge Management and is the Editor of the new Emerald monographic series, Working Methods for Knowledge Management. Her educational background includes a B.A. triple major in Intellectual History, Russian Language, and German Language; an M.A. in Russian and East European History; an M.S. in Information Science; and a Ph.D. in Information Science with focus on Systems Analysis and Design, and Economics of Information.

Wioleta Kucharska, Ph.D. Eng., holds an Assistant Professor position at the Management Department of the Management and Economy Faculty of Gdańsk University of Technology, Poland. She is involved in multiple knowledge cultures, knowledge management, including tacit knowledge sharing scientific projects. She published many peer-reviewed studies with Wiley, Taylor & Francis, Emerald, and IGI Global. Next to scientific achievements, she also has 12 years of managerial experience.

Index

21st-century knowledge 60, 300, 303

A

administrative units 104, 110, 149

B

business cultures 1, 4, 15-16, 41, 59, 82-83, 112, 124, 126, 131, 138, 145, 147-148, 160-161, 172, 205, 236, 240
business information 1, 60, 62-63, 65-66, 136-137, 276-277
business managers 6, 63, 65, 67, 82, 137, 141, 169, 172, 180-181, 205-206, 239, 269
business strategies 1-2, 4-5, 9, 14-16, 38-40, 42, 45, 51, 58-61, 65-66, 74, 126, 161, 163, 167-169, 171-172, 177, 182, 191, 202-204, 207, 211, 236-239, 244, 250, 269-270, 275, 290, 297

C

critical business asset 58, 60
cultural analysis 13, 16, 173, 175, 178, 203, 205-207, 237, 241, 279, 287
cultural artifacts 20, 25, 31, 86, 149
cultural attributes 112-114, 161, 177-178, 275, 300
cultural capacity 296-303
cultural factors 45, 107, 111, 202-203, 205, 225, 237, 240
cultural Leverage Points 177, 206, 240-241
cultural risk 5, 7, 9-10, 13, 40, 50, 178, 207, 268, 274-275, 286-287, 290, 294

D

decision making 41, 60, 107, 125, 135, 143, 300

E

essential elements 20, 23-24, 82, 129, 176
essential management 40, 42, 178
extensive exploration 132, 138

H

high-risk strategy 161
holistic view 51, 67
human resource 43, 45

I

information behaviors 70-71, 73-74, 127-130, 135, 137, 141, 146, 148, 152, 177, 207, 268, 274
information cultures 4, 16, 38, 59, 124-127, 129, 131-133, 135-138, 141, 144-145, 147-149, 152, 161, 167, 176-177, 207, 241, 268, 274, 280, 299-301
information management 58, 60-63, 65-67, 70, 72, 85, 124-125, 127-132, 134, 137-141, 144, 147-148, 168-169, 172, 177, 207, 209
information risks 287, 290, 293-295
information strategies 3-4, 7, 15-16, 46, 58-62, 66-68, 70-72, 74, 89-90, 100, 125-126, 133, 152, 160-164, 167-169, 171-172, 175, 178, 202-203, 205, 236-237, 239-241, 268-270, 279-280, 287, 303

information strategy 15-16, 58-62, 66-67, 70, 90, 124, 137, 149, 161, 167, 169, 172, 180, 205, 209, 239, 241

K

knowledge capital 1-3, 6, 63-64, 258, 299-302
knowledge economy 1-6, 8-9, 11, 15, 38, 49-50, 58-60, 124-126, 135, 161, 219, 226, 244, 248, 270, 274, 300, 303

L

life cycle stage 92, 102, 136, 139, 225

M

management process 38, 178, 203, 207, 237, 241, 268, 281

N

next generation 21

O

organization level 3, 42-44, 58, 61-62, 65-66, 71, 88-90, 100, 102, 125, 127, 132, 134-137, 146, 160-161, 163-164, 167-168, 172-173, 176, 178-179, 202-207, 225, 237, 239-241, 257
organizational culture 8, 21-25, 28, 31, 49-50, 65, 83-85, 88, 90, 93, 96-97, 99-100, 105, 132-133, 175, 180, 247, 256, 301

S

science literature 58, 70, 74, 124-125, 129-130
strategic planning 3, 11, 14, 23, 38-39, 41-42, 46, 61, 67, 163, 203, 237, 268, 271, 279-282, 287
strategic planning process 14, 38, 67, 268, 279-282, 287
strategy development 3, 11, 13, 16, 41, 67, 83, 178, 203, 207, 237, 241, 250, 279

U

underlying assumptions 20-22, 24, 26-27, 134, 250
unit-level business 205, 207, 239

www.ingramcontent.com/pod-product-compliance
Lightning Source LLC
LaVergne TN
LVHW081337300926
849161LV00008B/1994